The
Wenner-Gren
Foundation
for Anthropological Research, Inc.

Sensible Objects

WENNER-GREN INTERNATIONAL SYMPOSIUM SERIES
···

Series Editor: Leslie C. Aiello, President, Wenner-Gren Foundation for Anthropological Research, New York.

ISSN: 1475-536X

Since its inception in 1941, the Wenner-Gren Foundation has convened more than 125 international symposia on pressing issues in anthropology. These symposia affirm the worth of anthropology and its capacity to address the nature of humankind from a wide variety of perspectives. Each symposium brings together participants from around the world, representing different theoretical disciplines and traditions, for a week-long engagement on a specific issue. The Wenner-Gren International Symposium Series was initiated in 2000 to ensure the publication and distribution of the results of the foundation's International Symposium Program.

Prior to this series, some landmark Wenner-Gren volumes include: *Man's Role in Changing the Face of the Earth* (1956), ed. William L. Thomas; *Man the Hunter* (1968), eds Irv DeVore and Richard B. Lee; *Cloth and Human Experience* (1989), eds Jane Schneider and Annette Weiner; and *Tools, Language and Cognition in Human Evolution* (1993), eds Kathleen Gibson and Tim Ingold. Reports on recent symposia and further information can be found on the foundation's website at www.wennergren.org.

The
Wenner-Gren
Foundation
For Anthropological Research, Inc.

Sensible Objects

Colonialism, Museums and Material Culture

Edited by

Elizabeth Edwards, Chris Gosden and Ruth B. Phillips

BERG

Oxford · New York

English edition
First published in 2006 by
Berg
Editorial offices:
1st Floor, Angel Court, 81 St Clements Street, Oxford, OX4 1AW, UK
175 Fifth Avenue, New York, NY 10010, USA

Berg is the imprint of Oxford International Publishers Ltd.

Library of Congress Cataloging-in-Publication Data
Sensible objects : colonialism, museums, and material culture / edited
by Elizabeth Edwards, Chris Gosden, and Ruth B. Phillips.—English ed.
    p. cm.—(Wenner-Gren international symposium series)
    Includes bibliographical references and index.
    ISBN-13: 978-1-84520-324-5 (pbk.)
    ISBN-10: 1-84520-324-0 (pbk.)
    ISBN-13: 978-1-84520-323-8 (hardback)
    ISBN-10: 1-84520-323-2 (hardback)
    1. Material culture. 2. Senses and sensation. 3. Body, Human—
Social aspects. 4. Ethnographic museums and collections. 5. Colonies.
6. Postcolonialism. I. Edwards, Elizabeth, 1952- II. Gosden, Chris,
1955- III. Series: Phillips, Ruth B. (Ruth Bliss), 1945- IV. Wenner-
Gren international series.

    GN406.S48 2006
    306—dc22
                                                            2006004166

British Library Cataloguing-in-Publication Data
A catalogue record for this book is available from the British Library.

ISBN-13 978 1 84520 323 8 (Cloth)
  ISBN-10 1 84520 323 2 (Cloth)

    ISBN-13 978 1 84520 324 5 (Paper)
    ISBN-10 1 84520 324 0 (Paper)

Typeset by JS Typesetting Ltd, Porthcawl, Mid Glamorgan
Printed in the United Kingdom by Biddles Ltd, King's Lynn

www.bergpublishers.com

Contents

Part 3 Museums

List of Figures

Notes on Contributors

Ngahuia Te Awekotuku is a Professor of Research at the University of Waikato. She describes herself as a cultural activist, concerned with the arts and social change. She has published works of fiction, poetry and non-fiction. Her next book is a major study of Ta Moko, traditional Maori tattoo.

Tim Barringer is Paul Mellon Professor in the Department of the History of Art at Yale University. He has published widely on nineteenth-century art, museums and colonialism and was curator, with Andrew Wilton, of "American Sublime" (Tate Britain, 2002). His book *Men at Work: Art and Labour in Victorian Britain* appeared in 2005.

Liam Buckley teaches anthropology at James Madison University. His research and teaching interests focus on the relationship between visual culture and postcolonialism, employing methods of research and analysis from the fields of political anthropology, studies in cross-cultural aesthetics, and material culture studies. His publications include "Self and Accessory in Gambian Studio Photography" (*Visual Anthropology Review* 16(2):71–91), "Objects of Love and Decay: Colonial Photographs in a Postcolonial Archive" (*Cultural Anthropology* 20(2):249–70).

Constance Classen teaches in the Department of Sociology and Anthropology at Concordia University, Montreal. She has authored numerous books in the cultural history and anthropology of the senses, including *Worlds of Sense: Exploring the Senses in History and Across Cultures* (1993), *The Color of Angels: Cosmology, Gender and the Aesthetic Imagination* (1998), and (together with David Howes and Anthony Synnott) *Aroma: The Cultural History of Smell* (1994). Her latest work is an edited collection, *The Book of Touch* (2005). She continues to research the sensory and social life of collections.

Elizabeth Edwards is Professor and Senior Research Fellow at the University of the Arts, London. She was formerly Head of Photograph and Manuscript Collections at the Pitt Rivers Museum and Lecturer in Visual Anthropology at the University of Oxford. She has written extensively on the relationship between photography, anthropology and history and on material culture. Her most recent books are *Raw Histories: photography, anthropology and museums* (2001) and a co-edited volume with Janice Hart, *Photographs Objects Histories: on the materiality of images* (2004).

Jeffrey Feldman Jeffrey David Feldman is a cultural anthropologist who lives and teaches in New York City and writes widely on museums, colonialism and material culture. His most recent publications include "The X-Ray and the Relic: anthropology, bones and bodies in modern Italy," in L. Podezzi (ed.) *In Corpore: bodies in post-unification Italy* (forthcoming) and "The Jewish Routes and Roots of Anthropology," *Anthropological Quarterly* (2004). Dr Feldman is currently Assistant Professor and Acting Director of Museum Studies at The City College of New York.

Kathryn Linn Geurts earned her doctorate in anthropology from the University of Pennsylvania and teaches at Hamline University in St. Paul, Minnesota. She is author of *Culture and the Senses: bodily ways of knowing in an African community*.

Elvis Gerson Adikah graduated from the University of Ghana, Legon, in 2003 with a B.A. in Political Science. He is currently the Research Manager at Forest Watch Ghana, a coalition of local and international NGOs campaigning for sustainable harvesting and management of Ghana's forest sector.

Chris Gosden is Professor of Archaeology and a curator at the Pitt Rivers Museum, University of Oxford. He has published widely on issues of archaeology, anthropology and colonialism. Recent books include *Archaeology and Anthropology: a changing relationship* (1999), *Collecting Colonialism: material culture and change in Papua New Guinea* (with Chantal Knowles) (2001), *Prehistory: a very short introduction* (2003) and *Archaeology and Colonialism* (2004). He currently directs the Relational Museum project looking at the sets of connections composing the Pitt Rivers Museum.

David Howes is Professor of Anthropology, Concordia University, Montreal. He has published numerous books on the history and anthropology of the senses, including *Sensual Relations* (2003) and *Empire of the Senses* (2004), the lead volume in the Sensory Formations series from Berg. Other research interests include the anthropology of consumption and the sociology of law.

Aldona Jonaitis studies Northwest Coast Native art. She has published several books on aspects of the art, including *From the Land of the Totem Poles: Northwest Coast Art at the American Museum of Natural History* (1988), *Chiefly Feasts: The Enduring Kwakiutl Potlatch* (1991), *The Yuquot Whalers' Shrine* (1999), and *Art of the Northwest Coast: An Introduction* (in press). Currently she serves as Director of the University of Alaska Museum of the North in Fairbanks.

Diane Losche teaches in the School of Art History and Theory, College of Fine Arts, University of New South Wales. She has worked at the Australian Museum on exhibitions, and her current research interest is in the history and culture of Museums and the Pacific. She is currently researching at the American Museum of Natural History.

Sven Ouzman is former Head of Rock Art at South Africa's National Museum, Bloemfontein and is currently at the University of California, Berkeley. His academic pursuits include archaeological ethics, politics and theory, graffiti, indigeneity, intellectual property rights, landscape, museology, origins, rock art, and social and symbolic landscapes. He has produced more than 100 academic and popular articles on these topics. Further, Sven is interested in how intellectually and practically to practice archaeology in postcolonial contexts.

Ruth B. Phillips is Canada Research Chair and Professor of Art History at Carleton University in Ottawa. She is a former director of the University of British Columbia Museum of Anthropology and has curated exhibitions of African and Native North American art. She is the author of *Trading Identities: the souvenir in native North American art from the northeast, 1700 to 1900* (1998), and co-editor with Christopher B. Steiner of *Unpacking Culture: art and commodity in colonial and postcolonial worlds* (1999).

David Sutton is Associate Professor of Anthropology at Southern Illinois University, Carbondale. For the past 15 years he has been conducting research on the Greek island of Kalymnos in the eastern Aegean Sea. He has published two books based on this research: *Memories Cast in Stone* (1998) and *Remembrance of Repasts* (2001). Current research focuses on food as gifts in US popular movies such as *The Godfather* and TV shows such as *Seinfeld*. He is co-editor (with David Howes) of a new series with Berg entitled Senses and Sensibilities, which will publish ethnographically based studies seeking to explore questions of the role of the senses in contemporary cultural practices and the structuring of the senses in the spaces of late capitalism and globalization.

Preface

Elizabeth Edwards, Chris Gosden, and Ruth B. Phillips

This book arose from a Wenner-Gren Symposium entitled *Engaging All the Senses: colonialism, processes of perception and material objects* which was held from September 26 to October 2, 2003 in Sintra, Portugal.

As the complex sub-title of this conference indicates "Engaging all the senses" was an attempt to tackle a range of connected issues, concerning how we sense objects, how different sensory orders clash in and through the encounters of colonialism, and to what degree we can evoke different orders of sensory perception in museums which are themselves institutions that arise largely from colonial histories. The participants were mainly anthropologists, but included also art historians and archaeologists who work variously on material culture, the senses, colonialism, and museums. Following the Wenner-Gren format papers were circulated in advance and discussed at the meeting in a series of sessions entitled "The Operation of the Senses," "The Senses and Artifacts," "The Colonial Encounter," and "The Postcolonial Museum and the Senses."

An overview of these discussions was provided by Frances Knight Larson, then a graduate student at the Pitt Rivers Museum, University of Oxford, facilitating a fifth session in which the group as a whole considered how it was possible to bring together the varying but linked problematics of the senses, colonialism, and museums.

The final form of the papers collected here as chapters, the structure of the volume, and the editors' introduction have all been further refined and enriched by the group interactions that were made possible by the Symposium. These changes developed in the course of the formal presentations and debates, the more informal discussions that took place over meals, strolls in the eighteenth-century gardens of the Hotel Palacio de Seteais, and the hilly walks down to the town of Sintra, as well as the subsequent editorial process. Elvis Gershon Ardikah and Constance Classen were not at the Symposium but are co-authors of chapters here with Kathryn Geurts and David Howes respectively.

We are very grateful to Richard Fox (then President of Wenner-Gren) for approaching us to organize the Symposium and for subsequent advice and support. Laurie Obbink has provided help in many ways, important to the intellectual content and the feel and style of the Symposium and later interactions. Fatima Pinto helped organize a range of events in Portugal which were both stimulating and enjoyable.

In addition to the team at Wenner-Gren the editors would like to thank Jeremy Coote, Jocelyne Dudding, and Mike O'Hanlon (all of the Pitt Rivers Museum) for various forms of support and intellectual stimulus. We are also very grateful to Frances Knight Larson who, as monitor at the Symposium, made such an excellent intellectual contribution.

Introduction

Elizabeth Edwards, Chris Gosden, and
Ruth B. Phillips

Readers and Shakers and Other Points of Departure

The Kwakwaka'wakw curator and anthropologist Gloria Cranmer Webster tells a story about an encounter she had with the Canadian anthropologist Wilson Duff in the early 1970s. Duff came upon her one day while she was working in the store room of the old University of British Columbia Museum of Anthropology. "He picked up a raven rattle, brought it over to me and asked, 'Isn't it beautiful?' 'Yes,' I replied, and went back to my typewriter. He then asked, 'But how do you read it?' Impatiently I said, 'Shit, Wilson, I don't read those things, I shake them.'"

This casual exchange between a woman who would become a leading figure in the late twentieth-century renewal of Northwest Coast cultural and ceremonial traditions and a noted academic expert on that region's material culture (as well as an influential promoter of its status as fine art) introduces the two central problems addressed by this volume: the pervasive colonial legacies which have privileged the Western sensorium and the role that museums have played in the continuing inscription of this particular way of being-in-the-world. As an opening salvo in Kwakwaka'wakw efforts to repatriate chiefly regalia as part of the revival of community potlatching, the anecdote also represents the many late twentieth-century campaigns of anticolonial activism aimed at museums in their role as custodians of the objects amassed through colonial programs of collecting. The cumulative impacts of these challenges are being felt ever more strongly today in academies, museums, and other institutions, and they constitute an important stimulus for the intellectual work of volumes such as this. Webster has

1

glossed her own account of her encounter with Duff by commenting: "For me, that's how the world is divided: there are the shakers and the readers. The shakers just keep on shaking, regardless of what the readers have to say, and both are happy." Whether this structural divide between different sensory orders continues, or whether the pressures of increasingly hybrid and multicultural citizenries will result in the merging of sensoria is, in the large sense, the still open question that our book raises.

An important sign of convergence is the far-reaching academic critique that has been stimulated by, and developed in tandem with, indigenous activism. This critique, which problematizes the colonial and modernist empowerment of visual inspection and experience as primary modes of understanding and pleasure, has acquired increasing empirical grounding and theoretical force through the work of scholars in a number of areas, especially the anthropology of the senses, material culture studies, psychology, critical museology, history, and art history. To a large extent, however, the multidisciplinary strands of description and analysis have remained separate. While the senses are the means by which the human body perceives and responds to the material world, the critical nexus they form around material culture has yet to be adequately described and, following on from that, its impact for museological practices assessed. It was with this position in mind that the symposium "Engaging All the Senses: colonialism, processes of perception and material objects" was convened. The participants brought different methodologies to the problem, from anthropology, art history and history and from different positions within these disciplines. These approaches resonate through the volume, suggesting at the same time the possibility of cross-fertilization, if not synthesis. It has been our intention nonetheless to keep these different strands discernible so as to demonstrate the the rich and eclectic possibilities which can be brought to a consideration of material culture and the senses. What emerged strongly from the discussions at the symposium was the way in which thinking through the senses extended and rebalanced extant ways of thinking about material culture in a vast array of contexts, and suggested new approaches. Indeed it extended the concept of material culture itself, beyond "things" to materially expressed and phenomenologically expressed ideas such as elegance or balance, creating a more holistic approach to material culture which can more closely approximate many indigenous traditions.

Within this interdisciplinary context, the purposes of this volume are, then, threefold. It explores the different sensory ratios and registers through which material culture is understood in different societies; it examines the ways in which material culture and the social relations invested in it have been mis-apprehended through clashes of sensory systems within the colonial encounter, and it analyzes the role of the museum in institutionalizing Western assumptions about how we apprehend objects through cultural processes.

Our discussion proceeds from two critical apprehensions about material culture. First is the recognition that colonialism was profoundly material and that colonized and imperial centers were critically linked by a traffic in objects that was the sensorially figured: raw materials, crafted artifacts, foodstuffs, photographs, documents, bodies, and body parts (Brewer and Porter 1993; Clifford 1988; Marcus and Myers 1995; Edwards 2001; Myers 2001). Crucially, we argue that colonialism was experienced through multiple forms of sensory perception. Distinctions of hierarchy, class, and caste were created and represented not only through clothing, buildings, representational forms, and the organization of the landscape, but also through the formation of new conventions and distinctions around food, odors, sounds, and the bodily contacts in which material objects were, and continue to be, entangled. Indeed, both colonial and indigenous categories were often generated viscerally, out of responses of desire or disgust that could mutate in different kinds of social relations (Stoler 1995).

Our second point of departure is a re-consideration of the whole sensory register in relation to material culture. This position might be seen as a specifically focused response to broader contemporary concerns with visuality as a condition and mode of analysis. Ann Brower Stahl has identified a parallel problem in her discussion of the tension between the argument for the constitutive role of material culture in social relations and the linguistic bias of much recent theory:

> Anthropological analyses of colonial entanglements often direct attention to the problem of meaning logocentrically conceived and analysed. This privileges language both as a site of meaning formation and as an entry point into the analysis of meaning. As a result, we have not fully delivered on the promise implied in the recognition of object worlds as *active sites of cultural production.* (2002:832)

While we acknowledge that, although Western ocularcentricism or visualism has undoubtedly been over-stated, over-determined, and reified (and also ignores visualist traditions in non-Western cultures from Papua New Guinea to South America) (Howes 2003 and Taussig

1993), it nonetheless resonates through the arguments in this volume. Yet visualism here figures as a critical trope rather than an "ethnographic reality". As Taussig has argued, vision itself needs to be reconceptualized as integral to other sensory modalities (1993:26). The recent reinvigoration, redefinition, and proliferation of subdisciplines and interdisciplines that focus on visual and material objects of study, such as visual anthropology, material culture studies, and reformulations of art history as "visual culture" seem to us to reproduce the problem rather than addressing its limiting nature. For while the formulators of these new scholarly approaches argue that modernization, globalization, and electronic "media flows" have enhanced the power and dominance of the visual media in contemporary knowledge economies (Appadurai 1996; Mirzoeff 1999; Mitchell 1995; Miller and Slater 2000), the renewed emphasis on the defining power of the visual is paradoxical in relation to countervailing movements that seek instead to recover and reaffirm alternative economies of the senses. This volume, for example, communicates, for better or for worse, through the traditional academic mode of "seen text", although its arguments and critique might perhaps be made more compelling if they were expressed as, or in conjunction with, oratory, dance, and song or the manipulation of odors, tastes, temperatures, and textures.

A broader view of the senses, including the sensory integration of vision, not only brings with it a more holistic view of the role of material culture in human relations, but also extends our understanding of the integrated field of the material as phenomenologically experienced. It creates a domain of knowledge of and about the world which is "inseparable from the ways in which people actually live and act," and which, through what Jackson has described as radical empiricism, tries to "rectify the loss of plenitude of experience under a unifying rationale" (Jackson 1996:4, 7) More specifically, it generates new understandings of the degree to which past colonial regimes engendered conflicts around material forms that necessitate, in the present, a range of projects that attempt to come to terms with these histories. In order to address any of these deep and difficult issues, we need to start with a question that is simple, but not easy – "what are the senses?"

What are the Senses?

The senses form a bridge between the inwardness of the individual consciousness and the material and social worlds in which he or she exists (Jackson 1996; Ingold 2000).[1] Perception sounds a somewhat passive activity, but it is not. Many neuroscientists are now pointing out that action and perception are closely allied, so that patterns of action deeply influence the manner in which we are sensitized to the world (Lakoff and Johnson 1999; Clark 1997). It is now accepted that people learn how to use their senses, rather than merely deploying the natural capabilities of the body (Howes 1991, 2003; Classen 1993).[2] The human senses can be seen, then, as part of the set of physiologically grounded human skills which render a world intelligible and workable. This point is central to the chapters in this volume, for all explore specific ways in which culturally inflected constructions of the sensory resonate through the particular practices of material engagement. For instance, David Sutton's chapter 3 explores the skills of cooking and eating in a Western context, and he emphasizes sensory skills of consumption alongside the better-understood skills of production. Other chapters, especially those of Buckley (ch 2), Barringer (ch 6) and Guerts and Adikah (ch 7), explore the different sensory skills intrinsic to the embodied experience of "feeling" social praxis. The argument that a deep mutuality exists between our sensory apparatus and material things – that the sensory and the material call each other into existence – emerges from such studies. Material culture is, after all, the general name given to the elements of the world with which people work most closely. The forms that things are felt to take, the general sense of what it is possible to do with things, and the ways of being-in-the-world, derive from sensory interaction with the world.

Different cultures, then, create their own material orders and in the process make slightly different senses. These differences are manifested in the division, location, and naming of the senses and the sensations and attributes which are defined as constituting the senses in any given culture. As many commentators have noted, the so-called five-sense model of sight, hearing, touch, taste, and smell that has developed to make sense of the world in Western cultures is only one such ordering, and it is relatively recent in European history (Classen 1993). Several contributors to this volume take a critical stance within a five-sense model, notably Barringer (ch 6) in relation to hearing and Sutton (ch 3) and Jonaitis (ch 5) in relation to taste and smell, while others explore divergent sensory models and, in so doing, extend conventional understandings of the senses. Pain, for example, can be conceptualized as a generalized but powerful sense, both physiologically and culturally. Ngahuia Te Awekotuku's chapter 4 in this volume raises this issue through an exploration of the Maori cultural construction of pain in *moko* (tattooing). Can speech also be considered a sense? The production of sound is, after all, a physical and embodied process just as much as hearing. That hearing itself is given intentional bodily focus through the act of listening (Carter 2004:44) is made clear in Barringer's account of observers' descriptions of the visceral effect of the music composed for the Delhi Durbar of 1911.

Another strand of this discussion is demonstrated in chapters which describe the constitution of the senses through broader notions of embodiment which both extend and refigure the relationships between body, sensory perception, and cultural praxis. To what extent should our feeling for the position and actions of our bodies in space – proprioception – be understood as a sense? As Guerts and Adikah argue in chapter 1, for instance, Anlo Ewe people regard a feeling of balance as the unifying concept in a person's orientation to the world and its things (See also Shore 1996.) Similarly, Buckley's discussion (ch 2) of elegance and *ya ma sagal* – the feeling of being cherished and thus belonging – reveals this concept as an all-encompassing phenomenological engagement with the world for people in The Gambia. Conversely, it is precisely the denial of this kind of embodied engagement with the world that emerges as problematic in Feldman's exploration of the suppressed body in the museum, treated in chapter 9.

These studies also raise the question of how far the senses operate separately from each other and how far the senses combine to give a feel for the world. The everyday apprehension of objects through touch, vision, or smell can be understood as discrete acts or as engaging multiple senses simultaneously. The act of reaching for something, for example, requires a complex combination of locating the hand and arm in space through the feel and tension of the muscles and looking to see where the hand is. There is a strong possibility that different cultures have their own foundational schemas through which the world is put together, or, rather, sensed as a continuous whole.

Alternate conceptualizations of the senses and the importance of knowledge acquired through them are being documented and investigated in an ever-growing historical and anthropological literature (Classen 1993; Howes 2003; Stoller 1989; Feld 1982; Geurts 2003). Anthropologists such as Howes (1991), Classen (1993), and Seremetakis (1994) have drawn attention to the problems of the five-sense model and the ways in which perception can be differently conceptualized and articulated within cultural practices. Within a framework of thought more focused on the West, the work of Marshall McLuhan (1964) and his pupil Walter Ong (1982) has had a foundational influence. In considering the impact of new media, they argue broadly that the sensory model within a society is determined by its specific technologies of communication and, further, that each society has its own balance of emphasis – its ratio – of the senses. In their turn, anthropologists of the senses (Howes 2003; Classen 1998:403) have argued that while such analyses are important, they are technologically over-determined and universalizing in that they do not allow sufficiently for cultural variation and the different sensory environments and registers of different cultures. This is demonstrated, for instance, by Howes (2003:61–94), who has carried out the most convincing analytical work on cultural differences in the education of the senses, revisiting Malinowski's work on the *kula* in the Massim area of Papua New Guinea in terms of food, smell, and sound, and adding greater density to our understanding of *kula*.

As noted earlier, the over-determined concentration on visualism in contemporary cultural theory poses something of a stumbling block for understanding the full range of interactions with material culture. Importantly, the concern of all contributors is not so much with the suppression or denial of the visual but with the importance of acknowledging its sensory embeddedness. The modernist and post-modernist discourses of vision, played out especially through the key analytical tropes of the spectacle and the controlling gaze as theorized by Benjamin (1973), Debord (1970) and Foucault (1977), for instance, have been extensively explored and do not need to be revisited here. What needs emphasis, however, is the way in which, since Plato and Aristotle, one particular hierarchy of the senses has been used to legitimate certain forms of authority (Stoller 1989:81). The Western valuation of seeing and hearing as primary senses for the production of rational knowledge and the keying of touch, smell, and taste as lower and "irrational" (Classen 1998:405) is fundamental to the Western sensory schema. Seremetakis, writing of the relations between history, memory, and the senses, has identified the ways in which visualism, together with other imported or imposed theories, has proved seductive because of its ability to hide the sensory dispositions of the cultural periphery (1994: x). The strategies of stratification and specialization that result have had the effect of marginalizing the sensory intelligence of numerous groups struggling within world systems of discourse and knowledge, a process that has been integral to colonialism and the concomitant practices of museums and other institutions. Similarly, as Stoller (1989: xiii) argues, the impact of the disembodied rationalism of Western discourse constitutes a masculine theory of knowledge in opposition to a more embodied and multisensory "female" approach to the world. Such a point is especially pertinent to Barringer's discussion in chapter

6 of the "feminized" texture and color of Mughal culture in India as emphasized by British colonial commentators.

This and other discussions in the volume offer critical conceptualizations, responses, and configurations of the senses which illuminate the cross-cultural instability of sensory categories. As such, all seek to "re-carnalize" objects by articulating the non-discursive ways in which people and objects exist in the world, rather than reducing them to linguistically modeled semiotic bundles. As Pinney (2002:82) has pointed out, "the stress on the cultural inscription of objects and images has erased any engagement with materiality except in linguistic terms."

A multisensory approach, we would argue, integrates the visual into a holistic sensory perception which allows a richer and more ethnographically adequate multivalency of meanings to emerge as "the sense of things is constructed across a complex of exchanges between [the] various registers of representation" (Burgin 1986:58). Cross-cultural approaches can, thus, put vision in its place, as only one way of apprehending the world even if central and variously privileged.[3] Rather than understanding objects as possessing an unproblematic concrete existence that can be apprehended visually, or flattening their unique properties by considering them only as sites of social inscription,[4] the contributors argue for the necessity of thinking of objects as bundles of sensory properties which respond to specific sets of relationships and environments. Even photographs, as Buckley demonstrates in chapter 2, are phenomenologically inflected in The Gambia, and occupy a non-discursive position that links their visual properties to other sensory registers and to the embodiment of emotion. Such an approach addresses, at least in part, Alfred Gell's argument that objects cannot be apprehended exclusively within a visual/aesthetic response-theory. Rather, he argues, objects represent "unfolding patterns of social life" (Gell 1998:6) and constitute embodied emotional and sensory responses – of terror, awe, fascination, or desire – that are inherently entangled within specific dimensions of temporality.

Materiality and the Senses

Objects become sensible, as suggested by the title of this book, when they are embedded in a discourse which links things available as discrete entities to the senses (Dant 1999:11), to the physicality of concrete existence in the phenomenologically experienced world, and to ways of thinking about the world in which the senses constitute material objects as a series of fluid markers, designs, desires, and energies (Ingold 2000:

162–9). As Jackson has argued, many of the leitmotifs of anthropological analysis which have been used in relation to the sociability of objects and material culture studies – "practice, embodiment, experience, agency, biography, reflexivity, and narrative" – are drawn from the phenomenological tradition of Husserl and Heidegger (Jackson 1996: vii). Modern reworkings of this tradition resonate through the chapters in this volume. Attending to the senses is thus a useful and, we believe, a necessary further stage in the evolution of thinking about material culture, a field that has since the 1960s gradually reassumed centrality within anthropology. While this is not the place to review in detail the major re-theorizations of material culture of recent years (see for instance Buchli 2002; Brown 2001; Miller 1987; Tilley 1999; Lubar and Kingery 1993), it will be useful to provide a brief overview of the theoretical genealogy that has prepared the ground for thinking about material culture through the senses over a number of disciplines.

Within anthropology, the structuralism of Mary Douglas, Lévi-Strauss, and others reconfigured material culture as text, while post-structuralism, although maintaining the textual metaphor, insisted on the semiotically constructed and multiple meanings attributed to objects by different viewers and users. A marked neo-marxist turn toward processes of exchange and commodification was introduced by Arjun Appadurai, Igor Kopytoff and others in the 1980s, and this approach was further linked to colonial process a few years later in the work of Nicholas Thomas (1991, 1994). The circulation and reclassification of objects through different kinds of exhibitionary spaces and markets, and the contestation of the ways in which objects have been recontextualized in museums, have been illuminated by the work of scholars such as Sally Price (1989), James Clifford (1988, 1997), Fred Myers (2001), Barbara Kirshenblatt-Gimblett (1998) and Chris Gosden and Chantal Knowles (2001), and has also been the subject of several edited volumes (e.g. Marcus and Myers 1995; Phillips and Steiner 1998). Deriving inspiration from Hegel rather than Marx, Daniel Miller (1987) has emphasized the processes of self-creation through the consumption of material objects. Still more recently, material culture studies have responded to the work of Bruno Latour and to actor-network theory (1993), which dislodge embedded evolutionary narratives and stress the hybrid nature of people and objects. Simultaneously, theorists of the anthropology of art have returned attention to the formal analysis of objects in order to understand how their specific qualities operate in interpersonal and cross-cultural communication. Howard Morphy (1991) has focused on the role of art and the aesthetic in the creation and transmission of social meaning, while Jeremy Coote and Anthony Shelton (1992) have expanded understandings of how aesthetic objects shape social relations. Alfred Gell (1998) extended this discourse still further with his provocative theorization of the specific technologies through which art objects exert social agency, as we shall see later in this introduction. Within these debates, the sensory and the embodied – from the performance of praise songs to the visual beauty of Dinka cattle (Coote 1996:267–8) to Morphy's formulation of aesthetics as sensory engagement with the world (1996:255) – are implied without coming into full analytical focus.

These recent theorizations by anthropologists working on visual and material culture resonate strongly with the revisionist thrust within art history which has resulted both in a renewed interest in the social history of art and in the creation of the far more inclusive field of objects and images that makes up the interdiscipline of visual studies. As formulated by W.J.T. Mitchell, Nicholas Mirzoeff, James Elkins, Michael Ann Holly and others, visual studies has displaced or enfolded art history (e.g. Holly and Moxey 2002; Dikovitskaya 2005). However, despite the inclusive nature of the approach and the democratization of hierarchies of art that had been governed by gendered, racist, and classist assumptions there is nonetheless a tendency to subsume the multisensory facets of complex art works, compressing aspects of performance and ritual that are auditory, kinetic, or olfactory. For instance, in what ways might the sensory extend our understanding of altarpieces as the focus of gesture, movement, and prayers; the icon smoothed by kisses; the statue worn away by generations of supplicants?

Such questions bring objects back to the foundational tradition of Western aesthetic thought that has directly addressed the interrelationships among the senses, "art" and arts, and technologies and techniques. As Jean-Luc Nancy points out, Plato's codification of ancient Greek aesthetics established a fundamental separation between *tekhne*, the technologies of artistic creation (which are linked to specific senses) and the ultimate, synaesthetic goal of artistic creativity, *poiesis* (1996:6). In the Idealist aesthetics of Kant and Hegel (whose legacy visual studies seek to dismantle, at least in part), the central goal of art became identified with a striving to overcome the conditions of art's own materiality in order to express pure thought. For Hegel, however, "art, too, is there for apprehension by the senses, so that, in consequence, the specific characterization of the senses and of their corresponding material … must provide the grounds for the division of the individual arts" (quoted in Nancy 1996:9). A distinctive quality of each of the arts is its achievement of a "sense of the world," in Nancy's phrase, which opens into other sensory realms. "Each work is in its fashion a synesthesia and the opening of a world" (1996:31). The conventional privilege accorded to the visual in Western aesthetic thought is, thus, partly explained by the way in which other senses are engaged through processes of mental ideation.

Art-historical work on non-Western art during the past three decades has manifested a particularly marked tension between such fundamental assumptions of Western art history and the alternate sensory economies observed by Western scholars in the course of fieldwork-based research. This tension is exemplified by the influential work of Robert Farris Thompson on African art. In the introductory passage to his landmark exhibition catalogue, *African Art in Motion*, he strove to reconcile the relevance of the Greek notion of *poiesis* with a new understanding that the aesthetics of African sculpture were controlled as much by their function in dance and ritualized movement as by acts of static contemplation. "The famed unity of the arts in African performance," he wrote, "suggests a sensible approach in which one medium is never absolutely emphasized over others. Sculpture is not the central art, but neither is the dance, for both depend on words and music and even dreams and divination" (1974:xii).

What do Objects Want?

Thompson's work was both influential and precocious. The approaches of scholars in the social sciences and humanities over the past thirty years exhibit a series of "turns"– textual, linguistic, pictorial, and material – each of which has imposed a new framework and yielded new insights into the operation of objects and images in Western and non-Western cultures. The advent of a "sensory turn" in new work in anthropology, archaeology, history, art history, psychology, and neurophysiology is a notable development of the past few years, but it has yet to engage fully with material culture. As the chapters in this volume demonstrate, however, a sensory approach to material culture has the potential for articulating emergent subjectivities which encompass reality, imagination and reason, difference and commonality. Mitchell's remark that objects emerge as the terrain "on which political struggle should be waged, the site on which new ethics is to be articulated" (1996:73–4) resonates particularly strongly with the chapters by Buckley, Joanitis, Ouzman, and Te Awekotuku (chs 2, 5, 10, and 4 respectively). Their commentaries suggest ways in which the sensory opens up precisely such a terrain, where different sensory ratios configure objects, and allow objects to make their demands through their sociality, whether in the postcolonial modernity of Gambian politics as explored by Buckley, or the representational politics of an archaeological site description by Ouzman.

The sensory approach to objects thus positions them as integral to human behavior. It accentuates the relational qualities of objects as "categories (e.g. subject/object) or entities (e.g. person/thing) which work in *relation* to one another to produce further sets of relationships or understandings that, at their broadest, might be termed 'culture,' 'society' or 'locality'" (Geismar and Horst 2004:5–56 original emphasis). Bruno Latour has taken this function further, arguing that "things do not exist without being full of people" – that is sensing beings – and that it is no longer in fact possible to think in terms of dialogically structured categories that result in the mixing of "pure forms" such as "society" and "thing." Rather, in his view, we need to think in terms of "circulations, sequences, transfers, translations, displacements [and] crystallisations" (2000:10).

Dant, similarly, writes that, "we do not normally think of the relationship between humans and objects as "interaction" because human beings have intentions and construe meaning while things do not" (1999:121). Yet, he continues, through systems of intentionality articulated through their design, manufacture, and function and through the system of values in which they are enmeshed, objects are formulated in a certain way to extend or replace embodied functions and connect with spiritual ones as active players. Values attached to objects thus come to overwhelm people to the extent that we can ask, paraphrasing Mitchell (1996) on pictures – "what do objects want?" What, that is, do objects demand in terms of human emotional and sensory responses? How do different perceptual situations elicit different sensual configurations (Burgin 1986:58)? These questions raise, in their turn, the idea of the agency of objects, articulated most cogently through the work of Alfred Gell (1998). If, as Gell argues, agency is "a culturally prescribed framework for thinking about causation" (1998:17) and a "factor of ambience as a whole ... rather than as an attribute of the human psyche" (1998:20), the reengagement with the sensory offers a more adequate framework through which the power of objects as mediators and active agents can be understood. As the chapters in this book amply demonstrate, different sensory registers deploy this power in varied ways in different cultures. They create a range of unique "ambiences" in which human/thing relationships are shaped and mediated. At base, however, objects function as social agents in a double dynamic that *both* extends human action *and* mediates its meanings. "Objects in the landscape," writes Dant, "are not undifferentiated but 'call out' various responses that the 'me' of the social self responds to" (1999:13, 122).

Akrich adds to these theorizations the notion that objects impose behaviors back on to humans through a process of "prescription." Although her discussion in some ways anticipates Gell's notion of objects as "secondary agents" which are endowed with the "formation, appearance, or manifestation of intentional actions" (1992:36), her notion of prescription bears more directly on the role of the senses. In her account objects presuppose a purpose, or "role expectation" which includes the sensory. Similarly, Spurling (following Merleau-Ponty) has argued that both emotions and the senses reveal intentionality – one is angry *at*, scared *of* and so forth (1977:7). Such an approach follows a general premise of phenomenology that human action is always intentional and that perception and action are conjoined processes directed by human will and intention.

One of the most fertile frameworks for the study of material culture during the late twentieth century has been the idea that objects have a "social biography." This approach, which posits a fundamentally dynamic understanding of objects that both is linked to and foreshadows the notion of agency, was introduced in Kopytoff's seminal essay published in Appadurai's influential edited volume *The Social Life of Things* (1986), and then further elaborated by Thomas in his *Entangled Objects* (1991). In a biographical model, objects cannot be understood in terms of a single, unchanging identity (such as "museum object"), but rather by tracing the succession of meanings attached to them as they move across space and time. This model emerged from a felt need to develop methodologies which "redirected the unit of analysis ... to multisided ethnographies" (Steiner 2001:209), and address the inherent instability of the meanings attached to objects as they had become elided through their placement in the disembodied and thus limiting spaces of museums (Steiner 2001:210). Although the behaviors objects "want" often call upon a range of senses, as Stoller notes (1997:81) visualism has imposed a linearity on the biographical model that limits its productivity. This problem is exemplified here by Feldman's chapter on the absent body in the museum and the presence of traces such as the plaster casts of the physical anthropologists or the shoes of victims of the Holocaust.

Increasingly biographies are judged "by the sensory fullness" of the understandings they produce (Backscheider 1999:230). The sensory thus presents us with a bundle of possible trajectories or biographies which enliven objects and give them meaning in different ways within historically dynamic environments of the colonial and the postcolonial. As Jonaitis's chapter 5 and Ouzman's chapter 10 suggest, for example, the senses open the museum or heritage object to multiple readings beyond those constituted by a linear biographical mode. Thus it can be argued that further biographical possibilities open up, giving a density, and indeed points of fracture, to the linear insistence of the conventional social biography model. More importantly, a multistranded and multidirectional biographical model connects to differently constituted, sensorially apprehended, historical trajectories in which transferred ownership and shifts in geopolitical contexts are only part of the power of biography.

The Sensory Economies of Colonialism

We have stressed above the importance of highlighting the sensory relations that exist between people and things, as well as the nature of the balance that exists within that relationship. In colonial systems, as noted earlier, material culture moves people, both culturally and physically, leading them to expand geographically, to accept new material forms, and to set up power structures around a desire for the material. Early colonialism, of the second and first millennia BCE, begins at the point when objects are starting to break out of purely local value systems. Much of the capitalist valuation of objects concerns quantitative measures: the skill and labor needed to make something; the emergence of standardized shapes, sizes, qualities, and weights of objects to facilitate exchange. Such valuations predate capitalism and become increasingly common in the first millennium BCE, notably in the Mediterranean world and China. The quantitative evaluation of objects offers new possibilities for detaching people from their local groups and moving them in search of new opportunities for personal advancement – in our terms, they can "get rich." By contrast, many groups value objects according to a range of their sensory qualities: variations in color, shape, texture, weight, and condition allow for a flexible evaluation of things, often in relation to cosmological values. In order to understand the ways in which Native North Americans first reacted to outsiders, for example, we must look at the sets of values they attached to material culture and to human and spiritual relationships. For indigenous peoples of the Northeast, the acquisition and use of ritually charged objects was vital to human well-being and the fertility of the natural world. Horned serpents, panthers, and dragon-like beings, for example, were associated with the realm of earth and water, and medicine societies became empowered through possession of materials related to them. In this context, wealth was more like medicine, ensuring health and well-being, than it was like the European category of riches, and the valuables that constituted wealth had to be used wisely. By a process of "transubstantiation" (Miller and Hamell 1986:318), the values adhering in local objects were extended to European trade items. Initially, Europeans were assimilated into the network of local relationships through the significance of the trade items they brought with them: materiality was the basis for particular forms of sociality.

French fur traders working in the Great Lakes region were, in contrast, interested in profit – in buying cheap and selling dear – and their material success was measured in quantitative terms. Native American successes were less personal or easily defined, and depended on the control of cosmologically charged objects, but by processes of translation common throughout colonial cultures, European forms for the valuation of objects began to coexist with or displace indigenous forms of valuation. The purest form of quantity is money, which sometimes has no intrinsic value other than as a manifestation of quantity. During the seventeenth and eighteenth centuries in northeastern North America, for example, one particular form of indigenous valuable, white shell beads known as *wampum* – which carried positive and constructive spiritual powers – began to be manufactured by the Dutch and the English in New York and circulated as currency. In many times and places colonialism has come about when people become detached from their local community in the search for objects of quantity encounter peoples for whom qualities are crucial. Distinguishing objects in this manner had implications for the senses, for the qualities under discussion were, by definition, sensory qualities which depended on how things looked, felt, smelt, or sounded. The standardization of quantities which accompanied quantification and commoditization also narrowed and dulled the appreciable range of variation. At the heart of the colonial desire for objects lie differential uses and valuations of the senses which, in the course of history, can be thought of as having flowed through into the broader, cosmopolitan education of the senses that has shaped us all.

The desire for quantity – revolving chiefly around broad economic value – did not, however, do away with the capacity for making fine sensory discriminations but, rather, displaced this capacity on to other realms, such as that of consumption. In all periods, many of the commodities sought for colonial consumption have been attractive to the senses. Tea, coffee, tobacco, spices, sugar, silk, and even the humble potato, all titillated the senses of the metropolitan consumer while adding to the bank accounts of producers and traders. Over the last few hundred years at least, colonialism has shifted the balance between quantity and quality, with producers desiring the quantitative return, and consumers looking for new qualities of food, drink, home furnishing, and gardens to the point of displacing aesthetic satisfactions from the realm of production to the arena of consumption. Confronted with these irresistible and transformative changes, the colonized creatively reordered their own aesthetic and sensory worlds, but maintained, where possible, an appeal to the senses in arenas of production, exchange, and consumption.

Colonialism has also had a complex relationship with the growth of modernity during the past few centuries. Modernity is, of course, a complicated phenomenon, eluding easy definition. But modernity is integrally related to the control of sensory experience, from the transformation of smell through sanitation, to the suppression of sound through the regulation of noise, to the control of embodied relations through the ordering of social space.

These dynamics are transnational and cosmopolitan in character (Harvey 1989:10–38). The invention of the idea of primitive society, understood as small-scale, static, bounded, traditional, and lacking in possibilities for personal development, enabled Europeans to define their own Enlightened modernity against the imagined disorder and lack of regulation of colonized others. The construction of a coexistent antimodernity served, as needed, both as escape from and validation of the West's modernity. Anthropology, by creating and documenting the primitive, played an important role in helping to define modern Europeans in terms of what they were not.

Postcolonial theory endows the colonies, which have appeared marginal to European history both in a geographical and in an intellectual sense, with a centrality that has been displacing older narratives, and brings new perspectives to bear on the transformative impact of colonial encounters on the ways objects are understood. More recently thinkers have come to see the colonies as "laboratories of modernity" (Stoler 1995:15). Mintz (1985) has argued that large-scale industrial production may have been worked out in the colonies before being tried in Europe. Many more examples could be added to reinforce his interpretation, from the influx of bullion from the Americas that began around 1500 with its powerful stimulus to the reinvention of European economic systems, to the impact of importing cotton on clothing, to the incorporation of

Indian loan words into English (Gosden 2004:127–30). We are coming to understand modernity not as a movement that began in Europe and was exported elsewhere, but as a phenomenon engendered by the complex of colonial encounters and innovations which circulated back to Europe and then out again to the colonies.

An understanding of the senses and their continual reordering helps throw extra light on the complicated histories of colonial relations in modernity. The changing and fluid configurations of self and other had a history, which ranged from the responses of wonder, speculation, and disgust engendered by Columbus's initial contacts with the Taino in the Caribbean (Greenblatt 1991), to more stable forms of perception, categorization, and valuation of colonial others. These more orderly, but perjorative, forms of colonial understanding centered on the evaluation of human bodies, especially through the classifications of sexuality and race (Stoler 1995). What are such categorizations but orderings of the senses that single out and fix upon visual appearances of color, body shape and facial type, smell, sound, or touch? The complex interrelationship of the dual births of modernity and colonialism thus both derived from the senses and helped to reeducate them, changing in the process all relations to the material world and to other people. Stoler (1995) has pointed out that, as desire took new forms in colonial processes, the links between emotional frameworks and the senses were critical. The microcosm (the body and its person) and the macrocosm (the state) are intimately linked through a politics deriving from the earlier colonial state and its reworking.

Food, like music and photography, is also shown to constitute a site around which sensory, social, and political values can be made and remade. Jonaitis describes how the strong and opposing reactions of distaste and enjoyment of Europeans and Kwakwaka'wakw for eulachon oil constituted a cultural boundary marker in the colonial era and continue, despite changes, to constitute a demarcator of identity. She also explores the obstacles that prevent modern museums, required to observe strict health and safety regulations, from representing in a fully sensory way the relationship to food that many Kwakwaka'wakw potlatch objects want. Such an example suggests how museums harbor many objects with the potential to subvert the sensory hierarchies and the broad structures of meaning put in place during the colonial era. As key modern institutions that order and control world cultures, they have imposed Western classifications of knowledge and hierarchies of the senses on the objects within their walls. As sites of resistance and self-expression, however, they also embody the two countervailing tendencies within modernity – the complex of science and bureaucracy versus the value of individualism and self-expression – that we posited earlier. Out of this inherent contradiction could come a movement, as yet unformed, that might restore to museum objects sensory dimensions that were suppressed through colonial encounters.

The Senses and Museums

The privileging and reproduction of Western hierarchies of the senses so informs the Western museum that they continue to control even exhibitions whose intentions are to decenter Western hierarchies. For example, the *Trade and Empire* gallery at the National Maritime Museum in Greenwich, England, re-visioned British imperialism through an explicitly postcolonial lens. In one installation that was mounted on a wooden platform shaped like a pointed oval, a female mannequin in Regency dress stood next to an elegant mahogany table set for tea. As the visitor's gaze ranged across this refined domestic scene it was arrested by the sight of a black arm reaching up behind the table from a hatch set into the floor boards. The supporting wooden platform was suddenly revealed as the deck of a slave ship, a visual doubling which drove home the curatorial message: imperial expansion was impelled by European yearnings for the material and the sensory – the softness of silk, the hard lustre of porcelain, the warmth of mahogany, the sweetness of sugar, the stimulation of coffee, tea, and chocolate – but the costs of these sense-enhancing commodities included the imposition of extreme forms of sensory invasion and deprivation on other people.

Given the prominence both of pleasurable tastes, textures, and aromas and of psychic and physical pain in this representation, the Maritime Museum's almost total reliance on visual technologies of communication was all the more striking. Visitors absorbed the messages of the installation entirely through their eyes, reading extended labels and gazing at an array of artifacts. This is, of course, entirely consonant with the conventions of the modern museum which, as Svetlana Alpers has put it, has evolved as a "way of seeing" (1991). Yet as Classen and Howes's chapter 7 in this volume illustrates with particular vividness, despite the dominant paradigm of visual inspection and pleasure, the eighteenth-century cabinets of curiosity and other sites of collection that were the ancestors of the modern museum regularly engaged the senses of touch, sound, or smell in the investigation of the objects on display.

The gradual proscription of multisensory forms of engagement was an artifact not so much, as is often implied, of an epistemic privileging of visual inspection (Foucault 1970), but rather of new needs for security and the disciplining of the populace that emerged as these private collections were opened up to broad publics during the nineteenth century. Museums were part of the sensory and political apparatus control of modernity to which we have already referred (Bennett 1995; Duncan 1995). As Duncan argues, regulations against eating, drinking, loud talk, and other sensory dimensions of ordinary life can be understood as forms of ritual avoidance that constitute the museum as a liminal and transformative space (1989) that also work to produce citizens for modern democratic states. Similarly, the need to ensure the security of the museum's objects was a corollary to the new disciplinary function of the museum that had been unnecessary in both practical and symbolic terms during the years when collecting institutions remained small, private, and exclusive in their visitorship. Many historic examples manifest these dynamics, such as Brandon Taylor's account (1999) of the unanticipated necessity experienced by the National Gallery in London to formulate rules against eating, running, changing babies' nappies, and other mundane activities in the years following its opening in 1824.

The proscription of nonvisual forms of sensory experience of objects was not, in fact, total. Rather, multisensory engagements with objects remained fundamental to the investigation of material culture, but – to continue Duncan's metaphor – they became part of the privileged access accorded to a new priesthood of curators and museum professionals. The expert status and superior knowledge these experts claim is created through and distinguished by their freedom to touch, manipulate, sound, and even sometimes wear the artifacts (Parezo 1998). Such activities, however, were normally relegated to closed-off areas of the museum located "behind the scenes," a spatial separation that inscribes the distinction between public and private that is a further dimension of modernity. Such privilege evidences the fact that knowing-through-sensing *beyond* the visual is still regarded as necessary to the achievement of adequate understandings of material culture. As Losche's chapter 8 discusses, an important role of the museum curator (at least in theory) is to translate his or her multisensory experiences of objects in the museum and the field to broad publics through a range of didactic practices that include the writing of texts, the delivery of aurally received lectures, the provision of visual images, or – increasingly – the production of multimedia electronic presentations. The broad public thus acquires its multisensory understandings at one or more removes from direct experience.

During the twentieth century, as museum work has become increasingly professionalized, the apparatus that ensures the separation of objects and humans has become steadily more elaborate and bureaucratized. Even researchers must usually handle objects wearing gloves which impede the embodied experience and knowledge that comes only from the senses of touch, smell, and sometimes also hearing. It is especially revealing of the Western paradigm of museum preservation which works to arrest change in the object's material state – that conservators have become the ultimate border guards, authorized to regulate the behavior of people toward museum objects and uniquely possessed of the right to change the material states of objects through touching, cleaning, dismembering, fumigating, freezing, and other activities. The practices they enforce isolate objects from contact with food (to prevent insect infestation), touch (to prevent breakage and the contamination of skin oils), and changes of temperature or humidity (through the isolation of the artifact in a glass case or closed storage area).

Both Feldman's discussion in chapter 9 and Ouzman's in chapter 10 point to the tensions between natural processes of organic decay, the Western preservationist imperative, and the needs of originating communities. Today, standard museum protocols are increasingly being challenged by members of the communities from which the objects originate. They argue that the Western museum's ritual practices of sensory isolation and enforced stasis are antithetical to indigenous forms of ritual correctness that may require that objects be fed, held, worn, played, danced, or exposed to air, water, or incense. That the politics of postmodernity and postcolonialism are beginning to bring change even to conservation, that quintessential tradition of the Western museum, is perhaps the most convincing evidence of the profound paradigmatic shift that is beginning to occur in anthropology museums. Clavir (2002) argues for these changes, and details experiments that have been occurring in Canada and New Zealand that attempt to reconcile indigenous concepts of cultural *preservation* (which may involve the activation of material objects and result in alterations to the object's physical state) with the Western paradigm of conservation as an absence of change.

Conservation is, however, only one of many debates that are unfolding around objects in museums. Others center on modes of display, storage, and forms of access appropriate to different groups of people. We argue that it is helpful to think about the politics of these debates as deriving in large part from sensory understandings and their cultural meanings. Forms of association, which include both people and objects, depend on definitions of what is object, what is person, what is nature, and what is culture. If modes of perception depend upon the education of the senses within a particular sensory milieu, then apprehension is a political matter. Put another way, a politics derives not just from relations of class, gender, or age, but also from processes of categorization that create particular forms of connection and division. An object or even a museum can thus be seen as a microcosm of general social practice. Similarly, Latour (2003) and others have made the point that representation of large aspects of life, such as the state, are only possible on the basis of images of smaller things, such as objects and persons. What appear to be scalar differences disappear somewhat in this view, because only more immediate and tractable things can be sensed, so that the politics linking people and the world through the senses is then projected onto a larger screen. The nature of representation involves an interaction between the habits and constraints of museum practice and the sensory expectations various visitors bring to exhibits, particularly those containing objects with which the visitor has some link.

The passive (though always political) role of the museum as a space for representing the world has been changing. A phase of activism has begun in which many museums are redefining their role as one of advocacy for social change. Currently, as we have seen and as Joanitis's chapter 5 demonstates through its discussion of Kwakwaka'wakw relations with the American Museum of Natural History, members of indigenous and diasporic communities are demanding the most significant modifications of the sensory environment of anthropology museums, using a range of legal and ethical arguments to challenge the custodians of their traditional material culture to handle objects in accordance with the practices and belief systems of the originating communities (for example Clifford 1997; Jonaitis 1991; Tapsell 2000).

These challenges have resulted in three different kinds of intervention that alter and reinvigorate the sensorial regime that has surrounded collections of material objects produced by colonial encounters: the sensory surrounds inside the museum have been broadened, objects have been removed from museums and recontextualized outside them, and forgotten technologies of manufacture have been recovered through embodied engagements with historical objects which may have major impacts on material culture outside the museums walls. Diane Losche in chapter 8 of this volume tells the story of Margaret Mead's long-term effort to design a Pacific Peoples Hall that would suggest the sensory surround of light, space, and music belonging to the

Oceanic objects on display. The resulting 1960s exhibition – created by Western anthropologists and designers – was, as Losche recounts, a brave failure. During the past decade or so there has been a proliferation of innovative museum installations that expand the sensoria surrounding museum objects, created largely, but not solely, through new forms of collaboration between museums and members of originating communities.[5] These new collaborative models are, in turn, indebted to the galvanic effect of the well-reported celebrations of Maori ritual that accompanied the tour of *Te Maori* through the United States and New Zealand during the mid-1980s. They have also been influenced by such examples as the published reports of Clifford (1997) and Jonaitis (1991) of the ways in which direct, embodied contact with historical objects from their communities stimulated Tlingit and Kwakwaka'wakw elders to articulate previously unrecorded oral traditions and songs related to them. In other museums tobacco and cornmeal mush have been offered to Iroquois *Gagoh'sa* (False Face masks), incense has been burned in the presence of Cantonese opera costumes, and museum-owned masks have been sent hundreds of miles away to be danced at ceremonies in indigenous communities. A compelling set of recent case studies from British and North American museums (Peers and Brown 2002) suggests that "what objects want" is often more than the silent gaze of the observer. These events demonstrate that potentials for use and reception, engaging a range of senses, were designed into museum objects by their original makers. They remain latent in contemporary museum collections and can be reactivated by contemporary users.

The removal and/or sequestration of sacred objects from museums forms a second form of intervention. Such interventions may take the form of the simple deprivation of visual access or of the re-placement of the object in another context which privileges senses of hearing, smelling, tasting, or feeling. The series of repatriations of war gods by the Zuni and of human remains by native Hawaiians and the Haida of the Northwest Coast of Canada have involved public rituals of various sorts, as well as the re-creation of song, dance, music, and ritual feasts associated with mourning, reemplacement, and reburial. The challenges offered by such interventions have much broader implications for museums, however. As already remarked, Feldman brings out in chapter 9 the special and delicate role played by Holocaust memorial museums because the extreme nature of the experiences of the victims and survivors of the Holocaust is so difficult both to convey and to assimilate within a museum setting. Ouzman, too, juxtaposes in chapter

10 the conservation-dominated ethic of modern museums with the fact that many objects were created in order to decay and he asks how far the rights of objects have been violated in not allowing them to live out their original life course.

A future process of assessment may well determine that the third kind of intervention has had the greatest impact on changing the kinds of sensory access we have to material objects and, conversely, on shifting the emphasis from visual contemplation of objects as the primary way of seeking understanding of cultural process toward a reliance on other sensory channels. This form of intervention involves the re-creation of the museum as a space in which lost or poorly remembered forms of embodied knowledge involved in making objects can be recovered. Today, indigenous people as often come to museums to study collections in order to retrieve the knowledge of lost technologies – embodied forms of knowledge that have been another casualty of colonial encounters and modernization – and to make new objects as to restore appropriate ritual behaviors to historic objects in the collection (e.g. O'Hanlon 1993; Herle 1998; McLennan and Duffek 2000; Marie and Thompson 2004).

Toward (and Beyond) a Sensible Material Culture

We began this Introduction by stating its own exploratory intention. The need to make connections among the study of the senses, the received traditions of Western material culture study and museums, and the histories of colonialism within which the latter are so tightly bound up is imperative. Such a discussion opens up new areas of inquiry which were debated at length at the symposium, but which academic and museum scholars are only beginning to explore. To attempt a summary would be at once redundant and premature. Rather, we end with a series of provocations to further thought on the part of ourselves and others. The following propositions – each deriving from the one that precedes it – seem to us worth more exploration.

1. The senses concern bodily engagement with the world, so that the manner in which the senses are shaped and educated creates a structure to the world both offering and constraining possibilities for the human subject.
2. The senses are usefully viewed as skills, as they are deployed actively rather than passively. The tastes of food, the feel of clothing, the

smell of human bodies are both sensed and valued, and it is through these valuations that skilled discriminations can be made. A large part of the variety of human life depends on the sets of sensory skills that exist in different parts of the world.

3. The senses are fundamental to personhood. Who we are and how we construct ourselves in varying social situations depends upon the comportment of our bodies and their actions of production and consumption. How far we feel ourselves to be unified beings and how far we stress that we are fragments of a larger association of people and things depends on our means of attaching values to ourselves and to others (where others include people and things). Larger-scale units, such as the state, are constructed in the image of personhood. Although the state exists at a larger level than the senses, the body and its senses are still materialized through the state.

4. The senses are political. Politics involves issues of representation in two meanings of this word – the ability that each thing or person has to represent the interests of another person or thing, and the images that are created to evoke states of affairs which are absent or not entirely present. The politics deriving from the senses are especially obvious to all parties in colonial situations where different constructions of the world through the senses clash or mingle.

5. Museums are political in that they are created of congeries of people and things in relationships of representation, in both of the meanings used above. The limits of representation are created in large part through the sensory environments allowed and encouraged within the museum.

6. The politics of change and liberation within the museum, as elsewhere, depend on critiquing the sensory relations it establishes between objects and people and encouraging active debates concerning such sensory relations. Immanent within each object or person is a world of relationships which can be explored in detail on a small scale or followed in broader outline into larger political structures.

As Latour has commented, "Ethnologists, anthropologists, folklorists, economists, engineers, consumers and users never see objects. They see only plans, actions, behaviors, arrangements, habits, heuristics, abilities, collections of practices of which certain portions seem a little more durable, and others a little more transient, though one can never say which one, steel or memory, things or words, stones or laws, guarantees the longer duration" (2000:10). While the discussions in this volume are unashamedly interested in behaviors, abilities, and habits, they also attempt not only to "see objects" but to "sense objects." Thinking through objects with the senses also reengages with objects at a very profound level. It moves them back into the center of our considerations and brings them back to the world of people.

To dignify and engage with the subjective experience of the senses is not to deny reality, nor is it a return to fetishism or romanticism. Rather it is a way better to appreciate human imagination and experience (Stoller 1989:89). The discussions here, whether they are grounded in indigenous or subaltern experience, the postcolonial nation-state, or the museum, suggest a fullness, encompassing reality, imagination, and multiple experiences of perception and evocation.

Notes

1. This is, of course, a reason why sensory deprivation or over-stimulation are common forms of torture.

2. As early as 1898 the Torres Strait Expedition came to similar conclusions, arguing that tactile activity, hearing, and vision derived from adaptations to particular environments and did not derive from racial differences (Haddon 1903).

3. Evidence for the advent of a post-visual era is offered by the large number of contemporary artists such as Bruce Naumann, Christian Boltanski, Joachim Schmid, Sharon Lockhart, Lori Novak, and Mohini Chandra who are currently working with such multisensory problems as the materiality of images or the construction of soundscapes in aesthetic discourse. In moving the representational beyond the visual to explore embodied forms of knowing, they are insisting on the vital link between the visual and other senses.

4. It should also be remembered that images are themselves part of this defining process, and that they cannot be reduced merely to "the visual" (see Edwards and Hart 2004; Wright 2004).

5. Again artists, especially indigenous artists, have made important contributions to museums in this way. For example Wong Hoy Cheong "Shifting Light" at The Pitt Rivers Museum, University of Oxford, 2004.

References

Akrich, M. 1992. "The De-scription of Technical Objects." In *Shaping Technology: Building Society,* ed. W.E. Bijker and J. Law, Cambridge, MA: MIT Press.

Alpers, S. 1991. "The Museum as a Way of Seeing." In *Exhibiting Cultures: The Poetics and Politics of Museum Display*, ed. I. Karp and S. Lavine. Washington, DC: Smithsonian Institution Press.

Appadurai, A. (ed.). 1986. *The Social Life of Things*. Cambridge: Cambridge University Press.

——. 1996. *Modernity at Large: the Cultural Dimensions of Globalisation.* Mineapolis: University of Minnesota Press.

Backscheider, P. 1999. *Reflections on Biography*. Oxford: Oxford University Press.

Benjamin, W. 1973. *Illuminations*. Trans. H. Zohn. London: Collins-Fontana Books.

Bennett, T. 1995. *The Birth of the Museum: History, Theory, Politics.* London: Routledge.

Bredekamp, H. 1995. *The Lure of Antiquity and the Cult of the Machine.* Princeton: Marcus Weiner Publisher.

Brewer, J., and R. Porter (eds). 1993. *Consumption and the World of Goods.* London: Routledge.

Brown, B. 2001. "Thing Theory." *Critical Inquiry* 28(1): 1–16.

Buchli, V. (ed.). 2002. *The Material Culture Reader*. Oxford: Berg.

Burgin, V. 1986. "Seeing Senses." In *The End of Art Theory: Criticism and Postmodernism*. London: Macmillan.

Carter, P. 2004. "Ambiguous Traces, Mishearing and Auditory Space." In *Hearing Cultures*, ed. V. Erlemann. Oxford: Berg.

Clark, A. 1997. *Being There: Putting Brain, Body and World Together Again.* Cambridge, MA: MIT Press.

Classen, C. 1993. *Worlds of Sense: Exploring the Senses in History and Across Cultures*. London: Routledge.

——. 1998. *The Color of Angels: Cosmology, Gender and the Aesthetic Imagination*. London: Routledge.

Clavir, M. 2002. *Preserving What is Valued: Museums, Conservation, and First Nations*. Vancouver: University of British Columbia Press.

Clifford, J. (ed.). 1988. *The Predicament of Culture*. Cambridge, MA: Harvard University Press.

——. 1997. *Routes: Travel and Translation in the Late Twentieth-Century*. Cambridge, MA: Harvard University Press.

Coote, J. 1996. "Aesthetics as a Cross-cultural Category." In *Key Debates in Anthropology*, ed. T. Ingold. London: Routledge.

——, and A. Shelton (eds). 1992. *Anthropology, Art and Aesthetics*. Oxford: Clarendon.

Dant, T. 1999. *Material Culture in the Social World: Values, Activities, Lifestyles*. Buckingham: Open University Press.

Debord, G. 1970. *The Society of the Spectacle*. Detroit: Black and Red.

Dikovitskaya, M. 2005. *Visual Culture: The Study of the Visual after the Cultural Turn*. Cambridge, MA: MIT Press.

Duncan, C. 1989. "Art Museums and the Ritual of Citizenship." In *Exhibiting Cultures: The Poetics and Politics of Museum Representation*, ed. I. Karp and S. D. Lavine. Washington, DC: Smithsonian Institution Press.

——. 1995. *Civilizing Rituals: Inside Public Art Museums*. London: Routledge.

Edwards, E. 2001. *Raw Histories: Photographs, Anthropology and Museums*. Oxford: Berg.

——, and J. Hart (eds). 2004. *Photographs Objects Histories: On the Materiality of Images*. London: Routledge.

Feld, S. 1982. *Sound and Sentiment: Birds, Weeping, Poetics and Song in Kaluli Expression*. Philadelphia: University of Pennsylvania Press.

Foucault, M. 1970. *The Order of Things: An Archaeology of the Human Senses*. London: Tavistock.

Geismar, H. and H.A. Horst 2004. "Introduction: Materializing Ethnography." *Journal of Material Culture* 9(1): 5–9.

Gell, A. 1998. *Art and Agency: An Anthropological Theory*. Oxford: Clarendon.

Geurts, K. 2002. *Culture and the Senses: Bodily Ways of Knowing in an African Community*. Berkeley: University of California Press.

Gosden, C. 2004. *Archaeology and Colonialism: Cultural Contact from 5000 BC to the Present*. Cambridge: Cambridge University Press.

——, and C. Knowles. 2001. *Collecting Colonialism: Material Culture and Colonial Change*. Oxford: Berg.

Greenblatt, S. 1991. *Marvelous Possessions: The Wonder of the New World*. Oxford: Clarendon.

Haddon, A. (ed.). 1903. *Reports of the Cambridge Anthropological Expedition to the Torres Strait*. Cambridge: Cambridge University Press.

Hamell, G.R. 1987, "Strawberries, Floating Islands and Rabbit Captains: Mythical Realities and European Contact in the Northeast during the Sixteenth and Seventeenth Centuries." *Journal of Canadian Studies* 21: 72–94.

Harvey, D. 1989. *The Condition of Postmodernity: an Enquiry into the Origins of Cultural Change*. Oxford: Blackwell.

Herle, A. 1998. "The Life-Histories of Objects: Collections of the Cambridge Anthropological Expedition to the Torres Strait." In *Cambridge and the Torres Strait: Centenary Essays on the 1898 Anthropological Expedition*, ed. A. Herle and S. Rouse. Cambridge: Cambridge University Press.

Holly, M. and K. Moxey (eds). 2002. *Art History, Aesthetics, Visual Studies*. Williamstown, MA: Sterling and Francine Clark Art Institute.

Howes, D. (ed.). 1991. *The Varieties of Sensual Experience: A Sourcebook in the Anthropology of the Senses*. Toronto: University of Toronto Press.

——. 2003. *Sensual Relations: Engaging the Senses in Culture and Social Theory*. Ann Arbor: University of Michigan Press.

Impey. O. and A. McGregor (eds). 1985. *The Origins of Museums*. Oxford, Clarendon.

Ingold, T. 2000. *The Perception of the Environment: Essays on Livelihood, Dwelling and Skill*. London: Routledge.

Jackson, M. (ed.). 1996. *Things as They Are: New Directions in Phenomenological Anthropology*. Bloomington: Indiana University Press.

Jay, M. 1993. *Downcast Eyes: the Denigration of Vision in Twentieth-Century French Thought*. Berkeley: University of California Press.

Jonaitis, A. (ed.). 1991. *Chiefly Feasts: The Enduring Kwakiutl Potlatch*. New York and Seattle: American Museum of Natural History and University of Washington Press.

Kirshenblatt-Gimblett, B. 1998. *Destination Culture: Tourism, Museums and Heritage*. Berkeley: University of California Press.

Kopytoff, I. 1986. "The Cultural Biography of Things: Commoditization as Process." In *The Social Life of Things*, ed. A. Appadurai. Cambridge: Cambridge University Press.

Lakoff, G. and M. Johnson. 1999. *Philosophy in the Flesh: the Embodied Mind and its Challenge to Western Thought*. New York: Basic Books.

Latour, B. 1993. *We Have Never Been Modern*. Trans. C. Porter. New York, London: Harvester Wheatsheaf.

——. 2000. "The Berlin Key or How to do Words with Things." In *Matter, Materiality and Modern Culture*, ed. P.M. Graves-Brown. London: Routledge.

——. 2003. *Politics of Nature: How to bring the Sciences into Democracy*. Cambridge, MA: Harvard University Press.

Lubar, S. and Kingery, W.D. (eds). 1993. *History from Things: Essays on Material Culture*. Washington, DC: Smithsonian Institution Press.

Marie, S. and J. Thompson. 2004. *Long-Ago Peoples Packsack: Dene Babiche Bags: Tradition And Revival*. Gatineau, Quebec: Canadian Museum of Civilization Mercury Series, Ethnology 141.

Marcus, G. and F. Myers (eds). 1995. *The Traffic in Culture: Refiguring Art and Anthropology*. Berkeley: University of California Press.

McLennan, B. and K. Duffek. 2000. *The Transforming Image*. Vancouver: University of British Columbia Press.

McLuhan, M. 1964. *Understanding Media*. New York: New American Library.

Miller, C.L. and G.R. Hamell. 1986. "A New Perspective on Indian-White Contact: Cultural Symbols and Colonial Trade." *Journal of American History* 73: 311–28.

Miller, D. 1987. *Material Culture and Mass Consumption*. Oxford: Blackwell.

—— and D. Slater. 2000. *The Internet: an Ethnographic Approach*. Oxford: Berg.

Mintz, S. 1985. *Sweetness and Power: the Place of Sugar in Modern History*. Harmondsworth: Penguin.

Mirzoeff, N. 1999. *An Introduction to Visual Culture*. London: Routledge.

Mitchell, W.J.T. 1995. "What is Visual Culture?" In *Meaning in the Visual Arts: Essays in Honor of Erwin Panofsky's 100th Birthday*, ed. Irving Lavin. Princeton: Princeton University Press.

——. 1996. "What do Pictures *Really* Want?" *October 77*, Summer.

Morphy, H. 1991. *Ancestral Connections: Art and an Aboriginal System of Knowledge*. Chicago: University of Chicago Press.

——. 1996. "Aesthetics as a Cross-cultural Category." In *Key Debates in Anthropology*, ed. T. Ingold. London: Routledge.

Myers, F. (ed.). 2001. *The Empire of Things: Regimes of Value and Material Culture*. Santa Fe, NM: School of American Research Press.

Nancy, J-L. 1996. *The Muses*. Trans. Peggy Kamuf. Stanford: Stanford University Press.

O'Hanlon, M. 1993. *Paradise: Portraying the New Guinea Highlands*. London: British Museum Press.

Ong, W. 1982. *Orality and Literacy*. New York: Methuen.

Parezo, N.J. 1998. "The Indian Fashion Show." In *Unpacking Culture: Arts and Commodities in Colonial and Postcolonial Worlds*, ed. R.B. Phillips and C.B. Steiner. Berkeley: University of California Press.

Peers, L. and A. Brown (eds). 2002. *Museums and Source Communities*. London: Routledge.

Phillips, R. 2004, "The Value of Disciplinary Difference: Reflections on Art History and Anthropology at the Beginning of the Twenty-First

Century." In *Anthropologies of Art*, ed. M. Westermann. New Haven, CT: Yale University Press and Clark Art Institute.

—— and Steiner, C. (eds). 1998. *Unpacking Culture: Art and Commodity in Colonial and Postcolonial Worlds*. Berkeley: University of California Press.

Pinney, C. 2002. "Visual Culture." In *The Material Culture Reader*, ed. V. Buchli. Oxford: Berg.

Pomian, K. 1990. *Collectors and Curiosities: Paris and Venice, 1500–1800*. Trans. Elizabeth Wiles-Porter. Cambridge: Polity.

Price, S. 1989. *Primitive Art in Civilized Places*. Chicago: University of Chicago Press.

Seremetakis, N. (ed.). 1994. *The Senses Still: Perception and Memory as Material Culture in Modernity*. Boulder: Westview.

Shore, B. 1996. *Culture in Mind: Cognition, Culture and the Problem of Meaning*. Oxford: Oxford University Press.

Spurling, L. 1977. *Phenomenology and the Social World*. London: Routledge and Kegan Paul.

Stafford, B. 1999. *Visual Analogy: Consciousness as the Art of Connecting*. Cambridge, MA: MIT Press.

Stahl, A., 2002. "Colonial Entanglements and the Practice of Taste: An Alternative to Logocentric Approaches." *American Anthropologist* 104(3): 827–45.

Steiner, C. 2001. "Rights of Passage: On the Liminal Identity of Art in the Border Zone." In *The Empire of Things*, ed. F. Myres. Oxford: James Currey.

Stoler, A. 1995. *Race and the Education of Desire: Foucault's History of Sexuality and the Colonial Order of Things*. Durham: Duke University Press.

Stoller, P. 1989. *The Taste of Ethnographic Things: The Senses in Anthropology*. Philadelphia: University of Pennsylvania Press.

——. 1997. *Sensuous Scholarship*. Philadelphia: University of Pennsylvania Press.

Tapsell, P. 2000. *Pukaki: A Comet Returns*. Auckland: Reed.

Taussig, M. 1993. *Mimesis and Alterity: a Particular History of the Senses*. New York: Routledge.

Taylor, B. 1999. *Art for the Nation: Exhibitions and the London Public, 1747–2001*. Manchester: Manchester University Press.

Thomas, N. 1994. *Colonialism's Culture: Anthropology, Travel and Government*. Princeton, NJ: Princeton University Press.

Thomas, N. 1991. *Entangled Objects: Exchange, Material Culture and Colonialism in the Pacific*. Cambridge, MA: Harvard University Press.

Thompson, R. 1974. *African Art in Motion: Icon and Act in the Collection of Katherine Coryton White*. National Gallery of Art, Washington, DC.
Tilley, C. 1999. *Metaphor and Material Culture*. Oxford: Blackwell.
Wright C. 2004. "Material and Memory: Photography in the Western Solomon Islands." *Journal of Material Culture* 9(1): 73–85.

Part 1

The Senses

Enduring and Endearing Feelings and the Transformation of Material Culture in West Africa

Kathryn Linn Geurts and *Elvis Gershon Adikah*

Herein the longing of black men must have respect: the rich and bitter depth of their experience, the unknown treasures of their inner life, the strange rendings of nature they have seen, may give the world new points of view and make their loving, living, and doing precious to all human hearts.

W.E.B. Du Bois, *The Souls of Black Folk*

Taking a drink of water is a familiar human experience. But the taste, feeling, and meaning of such an experience is far from universal. Let us consider the words of Mr. Wakefield Kofi Sorkpor, an Anlo-Ewe man from southeastern Ghana, as he held a dried gourd with two hands and described a local custom: *Le mia fe tsinonome la miezaa tre; fafa de fomevi le tsinono kple tre me*: "We use calabash when drinking water; there is a special coolness or peace that can be derived from drinking water from a calabash." Even before the water reached your mouth, Mr. Sorkpor explained, there was the feeling of expectant waiting. By comparison, you typically held a commercially manufactured glass with one hand, which created a feeling of uncertainty, as if you were not really drinking the water. But holding the calabash with both hands created an anticipation in your body, and a knowledge in your mind, that it would bring you back to life.

In the summer of 2003 we asked Mr. Sorkpor and a number of elderly Anlo-Ewe individuals to reflect on some of the changes that occurred in

35

Figure 1.1 Anlo woman drinking from a calabash

coastal Ghana during colonialism. We talked about specific landscapes, objects, and social relations transformed as African, Arab, and European people created colonial societies in the settlements of Keta and Anloga. We approached these conversations with the assumption that the encounter involved a kind of negotiation of differing sensory experiences and clashing perceptions, and we made the local term *seselelame* (feeling in the body) the center point of our investigation. Mr. Sorkpor was quick to point out that the importation of commercially manufactured glasses introduced a different method for drinking water – a practice he evaluated as unstable, awkward, and crass. A calabash necessitated the use of two hands and created the feeling of balance which he associated with an overall sense of pleasure and rejuvenation.

Mr. Sorkpor's attentiveness to the feeling of inner balance did not come as a surprise. In earlier research we had already established that in Anlo-Ewe society not only balance but other internal senses such as proprioception and kinesthesia were highly valued (see Geurts 2002a). In fact, a taxonomy restricted to five external senses – hearing, touch, taste, smell, and sight – was not particularly meaningful to many Anlo-Ewe people (see Geurts 2002b). Instead, they recognized an array of sensory fields including: *nusese*: hearing and aural perception; *agbagbadodo*: a sense of equilibrium and balance; *azolizozo* or *azolinu*: walking, kinesthesia, and a sense of movement; *nulele*: a complex of tactility, contact, touch; *nukpokpo*: seeing and visuality; *nudodo* and *nudodokpo*: tasting and "tasting to see"; *nuvevese*: smelling and olfaction; *nufofo*: "talking" or a vocal-oral sense (Geurts 2002a:37–69). Not only was their cultural category for sensation broader than the classic five-senses model, but links were often drawn among sensations, emotions, and dispositions. This contrasted with Western philosophical traditions built on the distinctiveness of four domains: the external senses of hearing, touch, taste, smell, and sight; internal senses such as balance, kinesthesia, and proprioception; a set of emotional states including anger, happiness, sadness, disgust, and surprise; and moral responses differentiating between conscience and consciousness. But in Anlo-Ewe traditions, people have tended to posit a domain of immediate bodily experience encompassing perception, emotion, disposition, and moral knowing.

But why should these seemingly peculiar details about an Anlo-Ewe sensorium matter to us? Were they not simply problems of language variation and translation? Was there something unique to be found in Anlo-Ewe configurations of feeling and sense? To begin with, this set of interviews prompted us to wonder how common a term was *seselelame*, and we found it to be more esoteric than we previously thought. Translating it has always been difficult (cf. Geurts 2002a:37–46) and we have resisted the gloss of "sensation" – opting instead for "feeling in the body, flesh, or skin." Indeed, Ewe linguist Felix Ameka has confirmed that the phrase *se-se-le-la-me* could be used for both emotion and sensing: "lower level terms for various experiences in Ewe, like the superordinate label *seselelame*, do not distinguish between emotion, sensation, perception, cognition, etc. Instead, there are components that link to a bundle of these things at one and the same time" (2002:44–5). One of the implications of all of this is that the five exteroceptive registers of hearing, touch, taste, smell, and sight did not constitute a closed category in Anlo-Ewe thought, and were not the basis for their theory of knowing. Instead, Anlo epistemology and ontology depended upon an indigenous schema of *seselelame* – a sensibility in which bodily feeling was foregrounded as a source of vital information about environment and self. In this chapter we postulate that *seselelame* may be a foundational schema, and as such it may serve as a possible source domain for an array of cultural models – including narrative, verbal formulas, and other language arts.

What do we mean by foundational schema? The terms "model" and "schema" are sometimes used interchangeably, but here we rely on Bradd Shore's notion (1996:53) that foundational schemas have an encompassing quality, they are general and abstract, while cultural models are more particular and concrete. "A foundational schema functions," Shore suggests, "as a kind of template, a common underlying form that links superficially diverse cultural models" while simultaneously contributing to the "sometimes ineffable sense of 'style' or 'ethos'" that is characteristic of a particular social group (1996:117). In technical terms, Shore explains, a foundational schema provides what is referred to as a "source domain" for the "creation of a family of related cultural models." These cultural models "have evolved by means of a usually unconscious "schematizing process," a kind of analogical transfer that underlies the creative life of cultural models" (Shore 1996:118). In Anlo-Ewe contexts, balance would be an example of a model that is derived from a universal somatic experience that is nonetheless culturally instantiated in daily practice and thought. *Seselelame*, on the other hand, is more abstract and it usually remains out of awareness.

Anlo-Ewe society developed over the past three centuries in a coastal area of West Africa that served as the epicenter of the transatlantic slave trade. Its major commercial center, Keta, was a booming port town during the height of British colonial rule in the Gold Coast. Several centuries of Euro-African negotiations took place in Anlo-land, and we can consider it a site (or cultural world) in which people who employed their senses in variable, perhaps clashing ways, were thrown together. For one set of actors in this situation we can point to the presence of *seselelame* as a foundational schema and thereby suggest that Anlo-Ewe people placed a premium on feelings and inter-subjectivity during the slave trade and in the context of colonial rule. This same *seselelame* schema continues to contribute to Anlo-Ewe assessments of materiality, which we hope to show through interviews concerning adornment and dress, naming practices, and so forth. We go so far as to suggest, in fact, that as a foundational schema reflecting feeling and bodily ways of knowing, *seselelame* is Africa's legacy to the contemporary world.

While *seselelame* is an Ewe language term for feel-feel-at-flesh-inside, the broader sensibility in question is akin to Henry Louis Gates's "black structures of feeling" (1987:165–276) and resonates with a consciousness that is arguably more pan-African than restrictively Ewe. Useful here is Paul Gilroy's anti-anti-essentialist account of a black Atlantic (1993:102) in which he takes issue with an analytic orthodoxy that dismisses "the pursuit of any unifying dynamic or underlying structures of feeling in contemporary black cultures" and any attempts to "locate the cultural practices, motifs, or political agendas that might connect the dispersed and divided blacks of the new world and of Europe with each other and even with Africa" (1993:80). Gilroy suggests instead that "weighing the similarities and differences between black cultures remains an urgent concern" (ibid.). If *seselelame* proves to be a foundational schema, we can begin to explore its characteristics as a source domain for such cultural models as an aesthetic of the cool (Thompson 1966), doing the dozens (Abrahams 1983), signifyin(g) (Gates 1988), the spirit work of autobiographical poetics (Baker 1991), and so on. To appreciate these claims, let us look more closely at the meaning of *seselelame*.

One of our Anlo-Ewe interviewees, Mr. Edward Agbemade, explained that *Seselelame enye nyagbe si woa dode amedokuime/amedzi*. "*Seselelame* is a collection of words that works on one's body." He stated that *seselelame* helped one to capture in language how things worked on the inside of a person. Another individual described it as *aleke nese le lame*: how you feel within yourself, or how you feel in your body (Geurts 2002a:40). However, *seselelame* is not a private matter nor restricted to language, and instead references experiences of embodied intersubjectivity. For example, Mrs. Beauty Axornam Banini (an Ewe language teacher at a secondary school in Anloga) stated that if she were trying to explain *seselelame* to her students, she might say: *Ne medzi be made seselelame gomea, mele dzesi dege vinyewo fe nukpokpo, wofe nusese, wofe nuwona kple amewodomenono*; or: *Ne mie be seselelamea, mietsoo nukpokpo, nusese enuwona kple hadomenono fofui*. This meant, "If I want to explain *seselelame*, I would ask my students to take note of the way they see things, the way they hear [listen to] things, and the way they live in groups." Sensibility was at the heart of Mrs. Banini's concern.

To illustrate what *seselelame* meant to her, Mrs. Banini posed a hypothetical situation in which she was incapacitated with a swollen foot. If she was attending a public event in this condition, and had to stay put in a chair even as the food was served on the buffet table, she surmised that a close sister-colleague of hers might collect two plates of food – one for herself, and one for Mrs. Banini who was grounded by the bad foot. After eating the food, Mrs. Banini indicated she might express, *Ne enyona fieku la eyae wonya na adzikula*: "If it goes on well with the tigernut harvester, then it will be well with the groundnut harvester." This proverb captures how she would share a feeling of union, oneness, or harmony with her fellow sister. An unspoken need or desire (for the food) was met with an unspoken response (presentation of the plate), and so, Mrs. Banini explained, because it was well with that sister, it also sat well with her – creating a profound sense of satisfaction (*dzidzeme* or *nudzedze*). Her account focused on how a feeling arose intersubjectively (on the part of both women) that this transaction should occur. The one took action, and it resulted in a deep sense of harmony and satisfaction.

In this chapter we take our understanding of *seselelame* further by contemplating its out-of-awareness characteristics and by using it to help account for how certain objects from precolonial times continue to possess the hearts and minds of some Anlo individuals. Anlo is a dialect of the Ewe language and Anlo-Ewe refers to a group of primarily Ghanaian Ewes whose homeland is considered the coastal area of the Volta Region and the terrain immediately around the Keta Lagoon (Figure 1.2). In 2003 we held discussions with Anlo elders about calabashes, straw mattresses, earthenware pots, hand-woven cloth, and so forth. This archive of intimate objects – a kind of living museum of materials from precolonial and colonial worlds – served as the focal point of discussions about their enduring and endearing feelings for fragments of Anlo material culture. Let us begin with adornment and dress.

The Feeling of What You Wear

Throughout Africa clothing served as a powerful force in the colonizing and missionizing project of remaking identities and subjectivities (Comaroff 1996). In colonial Anlo-land, "Western clothing was instrumental in the construction of modern identities, and hats, coats, polished shoes and accessories, such as walking-sticks, were the vital paraphernalia of modernity" (Akyeampong 2001:101). Shifting boundaries between materiality and spirituality have been noted as a hallmark of colonial change (on the Anlo context see Greene 2002), and we encountered this in the seemingly mundane topic of undergarments.

Before the introduction of Western-style panties, Anlo-Ewe women wore a form of protective clothing referred to as *godui* (see Figure 1.3). Sometimes translated into English as "loin cloth," the *godui* was a piece of red fabric folded into a pad, placed in the crotch (between the legs) and secured in place by draping the front and back portions over the wearer's waist-beads. Mrs. Ablewor suggested that, in the past, the measure of womanhood was closely tied up with your *godui*. She illustrated this by creating several hypothetical scenarios involving loss or theft of her *godui*.

Mrs. Ablewor explained that when traveling she would wear one cloth and carefully pack another two. But if she arrived at her destination

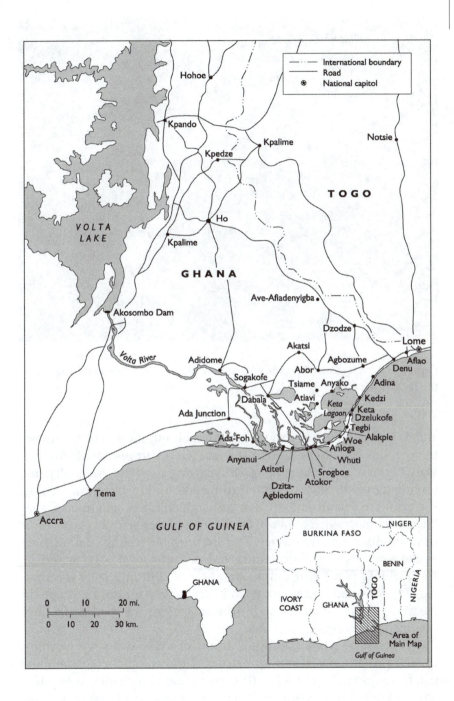

Figure 1.2 Map of southeastern Ghana

Figure 1.3 Woman selling *godui* and waistbeads (*yevugodui* are also hanging in the back of her stall)

and discovered that she had left the two behind, she would experience tremendous anxiety as though she had left a part of herself. Another story began with washing her *godui*, hanging it on the line to dry, and leaving for the market. Upon returning and finding her *godui* missing, she would feel panic and ask her husband, children, neighbors if they knew what happened to her *godui*. She would search for her *godui* more earnestly than for lost money. "An irrepressible feeling of uneasiness would awash me" she explained, out of fear that it was "stolen for spiritual foul play." Not simply an article of clothing, *godui* was more like an extension of the body, and Mrs. Ablewor indicated that the measure of one's womanhood, in Anlo society, was tied up in one's treatment and care of the *godui*.

A contrast between traditional forms of dress and sewn clothing, in fact, was an issue taken up by one of the colonial-era paramount chiefs. In 1906, Togbui Sri II (the new paramount chief) took office and initiated unprecedented change: "He repealed [a] ban on wearing European clothing in Anloga and put a stop to the burying of corpses in the deceased's house" while also opening up Anloga to "mission education and commerce" (Akyeampong 2001:113). Togbui Sri II "advocated a new image for Anloga and ... successfully divested kingship in Anlo of its superstitious cloak" in part by refusing to remain a "secluded priest-chief" and instead making himself a highly "visible, constitutional monarch who removed his office from the webs of religious constraint" (Akyeampong 2001:113). This was perceived by some as ushering into Anlo society a deeper commitment to colonial-style "progress." A shift toward Western-style dress and burial practices indicated further separation of material culture from its "spirit work" (cf. Baker 1991:76).

The spirit work of clothing also emerged as a detail in the discussion we held with the Nyigbla Priest (in position in 2003) as he described experiences that led to his holding this spiritual office. Togbui Nyigbla described a breakdown or a revelatory experience that he had in 1981 while he was staying in Abeka (a suburb of Accra). For forty days he was unable to eat, drink, or speak, and remembered hearing only the voice of a spirit. During this episode, he was taken from Abeka back to his family's home in Anloga, but the lineage elders were fearful of his capacity to communicate with spirits, and he was forbidden from living in the family home. He moved to a separate dwelling and lived alone until 1999 (when he was inducted into initiation as the Nyigbla Priest). During those years on his own he attempted wearing sewn clothing (i.e. Western-style trousers and shirt), but experienced intense itching and anxiety. He inevitably felt compelled to change back into calico.

Mr. Atsatsa also reported feeling differently in sewn clothing compared to how he felt in traditional garb. When he went to work on the farm he typically wore trousers, but when attending a funeral or public meeting, he preferred to wear *kete* (strip-woven) cloth. *Kete* was worn with a jumper (man's sewn short-sleeved collarless shirt) and African sandals, and in this attire he felt "very fine, confident, and comfortable." We discussed two different cloths that he had possessed in his life. His current cloth was a piece named *Tagbatsunku* which meant "housefly's eye" – referring to the pattern or weave of the threads – and he had owned it for approximately four years. Prior to that, however, he had *Takpekpe le Anloga* – a well-known cloth, popular among men, that meant "meeting at Anloga." Mr. Atsatsa reported that wearing his piece of *Takpekpe le Anloga* gave him a "particular dignity." We inquired about why he gave up that cloth, and whether changing cloth was akin to giving up one's *atsatsa* (a straw mattress, about which more later). It was true, he said, that when he got rid of the first cloth he did so quite unwillingly. His first reluctance was due to the fact that he had not yet found a good replacement. Secondly, he explained, it had been part of him for so long that it almost "blended into him" making the separation emotionally painful.

The Feeling of Who You Are: What's in a Name

Mr. Atsatsa related that when going out in public in *kete* cloth his experience was like that of having an added personality – particularly as some of his colleagues and friends would call out his *ahanonko* (drinking name). They would declare, *Katako gako, adawato tsitsixoxo be yeale da kple asi* (A very old mad man tries to catch a snake with his bare hands, yet when he catches it he will find himself bitten), pronouncing one of Mr. Atsatsa's drinking names. The cloth, he explained, actually affected the level of acceptance he experienced among his colleagues: when they spotted him in the traditional cloth, they would call his *ahanonko*, and he immediately had the feeling that he was among friends, contemporaries, or people with whom he shared the same sentiments.

Compared to walking in trousers, Mr. Atsatsa explained that he felt kinesthetically transformed when he donned *kete* cloth, experiencing a sense of pomposity and an elevated gait. He would walk *fiazoli* or *agozoli* – a chief's walk, a royal or majestic stroll (on ways of walking and Ewe terminology see Geurts 2002a, and b). These sensations along with the effects from his *ahanonko* made Mr. Atsatsa feel as if he was in another world, and if we were to see him in this state we would realize that "the man has arrived."

Ahanonko, indeed, was far more powerful than a mere nickname. For one thing, greetings that invoked *ahanonko* were multisensory – involving eye contact and elaborate handshakes, in addition to the aural dimension of singing out a poetically constructed name (Avorgbedor 1983). *Ahanonko* also exhibited some of the most interesting aspects of *seselelame* in that it linked sensation, emotion, and disposition. One of our interviewees, Mr. Zikpi, had an *ahanonko* of *Kpitiga abe yele Agbidime na fiawoo, nutsuwo tefe vovonatowo tui ehe xaxa* (Kpitiga said he is in Agbidime for chiefs; men's thoroughfare, cowards walked through and got stuck). Upon hearing that first word *Kpitiga*, Mr. Zikpi explained that he felt emotions and sensations welling up in his body. He stated that when a certain *ahanonko* was pronounced, *Ele nusea de kpoge le dokuiwome*: you will feel a peculiar kind of power within you. It can link you to a spiritual force inside of yourself. It can open the way for a man on a journey when he meets any blockade, and so one can even call out one's own *ahanonko* to tap into that inner strength.

Typically glossed as "drinking name," in the first instance *ahanonko* was simply an appellation given to a man in the context of meeting with his friends and colleagues over drinks. But it carried much more weight than a social nickname. As Togbui Zikpi explained, it showed that you were with a powerful force. Even when eating – holding a ball of *akple* in your finger, about to put it to your mouth – if someone called your *ahanonko*, you had to put the food down and respond. It would tap into something deep inside of you, and elicit very strong feelings. You had to leave anything superficial, anything you were doing, and respond. Mr. Atsatsa said, any time someone called his *ahanonko*, it was like *Eda fu tame nam* – "it felt as if feathers were being plucked from my skin; it raised the hair on my back."

The erasure of drinking names, in the context of colonial Anlo, poignantly highlights the ways in which spiritual-sensual phenomena were eroded. As a result of attending school under the Bremen missionaries, Mr. Sorkpor had never been endowed with a single *ahanonko* (see Figure 1.4). His life had taken a different course than that of Mr. Zikpi and Mr. Atsatsa. At the time we sat down with them, all three were in their mid-to-late seventies. Mr. Sorkpor had been a teacher, whereas Mr. Zikpi and Mr. Atsatsa had become fishermen-farmers. In their occupational contexts, Anlo naming practices were still rehearsed, and so Mr. Zikpi and Mr. Atsatsa each had about a dozen *ahanonkowo*.

Still, we were able to talk at length with Mr. Sorkpor about *ahanonkowo* – as he retained tremendous respect for the practice. Mr. Sorkpor explained that, "People use *ahanonko* to publicize their personality, to express their feeling about their life, their enemies, their attitudes about society and perceptions of daily life, etc. It provides a glimpse into their disposition." He also stated that *Wotsone bena yewo ade nutsunyenye afia*: Men or people who acquire *ahanonko* take it to exhibit their masculinity or manliness. For example, *Hateka metea nyi o* meant the rope used to pull pigs could not be used to pull cattle, and it was meant to exhibit the man's strength, masculinity, power. As a rule, then, it was men who possessed and used *ahanonko*.

However, masculinity per se was not the definitive property of *ahanonko*. Honor, dignity, and strength were the essential qualities, as was evidenced by Mr. Sorkpor's female cousin, Dzatugbui Sonefa, who had more than twenty *ahanonkowo*. A political activist, she was a member of the opposition party during Nkrumah's rule, and was imprisoned under the Preventive Detention Act. Mr. Sorkpor remembered her as a

Figure 1.4 Portrait of Mr. Sorkpor

very spirited woman, hailed by both men and women alike. She had the habit of wearing *atsaka* (men's knickers), and of joining the *asafo* dance group when they shot off muskets. She also reveled in calling out peoples' *ahanonkowo*.

Reinforcing the observation that these names provide a glimpse into the person's disposition, Mr. Sorkpor recounted several of his cousin's names. *Notsi mexoa dzudzo o; ne xoe ko ekema eku*: The nose never goes on leave; if you give it a vacation, you will surely die. Also, *Enye yae nye bolifomekpa etsi lae le nunye me goyim; ne mie koa togo koe woa sham* – indicating that she considered herself a *bolifomekpa* (I am *bolifome* tilapia or a *bolifome* fish). When the water level of the Keta Lagoon rose, the trenches between the shallot beds flooded, and tilapia fish would end up in those narrow waterways. The sun then evaporated the water and the fish died. Considering herself one of these fish – a *bolifomekpa* – reflected how she did not think of herself as anything big in life. It was only that small amount of water that kept her swimming, and when it disappeared, she would end up a dried fish.

Ahanonko drew out inner strength and character. *Avu adewo wona dzro, gake tso mele wo si oo*: Some dogs bark for nothing, yet they have no teeth. This *ahanonko* could be used when a man was passing a vicinity where some rogues were planning to attack him. As he moved along, someone who knew him might call out and say to him: *Hateka metea nyi o* (The rope used to pull pigs cannot be used to pull cattle – drawing out his strength, masculinity, power). He might then declare, *Avu adewo wona dzro, gake tso mele wo si oo* – signaling to the rogues that dogs without teeth may not be strong enough to harm him in any way. *Ahanonko*, Mr. Sorkpor explained, gave the feeling of being elevated, glorifying your soul. Because of this power, you could pronounce your own *ahanonko* when swearing an oath. I, Kodzo Ameka, *Hateka metea nyi o*, hereby swear that I will do this or that. This act would demonstrate your feeling of complete commitment – putting your honor on the line in swearing the oath. If wrongly accused of a crime, you might call out your own *ahanonko* as you swore an oath.

Ahanonko amounted to a cultural model for a naming practice – naming that occurred when a complex interweaving of emotions, sensations, sensibility, and disposition activated the practice of *ahanonko*. More deeply at work, however, was *seselelame* as a foundational schema – providing a base of feeling and bodily ways of knowing. *Ahanonko* was different than the given name which you carried since you were a child, because it was a label that you acquired while growing up, and Anlo people readily comprehended the difference between the two. *Ahanonko* represented what you had made of yourself. In instances when you felt an overwhelming sense of need to show force and say that "If I am not telling the truth, then the gods should take my life," this was a moment for *ahanonko*, not your given name.

Mr. Zikpi indicated that he believed *seselelame*, in part, sprang from the blood that you were made of; he described it as a kind of meeting between the external situation and the internal sensibility. And Mrs. Banini, we recounted earlier, indicated that *seselelame* combined the way you see things, the way you hear [listen to] things, and the way you conduct yourself in groups. *Ahanonko*, then, was a specific and concrete cultural model which was derived from how others saw you and how you conducted yourself; it summed up your honor, comportment, and sensibility. When you pronounced it in the context of an oath, you would be saying "All that I have become, all that I am, is on the line here as I swear by my *ahanonko*." As an emotional-sensual foundational schema of feel-feel-at-flesh-inside, *seselelame* served as a source domain described by Mr. Zikpi as a convergence of "the external situation and the internal sensibility" that gave rise to an Anlo-Ewe cultural model of assigning and performing *ahanonko*. We now turn to sensorial dimensions of the eating and drinking contexts from which these names sprang.

Drinking, Cooking, and the Feeling of How You Eat

While *ahanonkowo* were central to identity and identification, they traditionally came into being, of course, during moments when Anlo people (primarily men) got together to drink. This takes us back to the opening of this piece which focused on the feeling of taking liquid from a calabash compared to a commercially manufactured glass. In the final years of the nineteenth century, the material world of Keta was transformed by commerce. In 1906 it was designated the colonial headquarters of the Keta-Ada District, and in 1916 it became the major Gold Coast port east of the Volta River (Akyeampong 2001:75). At the turn of the century the area had a mixed economy revolving around copra, poultry, livestock, and agriculture, and was valued by the British in part due to the revenue from customs duties generated by liquor imports at the Keta port (Akyeampong 2001:79). The flood of alcohol into the Anlo littoral contributed to an increasing wedge between material and spiritual life. Historically alcohol was considered by Anlo to be a powerful and sacred material that could create a bridge between the spiritual and human world. Akyeampong (1996) has demonstrated how drink that was historically used for libations became secularized during colonization: young people assembled to get drunk, rather than engage in "spirit work" aided by alcohol.

Remembering the vibrant years when Keta served as a major port for the Gold Coast, one of our interviewees, Mrs. Edith Vuvor, described the day that her father brought home some drinking glasses and a bottle of beer. She was about six or seven years old, placing the event in the 1930s, and she indicated that they had never seen beer before, nor soft drinks – they only had *aliha* (a local brew made of maize or guinea corn). She remembered the store run by Mr. Barkley (a friend of her father's), and watching the unpacking of crates containing individual bottles of Heineken held in place with straw. That evening her father poured an inch of the beer into the bottom of a drinking glass and handed it to her mother. All the children watched while she drank, and begged for a taste, but to no avail. Not only the beer, but the drinking glasses too were off limits for the children and used only on special occasions or for guests. If one of the children broke a glass they would not receive school lunch money for a month – enough tuppence for her father to purchase another glass. Mr. Sorkpor, too, said that his father protectively kept the drinking glasses under the bed. The children would be beaten if caught disturbing them. Mrs. Vuvor indicated that to this day she never drinks water from a drinking glass when alone, but reserves them for guests. And Mr. Sorkpor echoed the sentiment that glasses were for guests, recalling that it was not until 1948 that he actually bought a drinking glass of his own, in Accra, and he admitted that in private he continued to drink water from a calabash.

Prior to and during the colonial era, cooking implements in the Anlo-Ewe area consisted primarily of *anyize* or *anyikutu* (clay or earthenware pots), *akpledati* (wooden paddle), *etsi* (wooden spoon or ladle), *wegba* (grinding bowl, plate), and *etre* (round gourd or calabash) (see Figure 1.5). The staple food – *akple* – was made by milling corn into flour on a grinding stone (called *ete*), mixing it with cassava dough, cooking it in a clay pot, and forming balls in a calabash. *Akple* has traditionally been served with soup (*detsi*) made of palm oil, tomatoes, peppers, shallots, vegetables such as okra, spinach, or eggplants, and fish, seafood, or red meat from cattle or goats. Mrs. Banini posited that Anlo cuisine today was much like it had been for her mother and even her grandmother's generation.

On the other hand, cooking implements and objects were quite different from how they were in her childhood. In place of earthenware pots, many people had switched to aluminum. For example, Mr. Zikpi explained that in his household they had recently stopped using *wegbawo* (earthenware plates) on a daily basis because the young people frequently broke them. However, he indicated that when he traveled alone and would stop to eat at a restaurant or roadside "chop bar," he always requested that his food be served in a *wegba*. It was more economical to stock metal or plastic plates at home. But Mr. Zikpi reported that eating from a *wegba* gave him a nostalgic feeling, a remembrance of the past, and he felt connected to his grandfather through the practice.

Milling of maize was traditionally accomplished with an *ete* (grinding stone). More recently corn mills were established throughout Anloland and flour was mechanically ground. The grinding stone or *ete* was still used for crushing and grinding pepper with other ingredients, but blenders could also be used. Several people mentioned that a very pleasurable activity was working with a *wegba* or at the grinding stone

Figure 1.5 Locally produced earthenware pots

mixing together pepper, salt, shallots, and fresh tomatoes into what is called *agbametadi*. The shallots in particular – grown in abundance in Anlo-land – would emit a pungent and fresh scent. Inspired by the grinding process and the aroma, people often took their *akple* and ate the *agbametadi* right from the *wegba* (not bothering with transfer to another bowl). Mrs. Banini described that when she had attempted to make *agbametadi* in a blender, the texture was completely transformed: *Blender na agbametadi woa kpotoo* (The blender made the *agbametadi* foamy). Such a light, airy consistency rendered *agbametadi* unappetizing.

Akple was traditionally eaten with the hands – you broke off a piece of the hot, doughy ball and dipped it into a peppery sauce or stew. During the colonial era, cutlery became more common, and Mr. Sorkpor reported that in boarding school (run by the Bremen missionaries) the students were compelled to eat with knife, fork, and spoon. Whenever the tutors were not looking, however, the students would seize the opportunity to throw away the cutlery and eat with their hands. Mr. Zikpi expressed recently that when consuming either boiled rice or porridge, he usually used a spoon, but for most foods – *akple*, *fufu*, *kenkey, abolo, yake yake* – he much preferred eating with his hand. He explained that when using his hand he felt he was truly eating for good health; he would get a special feeling that the blood in his veins was responding to his ingestion of food. He stated that if he used his fingers to take hot *akple*, he would feel the heat the moment he touched it, which produced the sensation that the food was already entering his body. By contrast, with a spoon, he did not really know he was eating the morsel until it dropped into his mouth. Mrs. Vuvor echoed this sentiment by looking at us incredulously when we suggested eating *akple* with a fork or spoon, and Mrs. Banini, too, laughed at the very notion. Mr. Zikpi reported that eating soup with a spoon, piece by piece, left him feeling as though he had not eaten at all.

Tactility and the use of one's hands also figured prominently in our discussions of drinking from a calabash. Drinking water (*zemetsi*) was traditionally stored in a large covered clay pot, the calabash set upside down on top of the lid. Mrs. Vuvor described how approximately once a month, she would carefully clean the pot by placing it upside down over coals. If you did not put it on the fire, then you at least had to set it in the hot sun, she explained, otherwise the bottom of the pot would become soft, with mud forming in your drinking water. Mrs. Ablewor described the same procedure, and explained that she often burned herbs in the clay pot. The oil from the herbs would seep into the clay, creating a pleasant aroma and making the *zemetsi* much tastier, according to Mrs. Ablewor.

Mr. Sorkpor reflected that while he might take the same amount of water from a drinking glass, the experience of taking it from a calabash was qualitatively different. An Anlo person would have the proclivity to reach for a calabash when drinking water in the same way a leech (*ahor*) would take to your skin, he explained. And just as the linguist would not laugh at the chief even when he stumbled, Mr. Sorkpor instructed, *Tre me dzea anyi agba kona o* – the earthenware plate should not laugh at the calabash (which is superior).

Using a calabash to drink water produced a sense of satisfaction (*dzidzeme* or *nudzedze*), and this wholehearted satisfaction was linked to the use of two hands. It reminded Mr. Zikpi, therefore, that during *vihehedego* (the naming or outdooring ceremony for newborns) the family or lineage elders declared, *Eva kple alo deka, mie xowo kple alo ve.* This meant, "You came with one arm, and we welcomed or received you with both arms" – signifying a wholehearted welcome (*miexowo dzifaa*). Taking something with one hand was dangerous, Mr. Zikpi explained, whereas when holding something with two hands, the safety and balance of the thing was guaranteed. Two hands provided a feeling of wholeness to what you were doing, Mr. Zikpi explained – be it drinking from a calabash, taking light soup from a *wegba*, or welcoming and receiving a newborn.

The pleasure of balance is probably universal as it stems from an inherently embodied experience (cf. Lakoff and Johnson 1999:291, on balance as a source domain for moral metaphors). But why an Anlo-Ewe cultural model of balance instantiates the desire to drink with two hands can be better understood through reference to the foundational schema of *seselelame*. Mr. Sorkpor described how using your hands for drinking and eating was like responding to *dzodzome* (providence or nature): you felt actively involved, your spirit was closer to the substance you were ingesting. He stated, *Enabe nakpo dzidzeme le nududuame*: It makes you draw satisfaction from eating the food. *Dzidzeme* literally meant the heart felt at ease, or it gave you your heart's desire. Drinking glasses, porcelain plates, and cutlery threatened radical alteration if not erasure of these sensations. Mr. Zikpi claimed that you felt as if you were actually doing something when using both hands: you felt sensations of wholeheartedness (*dzifaa*) and satisfaction (*dzidzeme* or *nudzedze*). Mrs. Banini used these same phrases to describe how she would instruct her students about what the complicated term *seselelame* was meant to capture. She noted that it activated a sense of satisfaction (*dzidzeme* or *nudzedze*) through the embodied intersubjectivity of agents or actors. Here the idea is transferred to the commingling of humans with objects. Balance is the more concrete and specific expression of the deeper source domain of *seselelame* (feeling in the body, flesh, or skin).

The Feeling of How You Sleep

Many people in Anlo-land slept on a thick straw mattress referred to as *atsatsa*. Constructed of reeds gathered from the lagoon and then laid out in the sun in the shape of a fan, the dried reeds were bundled together, tightly tied, and woven into a thick mat (see Figure 1.6). When interviewing Mr. Atsatsa, we asked him how he came to be known as "Mr. Mattress." His great-grandmother's first four children all died during childbirth, so when the fifth was born they gave him a repugnant name (*dzikuidzikui nko*) of Atsatsa to ward off spirits that might take his life. *Atsatsa*, in those days, was used to wrap the corpse and place it into the grave (as wooden coffins were not yet common in Anlo society).

We then discussed sleeping habits, and Mr. Atsatsa reported drawing a great deal of satisfaction from sleeping on a traditional straw mattress.

Figure 1.6 Locally woven *atsatsawo* (mattresses)

He got the feeling that when he lay down on *atsatsa* his bones and body parts were well laid out; the mattress did not allow one's limbs and torso to curve and contour and create a sensation of damage. *Atsatsa*, therefore, allowed him to feel very relaxed and comfortable. In a similar fashion, Mrs. Ablewor explained that she also preferred the *atsatsa* over a foam mattress. The foam mattresses, she stated, gave you an uncomfortable feeling of not being safe because of the way you bounced up and down, whereas the *atsatsa* provided a sensation of solidity and security.

Similar to his distress over giving up a favorite cloth, Mr. Atsatsa expressed a great deal of emotion when we talked about the process of replacing his straw mattress. He explained that it was not at all rational, but when he felt like throwing away his *atsatsa* and getting a new one, it was an extremely difficult event. The *atsatsa* had become a part of him, he explained; his body felt very comfortable on it, as he had been sleeping on it every night for several years. He indicated that when he needed to replace his *atsatsa* he did it unwillingly, but something in his body (a feeling) compelled him to make the change. Sometimes the color had changed, or he felt that aesthetically it no longer looked right in the room, but more than anything logical it was just an overpowering feeling that prompted him to search for a new *atsatsa* and discard the old. The final act was to set fire to the used *atsatsa*, thereby killing any insects or bedbugs harboring in the straw.

From holding a calabash with two hands, and sleeping on a woven mat, the sensation of balance came into play in evaluations of the experiences. Elsewhere we have developed in more detail the analogical extension of balance as a physiological phenomenon to the metaphorical realm (see for example Geurts 2002a:144 on personhood and the ritual reinforcement of balance). Here we are attempting to better understand the endearing and enduring feelings that people have for these objects. In addition to the pleasurable sensations of balance, which are readily articulated by people throughout the world, with Anlo people we must also take into account the emotional-sensual "feel-feel-at-flesh-inside" (referenced by *seselelame*) that may be a source domain or foundational schema for the more concrete cultural modeling of balance. Let us turn back to several questions we raised earlier about consciousness and language.

Feelingful Language as Thread and Threat throughout the Black Atlantic

If our work with *seselelame* was merely a problem of language variation and translation, we might expect to find this term used in Anlo-Ewe discourse as frequently as "sense" is used in the English vernacular. But it is not. We have not actually come across the term *seselelame* in many written texts produced by Anlo artists, poets, or scholars, but one rare instance of it in print is from the opening pages of Kodzo Ayeke's book *Hlobiabia* (*Vengeance*): *Ne atiwo kata atro zu nunloti eye atsiafu ha atro zu nunlotsi go la, nyemate nu anlo nye seselelamenyawo kata na wo o.* This means, "Even if all the trees in the world were writing sticks, and all the oceans were ink, it would not be enough for me to express all that I feel inside my body for you (all the words of *seselelame* that could express what I feel for you)." This passage underscores our claim that *seselelame* is typically out of awareness; it conjures experiences not easily put into words. Inherently viscerogenic, *seselelame* comes to be known not discursively, per se, but through its instantiation in diverse cultural models that cross-map and interpenetrate.

For example, in black Atlantic contexts relationships among words, feelings, and sounds are put together differently than in communicative contexts associated with Euro-America. Well documented is the prominence of the acoustic in various verbal arts throughout the African continent (see Peek 1994), as well as the ways in which African music can be understood as derived from language (Chernoff 1979). Kofi Agawu's (1995) rich soundscape of a northern Ewe village illustrates how narrative, dance, drumming, language, and song all interrelate – drawing our attention to the musicality and rhythm of a tonal language such as Ewe. Paul Stoller (1989) has demonstrated how in many West African contexts speech is believed to have a power and energy independent of its referential qualities (also see Geurts 2002b:190–4). In fact, we would suggest that in many African and black Atlantic contexts *speech is bodied forth* rather than cerebrally confined. An emphasis is often placed not so much on what you say but on how you say it. For Anlo-Ewe, at least, the distinction made in Western contexts between discursive and nondiscursive (mind versus body) does not work well, thus repositioning the whole relationship between embodied experience and meaning (see the example of *lugulugu* in Geurts 2002a:74–8). With speech exhibiting such multisensory characteristics, it becomes all the more imperative that we attend to what Gilroy identifies as the "dramaturgy, enunciation, and gesture" or "pre-and anti-discursive constituents of black metacommunication" (1993:75).

How then does our employment of *seselelame* help us to make sense of colonial encounters in southeastern Ghana? We have suggested that attending to *seselelame* opens a window on structures of feeling that go back in time in Anlo-Ewe worlds, and that it was certainly at play as Anlo people forged social relations with slave traders, missionaries, and colonial officials. This suggests that colonial meetings represented encounters not just between different cultural logics but rather between whole different ways of configuring experience. Here we will review several terms that provide a glimpse into the ways in which Anlo-Ewe people mediated their perceptions of precolonial and colonial contacts with Europeans.

An Ewe word *yevu* was usually used to represent Europeans or Americans, and a distinction was drawn between these people and those referred to as *ameyibo*. *Ame* meant person, and *yibo* referred to the color black, so *ameyibo* was used to describe or represent "black person." These days, if you ask most Anlo-Ewe people under the age of thirty or forty what the term *yevu* means, they answer that it simply denotes "white person." However, *yevu* contains neither the term for person nor the term for white. Instead, it is a contraction of the words *aye* (tricky) and *avu* (dog). Coined at some point during the slave trade, or in the context of colonial rule, this representation captured a feelingful perception Anlo-Ewe people held of those Europeans with whom they were in contact.

To this day, objects or things associated with Euro-American ("white") society are labeled with the term *yevu*. *Godui* – a female undergarment or loin cloth – has given rise to *yevugodui* for sewn or Western-style panties. *Abolo* is the term for a corn and cassava flour bread that has traditionally been steamed. Baked loaves of wheat-flour bread are called *yevubolo*. The point is that while most people do not reflect on the fact that they are saying "tricky dog panties" and "tricky dog bread" when uttering *yevugodui* and *yevubolo*, the poetics and significance are there for those who consider the deeper meaning. We can think of them as snapshots, or a kind of West African haiku, encoding perceptions from a particular historical moment when Anlo people were trying to make sense of their own sensations.

A second term – *akpeteshi* – serves to make a similar point about capturing certain feelings and perceptions evoked during colonization. The word refers to locally distilled alcohol, as distinct from commercially produced or imported gins or beers. This particular spelling and pronunciation – *akpeteshi* – is an Ewe word and refers mainly to brews made of sugarcane and produced in the Volta Region. But this Ewe term is a contraction and a modification of a phrase originally coined in the Ga language: *Ya kpata shishi* (Go under the shed). The colonial administration banned the local production of alcohol – while simultaneously allowing the importation of beer such as that described by Mrs. Vuvor. When people wanted locally distilled liquor, they would ask those who brewed it, "Do you have the stuff?" The customary reply was, "Go under the shed" and "You will find it hidden over there." *Akpeteshi* poetically captures this specific colonial experience and encodes cultural memories of having to take the local drink in secret. *Ahanonko* (a drinking name) does this same kind of work: crystallizing and then referencing a particularly powerful sensual-emotional moment in time.

The kind of verbal play highlighted here is known throughout the black Atlantic as Signifyin(g). In *The Signifying Monkey*, Gates points out (1988:xxiii) that "to rename is to revise, and to revise is to Signify," and he stresses that signifyin(g) essentially involves repetition with revision. Typically in African languages "the word for 'stranger' is the same as the word for 'guest'" (Chernoff 1979:158), but while Anlo people may have initially accorded European strangers the status of guests, revised perceptions led to renaming them *yevu* – thereby signifyin(g) Anlo people's sensations of consorting with "tricky dogs." What does this amount to or mean? It concerns the ways in which people give voice to sensations and feelings. In Anlo-Ewe contexts we have found that *seselelame* underlies a sentiment characterized by a profound attentiveness to feeling, intersubjectivity, full-bodied speech (in the form of proverbs, drinking names, signifyin(g), and so forth), and the interrelationship of sensation, emotion, and consciousness.

Elsewhere we have described how with *seselelame* integration of processes is valued so that a direct connection is perceived between ways of moving, sensations of motion, how you think and speak, your disposition and moral character (Geurts 2002b). Furthermore, with *seselelame* we are confronted with not only the nonuniversality of the five-senses model, but also with an Anlo theory of the nature of being and an Anlo theory of knowing which thoroughly and completely links knowledge and reason, along with the development of morality and identity, to the body and to feelings in the flesh. There is a fleshly consciousness in *seselelame* that suggests a sort of unique link between sensation, emotion, and language.

Earlier we claimed that colonial meetings brought about encounters not just between different cultural logics, but rather between whole different ways of configuring experience because meaning is not what we Westerners take it to be. Meaning in black Atlantic contexts involves an intermingling of body, language, and feelingful signification which is upsetting to all of those terms. It is not so much *what* you say (not the words themselves), but the *way* you say them – the spirit and feeling bodied forth through the words. Discourse is *of the body* as much as it is *of the mind*, which Anlo society brilliantly demonstrates in the production and performance of *ahanonko* (drinking names).

In *The Power of Feelings*, Nancy Chodorow reminds us that recognition of emotion and feeling poses a great threat (intrapersonally as well as socially). In a poignant anecdote she describes how one analysand (client) was so fearful of trying to claim his own feelings that he had an overwhelming need to *"bleach* the feeling out of words, to hold his breath and be vague" (1999:271). Signifyin(g) enacts the opposite: there is nothing breathless or vague about calling the colonial master a tricky dog. It is a dramatic phrase packed with emotion and color. Though generally out-of-awareness, *seselelame* (feel-feel-at-flesh-inside) nonetheless functions as a foundational schema enabling emotion and sensation to be marshaled precisely *because* feeling poses a powerful threat.

One common thread we can trace throughout the black Atlantic, without implying parallel histories or cultural homogeneity, is the continual existence of structural (racialist) inequality that can always be palpably felt by those subjected to its power. Throughout this context, "black identity ... is lived as a coherent (if not always stable) experiential sense of self. Though it is often felt to be natural and spontaneous, it remains the outcome of practical activity: language, gesture, bodily significations, desires" (Gilroy 1993:102). Gilroy goes on to invoke an "anti-anti-essentialism that sees racialised subjectivity as the product of the social practices that supposedly derive from it." Social practices ranging from subtle putdowns to "racial terror" produced a "subjectivity" that drew on feeling (rather than repressing it), and cultural models spawned by the cultivation of such "feeling" range from the aesthetic and expressive to the political. In fielding the interaction and interference between bodily ways of knowing and language, the sensory-emotional is not bleached out but rather used in displaying color and asserting power.

Conclusion

We have suggested that as a foundational schema *seselelame* (feel-feel-at-flesh-inside) reflects Africa's legacy to the contemporary world. While *seselelame* itself is an Anlo-Ewe word, we have suggested that it refers to a consciousness that is arguably more pan-African than restrictively Ewe, and that it should be considered a possible source domain for such black Atlantic cultural models as signifyin(g), doing the do, an aesthetic of the cool, spirit work, conjuring, and so forth. By suggesting the possible existence of a foundational schema at work throughout the black Atlantic, we do not mean to deny local variation or imply some kind of genetic basis for the style of feeling we have described. Rather, we are invoking a complex though nonetheless real phenomenon sometimes designated as "blackness without blood" (Gates 1992:151).

In revisiting the archive of intimate objects (what we called a living museum of colonial encounters on the Anlo littoral), it was the introduction of *seselelame* into our discussions that allowed the interviewees to reflect on certain sensual and emotional experiences. These were everyday rather than prestige objects, and yet people readily admitted a powerful attachment to many of the items. The draw was not to their visual qualities or to their monetary worth, but rather what stood out were the enduring and endearing feelings that resulted from interacting with these materials. Asking them to think about material culture in relation to *seselelame* (feel-feel-at-flesh-inside) prompted Mrs. Vuvor's nostalgia in recollecting the first drinking glass she touched, and Mr. Sorkpor's account of holding his calabash with two hands. It allowed Mrs. Banini to imagine the pungent aroma of shallots when grinding them with tomatoes and peppers for *agbametadi*. *Ahanonkowo* (drinking names) surfaced as an unexpected object in our discussions about the feeling of what you wear. But it provided a powerful illustration of the blending of language, consciousness, materiality, and meaning that emerges when we attend to cultural models spawned by the foundational schema of *seselelame*. We can conclude that for Anlo-Ewe people, bodily ways of knowing were undoubtedly as powerful as cognitive and discursive ways of making sense in colonial Africa. Congruences between the role of *seselelame* in Anlo-Ewe accounts of the past and in other sensory histories from the black Atlantic are yet to be explored.

References

Abrahams, Roger D. 1983. *The Man-of-words in the West Indies: Performance and the Emergence of Creole Culture*. Baltimore: Johns Hopkins University Press.

Agawu, Kofi. 1995. *African Rhythm: A Northern Ewe Perspective*. Cambridge: Cambridge University Press.

Akyeampong, Emmanuel Kwaku. 1996. *Drink, Power, and Cultural Change: A Social History of Alcohol in Ghana, c.1800 to Recent Times*. Portsmouth, NH: Heinemann.

———. 2001. *Between the Sea and the Lagoon: An Eco-social History of the Anlo of Southeastern Ghana c.1850 to Recent Times*. Oxford: James Currey.

Ameka, Felix K. 2002. "Cultural Scripting of Body Parts for Emotions: On 'Jealousy' and Related Emotions in Ewe." *Pragmatics and Cognition* 10: 27–55.

Avorgbedor, Daniel K. 1983. "The Psycho-social Dynamics of Ewe Names: The Case of Ahanonko." *Folklore Forum* 6: 21–43.

Ayeke, Kodzo. 1989 [1973]. *Hlobiabia*. Accra: Bureau of Ghana Languages.

Baker, Houston A. 1991. *Workings of the Spirit: The Poetics of Afro-American Women's Writing*. Chicago: University of Chicago Press.

Chernoff, John Miller. 1979. *African Rhythm and African Sensibility: Aesthetics and Social Action in African Musical Idioms*. Chicago: University of Chicago Press.

Chodorow, Nancy J. 1999. *The Power of Feelings: Personal Meaning in Psychoanalysis, Gender, and Culture*. New Haven, CT: Yale University Press.

Comaroff, Jean. 1996. "The Empire's Old Clothes: Fashioning the Colonial Subject." In *Cross-cultural Consumption: Global Markets, Local Realities*, ed. David Howes. London and New York: Routledge.

Gates, Henry Louis. 1987. *Figures in Black: Words, Signs, and the "Racial" Self*. New York: Oxford University Press.

——. 1988. *The Signifying Monkey: A Theory of African-American Literary Criticism*. New York: Oxford University Press.

——. 1992. *Loose Canons: Notes on the Culture Wars*. New York: Oxford University Press.

Geurts, Kathryn Linn. 2002a. *Culture and the Senses: Bodily Ways of Knowing in an African Community*. Berkeley: University of California Press.

——. 2002b. "On Rocks, Walks, and Talks in West Africa: Cultural Categories and an Anthropology of the Senses." *Ethos* 30(3): 178–98.

Gilroy, Paul. 1993. *The Black Atlantic: Modernity and Double Consciousness*. Cambridge, MA: Harvard University Press.

Greene, Sandra E. 2002. *Sacred Sites and the Colonial Encounter: A History of Meaning and Memory in Ghana*. Bloomington and Indianapolis: Indiana University Press.

Lakoff, George, and Mark Johnson. 1999. *Philosophy in the Flesh: The Embodied Mind and its Challenge to Western Thought*. New York: Basic Books.

Peek, Philip M. 1994. "The Sounds of Silence: Cross-world Communication and the Auditory Arts in African Societies." *American Ethnologist* 21(3): 474–94.

Shore, Bradd. 1996. *Culture in Mind: Cognition, Culture, and the Problem of Meaning*. New York: Oxford University Press.

Stoller, Paul. 1989. *The Taste of Ethnographic Things: The Senses in Anthropology*. Philadelphia: University of Pennsylvania Press.

Thompson, Robert Farris. 1966. "An Aesthetic of the Cool: West African Dance." *African Forum* 2(2): 85–102.

two

Studio Photography and the Aesthetics of Citizenship in The Gambia, West Africa

Liam Buckley

A house is first and foremost a geometrical object, one which we are tempted to analyze rationally. Its prime reality is visible and tangible, made of well-hewn solids and well-fitted framework. It is dominated by straight lines, the plumb line having marked it with its discipline and balance. A geometrical object of its kind ought to resist metaphors that welcome the human body and the human soul. But transposition to the human plane takes place immediately whenever a house is considered a space for cheer and intimacy, space that is supposed to condense and defend intimacy.

Bachelard, *Poetics of Space*

In The Gambia, West Africa, studio photographers practice a style of portraiture that depicts the sitter within a parlor (see Figure 2.1). Sometimes, a person will visit a studio known to look like a parlor. On other occasions, the photographer will leave his studio and walk to a nearby compound, responding to an invitation to photograph a client in an "actual" parlor. In both locations, the arranged environment contains the same items – air fresheners, the sofa, the chair, the table, the telephone, the lacework hanging over the back of the sofa, over the arm rests of the chair, over the top of the table, the curtains hanging on the wall, the television set, the radio, the calendar on the wall. Studios look like parlors and parlors look like studios.

Figure 2.1 Parlor portrait, purchased in Banjul, The Gambia, 2000

The photographers' clients describe the experience of appearing in a parlor with the expression "*ya ma sagal*," meaning "you make me feel cherished." Indeed, clients often choose "*ya ma sagal*" as a caption for their portraits to be inscribed at the bottom of the photograph.[1] In a wider cultural context, this feeling of being cherished usually occurs when one receives a treasured gift, and has a double connotation – in receiving the gift as an honored recipient, the person feels luxurious and gift-like. Cherished and portrayed people sense that they are elegant as they engage a relationship of intimacy and trust with their material environment. In turn, elegant surroundings generate the experience of comportment within the sitters' bodies and the sense of being well composed. As such, portraiture distributes people in a visual field of tension with the world, and makes them look taut in the same way that the tuned guitar string is taut. The photography involved in this portraiture is not merely a visual process but also a phenomenological and nondiscursive position that links the visual to other sensory registers, including the embodied emotion of elegance.

Parlors in The Gambia have not always been elegant places. My elder hosts told me: "We had them [parlors in the past], but not like today, not all the furnishings that there is today – just wooden chairs, a table … but no lace, no television sets obviously." This chapter, then, considers the genealogy of the parlor aesthetics and sensations, and how portrait studio layouts have reflected changes in the types of environment that lend themselves to the bearing of elegant appearance in The Gambia. According to what social dynamics does elegance currently inhabit parlors? With what sensibilities and interpretative practices have people looked for and located the potential for elegant appearance since the end of colonialism? What is the globalized modernity and postcoloniality of the social relations constituted through the materiality of elegance in parlors and studios? Analyses of African styles of arranging domestic space have tended to process household data as indicative of cosmological, traditional, and kin-based realms of life sealed off from other categories of social experience (see Fortes 1949; Douglas 1972; Cunningham 1973; Kent 1990). Developing on this work, I examine the practice of arranging elegant settings as a record of how Gambians have *sensed* their experience of social change and political events occurring in a public world that is not so clearly separate from the private (see de Mare 1999).

The aesthetic that appears today in parlor portraits followed the colonial period and emerged during the early years of Independence (1965) in a space of "pure distance" (Foucault 1977) that separated people from the material culture and administrative instruments of decolonization. This disjuncture located people and their elegant appearances according to the photographic work of national census-taking in the late 1960s. On this occasion, two styles of dwelling, of letting-live and "being at peace" (*jamm rekk*) and two ways of making promises to safeguard life (see Bourdier and Minh-Ha 1996:xii), confronted each other in a place transitioning from being a colony occupied by the ideologies of imperialism into a new nation occupied by Independence. Gambian postcoloniality is a process of uprooting and relocation that has dispersed the creativity and tension of this confrontation across a series of arranged layouts – each one of which has been re-arranged in portrait studios by photographers who are always anxious to stay up to date and in fashion.

The studio names of the early days of Independence reflected the dynamic that related portraiture to the experience of living through social change. In Bathurst, the capital city, there was "*Tarru*," meaning, "to make beautiful," and "*Ifange*," a Mandinka term meaning "to look at oneself." Portraiture and Independence came together in the practice of making society look beautiful and encouraging a civic participation based on acts of maintaining well-groomed appearances. Today, the sensual folds and twists of lacework covering a sofa in a parlor, or the curl of an extension cord leading to a telephone in a studio set up to look like a parlor, manifest an account of how local standards of elegance modernized nationalism and Independence in The Gambia.

Occasions for Elegance

The sensation of being cherished, as experienced during the time one spends as a sitter in a furnished portrait studio – or as a honored guest in an elegant parlor – begins with an invitation: to look at the camera, to sit down and stay for a while. As such, the visit to a studio or to a parlor belongs to a category of occasion during which a person feels his or her presence to be desired by others, and in turn feels ready to be photographed. This category is known as *xew*, which literally mean a "happening" – the term is used in the greeting *lu xew?* "what's up?" These events include naming ceremonies (*nginteh*), baptisms (*botiseh*), birthday parties (*magal besi judu*), as well as "programs" such as nightclub dance competitions and pop concerts. People consider these occasions as suitable staging areas for portraits because, first, they are joyous occasions (*content xew*), and secondly, these are events to which guests are personally invited. Thus, a funeral (*daigh*) is not a *xew* and therefore not a place for cameras because the event is sorrowful (*nahal*) and because the mourner's attendance is not in response to an invitation, but to an announcement, made over the radio or in a newspaper obituary, to an unnamed audience of potential sympathizers.

The postcoloniality of being cherished places contemporary parlors and studios along an embodied aesthetic continuum that links portraiture with the administration of new nation building. The relationship between the invitation to be photographed and the feeling of being wanted originated during Independence and the first national census, which was the first opportunity that most Gambians had to stand in front of the camera. Since Independence, this invitation has been issued in a range of ways and settings. Whether the invitation is to appear in a portrait or to consider oneself a citizen, it is modern to the extent that it asks that it makes people feel *elegantly* at home and comfortable – that is, elegantly, not merely in an abstract manner, but in a way that has been strongly embodied and materially articulated.

Portraiture and the Elegance of Nationhood

One of the first studios to open after Independence (1965) was "Tarru," owned and operated by Ousman Njie. Njie had started taking photographs when he was in school in the 1940s – he bought some developing chemicals and a tank, and set up a darkroom in his bedroom. He painted the light bulb to dim it, and used bed sheets to stop light coming in through the windows. On weekends, when he was free from work, Njie would work on photography at his home until the sun went down, using natural light: "I didn't know the flash back then." The place where he took photographs, his proto-studio, was his bedroom. It was so small that people sometimes had to sit on the bed to be snapped. Eventually his client-base got too big for his bedroom, and he rented his first proper studio.

Most of Njie's photographic work was related to the establishment of the administrative infrastructure of government during the early stages of decolonization. By Independence in 1965, he was well known as one of the few professional photographers in Bathurst. In addition, he was a supporter of the PPP (People's Progressive Party) Government, and his uncle was the Minister of Foreign Affairs. With this connection, Njie received contracts to photograph all the Members of Parliament in their offices, as well as all the PPP candidates. His professional background was so respected that he would even receive contracts to photograph the opposition candidates.

The PPP government hired Njie to take the registration photographs for the first national census. Using a constituency boundary map, Njie traveled from village to village, following the routes previously taken by the Public Relations Office Mobile Cinema vans during World War II. Njie photographed the citizens of the new nation during the dry season, before people began to trade and travel from home. To the people in the villages, Njie's arrival in a Land Rover on official business would have been part of the stream of officials from the capital city making entrances in motorized vehicles, which dated back and formed a continuum of mediated encounters linking the colonial with the postcolonial.

During the daytime, the photographer could snap up to a thousand people in a large village, by photographing five people in a single print that would be later cut into five separate identification photographs. In the evening he would drive out to pay "house calls" on the older people who could not make it to the registration center, and to photograph those women who were reluctant to leave cooking fires unattended and run the risk of starting a dry-season bush fire. At sunset, Njie started to make his prints – he would collect his water at the well, and develop the film, using his electric fan to dry the negatives. Later at night, Njie ran his generator to power strings of lights set up around his Land Rover – this attracted the villagers and staved off his loneliness. Sometimes, the locals would take advantage of the unusual presence of lights and stage late-night wrestling competitions or have dances, attending in the good clothes they had worn for their pictures.

National census photography could only take place during the dry season – this was the time when the roads were passable and when people were not busy working in the fields. It was also the time of feasts and dances. The timing of the census raises the question of how people actually experienced being photographed for identity cards and how they may have reflected on the advent of Independence. If we conceptualize the census according to a metropolitan model that posits a relationship between portraiture and governmentality, then Njie's camera was part of the budding administrative technology of nationhood. However, if we privilege the local calendar to which the census necessarily submitted, then the camera contributed to a "festive technology" (see Bourdieu 1990:20). As such, the official photographer joined the ranks of exotic visitors who entered villages during this season and gave cause for further celebration – the masques, the itinerant traders, and the showmen wheeling magic lanterns. Indeed, the association of photography with festive celebration had a village history dating back a quarter century. For example, in 1941, the Commissioner for the North Bank Province reported on the joy with which villagers consumed imperial publicity. An exhibit of photographs, distributed by the Ministry of Information, provided the occasion for people to dance and sing, "The British are fighting with guns and beating the enemy, and all the time they are taking photos!"[2]

The act of being photographed – the full sensual experience and emotion of getting dressed, of feeling dressed-up, of assembling with and looking at others who were similarly well-dressed – mediated most people's first experiences of articipating in the administration of an independent Gambia. The occasion of this engagement with nationhood clearly conformed to the characteristics of *xew* – it was joyous and people's attendance depended on their being invited. That they were invited as *individuals* fitted neatly with the administrative rigors of census taking and citizenship. The modularity of nationhood – its capacity to be replicated in different settings – depended on its ability to generate analogues with local ideas regarding the forging of substantial relationships (see Anderson 1991:4). During the portrait work of the National Census, the concept of citizenship – the relationship between individuals and the nation-state – materialized according to an ethos of elegance which allowed people to feel cherished and wanted, and secure within their encompassing environments.

Elegance after Independence

How did the encounter with the administrative work of the National Census affect portrait photography in The Gambia? What did portraiture feel like after Independence? What were the possibilities for new sensory engagements with photography after colonialism? The census contracts bankrolled the first studios in the new nation and enabled the first generation of professional photographers to emerge. Previously, people had taken portrait photographs as a hobby that occasionally brought in enough money to buy more film and maybe a new camera. Their photography had not supported their families. Indeed, most of the people taking photographs were employed as civil servants whose work contracts prohibited any form of moonlighting or sideline work. This photography concentrated on the public life of the capital city as it prepared for Independence, focusing almost entirely on the lives of high-ranked men with whom the photographer was already socially acquainted. During the National Census, a city photographer such as Ousman Njie had his first experience of photographing people with whom he had very little in common. In contrast to the photographic work of the colonial period, women and people living up country appeared in front of the camera at the same rate as men and the inhabitants of Bathurst.

The most significant effect of the National Census on photography in The Gambia was that the burden of portraiture, like the concept of citizenship, was to make people feel cherished. Even during this period of state-oriented regulation, photography was not simply a matter of disciplinary surface description. Portraiture restored people to a state of grace that accompanies the end of colonial occupation. The portrait work of the census was national to the extent that it had been a joyous and celebrated occasion – to which all were invited. Still today photographers often name their studios out of loyalty to their nation ("Uprising Studio Ready to Serve the Nation" in Brikama), and to their provinces (Dandemayor Photo Studio in Serrekunda, Niamina Photo Studio and Cosmetics in Banjul, Jarumeh Photo Studio in Brikama). In the studios that sprung up after the census, photographers worked to arrange environments in which the sensoria of their clients could feel as comfortable as citizens might feel at home in the new nation. The relationship between the sitter and portrait photographer mirrored that of the citizen and the nation, not according to an affinity based on blood and honor, but on the embodied sensation of elegance.

The new studios shone out loud at night. As in the space around Njie's Land Rover, electricity played a central role in fostering a modern atmosphere of welcome and celebration in the studios that emerged in the early years of Independence. As an emblem of nation building, electricity enabled schoolchildren to do their homework in the evening under the new floodlights at the pier in Bathurst. The current also powered the lights and the record player that made a studio such as "Afro Beauty" owned by Peter Kwesi Adjei seem so appealing at night. In 1967, Adjei arrived from Ghana in Bathurst and worked at Darling's Studio, assisting his fellow Ghanaian with the darkroom work. In 1969 he moved into his own studio "Afro Beauty," snapping portraits with a Minolta 303 and 101V, and stamping the back of his prints with a palm tree logo. Adjei's fluorescent lights with filters made "Afro Beauty" the talk of the town.

The new sounds on the record player made people want to sit and stay a while. Adjei had an elder brother in Europe who sent LPs in the mail: Otis Redding, James Brown, Sam and Dave, Diana Ross and the Supremes, Jimi Hendrix, Marvin Gaye, and Wilson Picket. City hipsters, some wearing flared trousers (*fadeleph* "elephant leg"), some of them slicking their hair down into Beatles-style mop-tops, wearing winkle-picker shoes, would sit watching the records turn, listening to the sounds, reading *Ebony Magazine* and *Flamingo*. They listened to American music, to music from The Gambia: the Super Eagles, the Alligators, Los Candiceros; to reggae: Jimmy Cliff, Desmond Decker; to British music: the Beatles, the Rolling Stones. The Super Eagles would play at the tennis lawn near the house of parliament, at the Alliance Française, at the Adonis Hotel, at the Blackstar Bar and the Ritz Cinema. People on their way to a show would drop by to have their portrait snapped.

Locally, the "scene" at "Afro Beauty" would have been known as a *vous* (as in "rendezvous"). A *vous* has a life of its own independent of the business near which it meets. Today there are flourishing *vous* at long-established studios where little photography is being practiced. In these cases, catering for the *vous*, selling drinks and food, keeps the photographer busy and in pocket. *Vous* usually have a main activity. While Adjei's was a music *vous*, Malik Secka ran a chess *vous* at "Ifange." At a *vous*, a person could meet up with people from the same village, region, country, or a person who followed the same fashion style. Unlike a women's credit association (*kompin*) a *vous* requires no formal membership. A *vous* is regularly a male domain, a place to play games (*marrias*, monopoly, drafts, bingo, ludo), drink tea or liquor, and chase girls. Adjei's crowd was so well established that when the studio closed down, the premises immediately reopened as a successful bar, famous for its "good music."

The elegance of "Afro Beauty" drew on the excitement of nightlife, of dressing up and going out to clubs and restaurants. In addition to the space where Adjei actually snapped his clients, the studio had a dressing room, a darkroom, an office, and significantly, a sitting room where people could hang out. This "parlor" with its ample supplies of *kana*, a locally fermented moonshine, was a sensory meeting place for a series of elements that did not encounter each other in the daytime. At night, the studio was a demimonde of people from the provinces, the ghetto, and the city. Part portrait studio, part nightclub – "Afro Beauty" was a Bathurst exotic whose cast of characters included hipsters, single "walkabout" women of the night (*chagan*), criminals and ruffians from the ghetto, married men with their mistresses. In front of the camera, surrounded by the bright lights and loud music, a young man might be standing. He would be dressed in a suit and holding a suitcase, and in need of a portrait that would confirm his urbane status and raise him in status and marriageability when he returned home to some village in the provinces.

In "Afro Beauty," a hipster discourse traveling from across the Atlantic merged with a nationalism posited on the potential of each individual to feel elegant. As Adjei put it, the studio only wanted "the beautiful people." Sorcerers, crossing over from the North Bank on the ferry, provided the portrait photographer with something magical to wear around his wrist and his waist, and a solution with which to wash: "People couldn't just walk by without coming in. It was like love. Everyone loved 'Afro Beauty.'"

Throughout the 1970s and well into the 1980s, portrait photographers frequently returned to "their roots," and took government contracts to snap registration photographs and to produce candidate portraits at election time. This work always improved the cash flow of their businesses when work was slow. Back at work, photographers began to change the look of their studios. Today, photographers associate this period of change with the work of Mansong Dambele. Older photographers now claim either to have trained Mansong or to have refused to train him. The younger photographers will claim to have been trained by him or by one of his original trainees. While the older men today voice a certain skepticism regarding Mansong, the younger guys have nothing but respect for the man. Mansong is known as a rascal, as a photographer who knew nothing about photography, and as the man who established studio practice as it occurs today. He is the stuff of studio folklore. He is the photographer who wandered the streets of Banjul during the bloody coup attempt of 1981 snapping armed rebels, the dead bodies, and the burned-out buildings and cars; the photographer who sold these photographs to the Information Office and invested the money in his studio; the photographer who was scared of the dark and could not bear to develop and print images.

The major change in studio layout during the 1980s was the gradual removal of the space devoted to the darkroom. The time, energy, and resources that the photographer had previously directed toward developing and printing photographs now went into furnishing and decorating the space where his clients were photographed. From the beginning of his career, Mansong outsourced his printing. He got a job working at the Atlantic Hotel, snapping identification photographs for the staff, and would employ other photographers to develop and print his film. Mansong was thus able to give the impression of working very quickly and efficiently, to expand his business into larger portrait work such as employee-of-the-month photographs, and to open a shop in the hotel selling film to tourists.

Between 1977 and 1979, Mansong won a series of lucrative government registration contracts. With the profits, he established a chain of studios, known for their bright yellow decor and the uniforms that his employees wore – bright yellow shirts and black ties. During the 1980s, Mansong played a key role in the establishment of the country's photo lab system, working with a group of Korean investors. In 1987, Photostar Lab opened on Clarkson Street in Banjul, and printed all of Mansong's work, charging 2.5 dalasi per print. Anyone else who wanted pictures "professionally printed" had to go through Mansong who charged 5 dalasi per print. At first Photostar did some of its snapping in its own small studio set up inside the lab. In 1992, however, portrait photographers organized – Photostar agreed to shut its studio if the photographers agreed to use its lab facilities. In the same year, Saffideen Lab opened, breaking Photostar's and by turn Mansong's monopoly on printing. Furthermore, Saffideen offered different rates for "amateurs" and "professionals" that favored studio owners who declared themselves to be "Saffideen Photographers," and encouraged non-professionals to upgrade and find themselves studio space. The events of 1992 formally separated portrait taking from developing and printing, and led to an increase in the number of studios in operation. Photographers closed down their darkrooms and entered into client relationships with the labs, which began to fund studio maintenance and decoration.

Today, older photographers will show the marks on their hands left by the stain of developing chemicals as they talk about the days before the labs. Like the old guard in any profession, they poke fun at the rising newcomers. Old Pa photographers will ask their juniors questions about exposure rates and focal distance, and laugh at the blank looks they get in return. They will also comment on the fact that the only light in the studio comes from a candle, and that the cassette-radio is powered by an extended series of barely charged batteries. While the elders will admire a studio nicely arranged like a parlor, they will pour scorn on the fact that the studio owner would rather buy furniture than pay his electricity bill. In the mystique of the studio, flashguns have replaced studio lights. Today the shine of the electricity that inspired the festive atmosphere associated with portraiture during the National Census and in hip studios such as "Afro Beauty" is diminished and temporary. As with a power failure when the national utility company cuts the supply, the momentary flash of the camera is always followed by darkness.

Accounts of how the practices and sensation of elegance were affected by the lab system center on the emblem of the flashgun. For example, older photographers in Brikama think back to Koriteh 1988 and the last days of black and white photography when the first studio devoted to color photography opened its doors. Senegalese photographers had been traveling into The Gambia since 1986 to get people interested in color photography. The Gambian photographers of the time had little interest in working with color film. "As a professional, it was of no benefit to me," one photographer noted. It was rightly feared that color would completely replace black and white and make the photographer, who was used to making his own prints in his own darkroom, dependent upon the color lab technician. The first color studio had a big campaign that became the talk of the town by offering one free snap for each person who came in: "at night there was just a flash bouncing everywhere, it was just like Christmas." In the days that followed, there was a quick turnabout in people's attitudes to the black and white portraits. When people came into Doudou Jeng's studio, "Image Hunter," and saw the samples of black and whites hanging on the wall, they said, "oh these are local photographs, they're a thing of the past, let's go to the other studio." By Tabaski-time that year everyone in Brikama, it seemed, was going to the color studio, willing to pay for these new-looking portraits. Many of the established photographers were not able to make the transition into color and shut down their studios. When enlargers broke, there were no longer any spare parts readily available. Jeng carried on printing black and white for passports, but eventually ran out of developing chemicals and paper, and finally made the move to color.

Maintaining Elegance

A parlor is like a studio in that they both require continual upkeep. Householders and portrait photographers follow the same annual cycle of decorating and updating the appearance of their parlors and studios respectively. In parlors and studios, the sensorium of elegance remains keenly aware of the world as long as it is dynamic. People renew their material environments and the feeling of being comfortable in those spaces, following an eye for change that keeps up with fashion. The season for decoration follows a religious calendar, beginning with the festival of Koriteh that marks the end of Ramadan, and reaching its peak sixty days later with the Tabaski festival. During the two-day Tabaski festival celebrants slaughter a sheep to commemorate the ram that God had supplied to Abraham, as he was about to sacrifice his son.[3] It is a day of fine dressing, of extended visits to the mosque, for visiting friends, giving charity, and for having one's picture taken. In the two months that follow Koriteh, householders buy new furnishings for their parlors and new clothes for themselves. People increasingly dress up in the evening and walk out to their local studio to have their portrait taken in their new finery. In the meantime, photographers decorate their studios with new furnishings and get ready for the newly updated and beautified appearances of their clients.

During my fieldwork Koriteh fell midway through January (2000). Gambians – although mostly Muslim – enjoy participating in the festivities of Christmas. The possibility of a visit from Santa Claus is an exciting prospect for children for whom this old man is but one of the many masked figures that enter compounds seeking out naughty boys and girls and handing out treats at this time of the year. During the time of my fieldwork, however, Christmas Day itself had been a slow occasion as it was still Ramadan. Not long after, however, Ramadan ended and Koriteh began with added enthusiasm, as it was this year coinciding with the millennium celebrations. Dodging the masks that roamed the residential areas, children went door to door, asking for their Koriteh present (*salibo*). People attended a schedule of dances, grand shows, and sporting events that mark the celebration of Koriteh.

After Koriteh, people settle down to the often-painstaking job of getting ready for Tabaski. It is a process of calling on and mobilizing one's credit-worthiness – both socially and economically. In the markets, merchants draw on all the credit they can access to increase their stocks of cloth, household accessories, and furnishing. At work, employees ask their bosses for advances on their salary, so they can go to market to make the biggest buys of the year.

To decorate and arrange a room into a parlor (*sal*) is to "make up" a room, (*defaru*) – an activity that refers to both the application of cosmetics, and the activity of house cleaning and dusting. The contents of the parlor belong to the general category of *mobil*, ornaments or furniture that "makes the house nice" (see Figure 2.2). While the words used to name the contents of the parlor are of French origin, they connote a foreignness that Gambians associate more with neighboring Francophone Senegal than with any Western nation. Chairs (*cis*) and a sofa (*cis bu mag*), made of wood with fabric-covered foam cushioning, face inward toward the middle of the room. Linoleum covers the floor – it is easy to clean and to transport should the occupant of the household move to a different residence. In one of the corners, a television sits on a small table. Some lace covers the top of the television – it is pulled down over the screen during the day and at night when the room is empty of people. Some ornaments, maybe a framed photograph, face the middle of the room from on top of the television. On a shelf below the television, a VCR and a tape-rewinder. Lace also hangs in the windows, on the backs and the arms of the chairs and sofa, and on the top of low table in the middle of the room. On top of the table there stands a vase holding plastic flowers, an ashtray, a pen, a pair of glasses. On a shelf beneath the tabletop are some old newspapers,

Figure 2.2 Parlor, Serrekunda, The Gambia, 2000

lottery sheets. Along the walls, standing on the floor, wooden cabinets (*cabinet*), and cupboards (*armoire*). The cabinets usually lock, and the cupboards are often open to display the contents on the shelves. Sliding glass sometimes provides a transparent covering for the contents of the cupboards. Curtains (*gridox*) hang in the doorway (*bunta*), the window (*parenti*), and sometimes on the walls.

The days running up to Tabaski are devoted to the activity of dressing and dressing up. At the markets, the streets are awash with waves of cloth – cloth for new clothes, for sofa coverings, for new curtains. Traders hire drummers to stand on the street and draw people to their end-of-Tabaski sales (*wanter*) with talking beats. The sound of sewing machines fills the air, day and night, as tailors try to keep up with their orders for new clothes.

On the morning of Tabaski day families fill the streets walking in their new clothes to the mosque. After the prayers, the men return to the compounds to slaughter the rams. The older men will change out of their *bubbu* to avoid getting blood on the new cloth. The young boys remain in the prayer-clothes as they huddle around to watch the older boys and men hold the ram's neck over a hole dug in the ground at the back of the compound, and the head of the compound making the sacrificial slices. The women remain in their fine clothes all day. The younger women change from outfit to outfit throughout the day, displaying the range of their wardrobes as they would at an important birthday party. By the end of the day, all are dressed up again as they step out of the compound to visit the studio.

The period running up to Tabaski is also a time of excitement and some anxiety for portrait photographers. A month before the feast, I visited the portrait photographer Abdoulie Kanteh in Brikama, and complimented him on how well-stocked his studio was. It looked like an overflowing emporium of furnishings and household accessories – a TV, a sofa, various cabinets, some toys, plastic plants, a globe, photographs in frames on top of every possible surface. Looking around his studio, Kanteh just shook his head and said that the contents needed to be changed in time for Tabaski. His clients were already well familiar with the items in his studio, and he would need to update its look to keep their business. He showed me a new piece he had just acquired – a corner cabinet. He was trying to figure out where he could put it – there wasn't much space left.

The photo labs play a central role in rallying the photographers to meet the challenge of the heavy workload associated with Tabaski-time. After Koriteh, the labs announce the annual Tabaski competition, offering prizes to those who bring in the most film. The lab records each film that the photographer drops off, and give "gifts" as "motivation" – a free enlargement with each roll of 36 exposures (that the photographer can either sell or use to decorate the display window of his studio advertising his products), new cameras, free film, cash prizes. Sometimes photographers pool their films under one name in an attempt to win the big prize. On Tabaski day itself, the photographer will get up early, get dressed in his new clothes, and go to the mosque with his camera. After participating in the prayers, and taking some pictures of families in the prayer ground, he will return home to quickly enjoy the day's feasting and get his studio opened up for business. Vans from the labs visit the studios throughout the evening, and late into the night, picking up film to be developed and printed. Tabaski day begins the most intense work period for the labs in the photographic year. For the next ten to fifteen days the labs will stay open and be busy around the clock, never closing their doors.

I visited Muntaga Jallow's Hollywood Studio in Serrekunda the day after Tabaski. He looked tired but happy: he'd been busy with work until 3 a.m. that morning. On the previous day, he had opened his studio around 2.30 p.m. and had snapped sixteen rolls of 36 exposures – a total of 576 portraits, at a rate of 48 per hour. The van from the Saffideen Lab made its last film run at 2.30 a.m. and had awarded him a new camera for his efforts. His doors re-opened at 9 a.m. for the clients who were eagerly awaiting the arrival of their prints and for those who did not have the chance to get to the studio the day before.

The fact that Hollywood Studio, with its Beach backdrops, was not set up for parlor-type portraits did not stop Muntaga Jallow from taking many parlor portraits during Tabaski. Two children walked into the studio and interrupted my conversation with Muntaga Jallow. They delivered a message that he should bring his camera to a nearby compound. The kids followed us across the street and into the compound, crouching down and imitating Muntaga Jallow's poses as a cameraman. Jallow worked quickly so he could get back to his studio. The first shot was of a woman in her room – it was not strictly speaking a parlor, as it contained a bed. But the bed was nicely made, with new covers. There were photos in the glass cupboards of the bed's headboard, and the room had enough space for a cushioned chair. The woman sat on the elegant bed in her elegant clothes and posed for Muntaga Jallow who was holding the door curtain with one hand and standing in the doorway, as there was not enough focal distance for him to remain inside the room.

Muntaga Jallow moved on to the second household, stood in the doorway of another elegant chamber, and took three snaps – one of the woman, and two of each of her children. At the third household, he had to wait a few minutes as the woman prepared her baby. When they were ready, Muntaga Jallow positioned them on the ornate bed, and snapped them. At the fourth and final household in the compound, Muntaga Jallow snapped a woman with her two children – two portraits – one of the three together, and one of the youngest child sitting on his toy bicycle. Muntaga Jallow worked quickly and was soon back at his studio.

As this account of Muntaga Jallow's Tabaski parlor-portraits suggests, the space of the parlor is a flexible concept. Maintaining a parlor requires a luxurious use of space that many people cannot afford, especially when people need somewhere to sleep. In that case, the parlor may in fact be a bedroom – this does not detract from its parlor status. Not all bedrooms are parlors, however. The parlor, then, is not fixed to any one residential space. The parlor might be better understood as an attitude to decorating and arranging household space – that is, as a sensual space, where persons participate in specific sensory relations with the material environment. It would make sense, then, to step into the front room of a household, and see a parlor even if the room contained a bed, as long as the bed conformed to parlor standards: for example, if the bed had cupboards built into the headboard, and cabinets built into its base. What finally and crucially distinguishes the parlor from bedroom is the question of whether or not the room is a "photographable" space. A bed can be said to exist in a parlor if it were considered to be a suitable place to pose for a photograph, as well as a place that one would decorate for Tabaski. Neither the kitchen nor the bathroom – nor a "plain" bedroom – could be a candidate for parlor status. The parlor contains a transportable disposition that touches many domains of life, and is found not only in studios but in the lacework and air fresheners that taxi drivers place over their dashboards, or in the cushions and comfortable chairs that hosts of dances and funerals bring outside for their honored guests as they sit in the heat.

Parlors, Studios, and Postcolonial Sensoria

With their flashguns, auto-focus cameras today yield portraits prized for the way that the sitters appear to shine and look as clearly in focus as the furnishings that surround them (see Buckley 2001). The profession of portraiture has established environments that have become jural entities in themselves (see Lévi-Strauss 1988:163–88). In these spaces, portrait sensoria have explored ideas of obligation, association, and membership in terms of an idiom that describes what it is to appear elegant and in tune with one's surroundings. In parlor-like settings today, people sense the types of things and desires – modern, global, and postcolonial – they must engage if they are to remain feeling wanted.

Within Western popular tradition, the parlor is a room one step away from the world. It is a place for conversation and entertaining, as well as a site of possible mischief, where people tempt social norms by breaking rules when playing games. The category of social skill developed in the parlor – the parlor trick – fulfils the obligations of amusement rather than those of work. It is a social accomplishment that is functionally useless, and is thereby capable of stimulating moral outrage. The regularity and seriousness of the society of the world outdoors comes indoors only when it can shrink itself, become light, and serve as a game that promises delight and does not require professional membership or training – parlor cricket, parlor billiards, parlor croquet, parlor tennis, parlor bowls, parlor quoits. The parlor is by definition handsomely furnished, full of elegant coverings. People inhabit its comfortable circumstances, sitting in cushioned chairs, supporting the projects of modernity at work in the outdoors (politics, social movements, anthropology) without having to participate directly – a parlor Socialist, a parlor Bolshevik, a parlor Fascist, an armchair anthropologist.

In the world outdoors, commerce takes on the look of the parlor (see Benjamin 1999), when the consumption of some services depends on affording the customer the nonparticipatory feeling of being at home, on providing first and foremost the chance to find some respite along the main street from the pressurized world of goods. In these cases, storefronts open into interiors that resemble elegantly fitted apartments. Here, in ice-cream parlors, tanning parlors, beauty parlors, manicure parlors, massage parlors, undertaker's parlors, customers can cool down, drop their guards, and let out the visceral sounds of relaxation and release (sighs, a heavy breath, a loud sob).

For people in The Gambia, the parlor is an "exhibition room" (Aspen 1986:20), a place to offer an especially appreciated form of hospitality (*teranga*) that is based mainly on the activity of showing (*woon*) and inviting the guest to see what is on display in this front stage. An appreciative guest will say "*chalit la*," a statement of gratitude that anticipates the future presence of *chalit* – the thing (an umbrella or a bag for example) that one leaves behind during the first visit – that necessitates a return trip. At all times, the host carefully manages the guest's viewing experience (see Rosselin 1999). Upon entering, the guest is able to see a level of display immediately open to anyone in the room – the furnishings, and the pictures, calendars, and photographs on the walls. At first there is little chance for the guest to inspect the display very closely. The good host, following etiquette, will almost immediately ask him to sit down (*toggal!*).

The guest participates in a second level of display when the host decides to turn on the TV set (first lifting up the lace covering) or to play a video. Another, more intimate form of display begins when the host offers the guest photograph albums for viewing, and the chance to listen to the narratives of travel, parties, dances, and previous visitors which accompany the images:

> The host's eldest sister, his eldest brother now in Angola, a shot of a woman sitting on a sofa in a parlor with a telephone in front of her on a coffee table, two photographs – a man sitting on a sofa holding a telephone, in the second a woman sitting on the same sofa holding the same telephone – later these two people were married. A double page of six photographs taken during a naming ceremony, all taken in the parlor of the host's eldest sister. A photograph of the daughter of his eldest sister – "the one you met in my sister's parlor when you first arrived." A photograph of his mother on her return from pilgrimage to Mecca, dressed in her *Ajaratou* white, sitting next to the host's eldest sister in her parlor. (author's field notes 4/14/00)

As the narrative progresses, the pages of the album turn over, moving backward and forwards. The viewer sees more portraits and appreciates more links between those in the portraits. The connections start to build up. As an arena for display, the parlor serves as both a room to show photographs and a room in which to pose for photographs. The activity of parlor viewing ascribes high household rank to the person who appears photographed in the parlor with the greatest frequency, the person with whom others always pose for photographs when they visit the compound.

The parlor in The Gambia has only recently become a site for re-presenting the consumption of goods and services that promise and guarantee good taste and fulfilling sensations. The majority of television commercials promote Gambian businesses and products that people can only engage when they step out of their compounds – banking and shipping services, European-style supermarkets, kiosks selling lottery tickets, wrestling competitions, pop concerts at hotels and the national stadium, for example. During my fieldwork, only two types of commercials depicted Gambians at home. In the first, a woman who chooses to use "Jumbo," a ready-made vegetable cooking stock, enjoys an easier and more successful life as a wife. Two men – one the head of the household and the other a guest – sit in a parlor enjoying a large food bowl of *bennachin*, making appreciative sounds of digestive approval. The woman who has chosen to use Jumbo walks into the parlor and is greeted by her head-of-the-household husband who praises how well the food tastes, her "tasty hand" (*saf loxo* – the sign of a expert cook) and her status as a good wife. In the second commercial, a man enters a parlor to ask his host for the loan of some money – he has bills that are piling up and no way of clearing them. The head of the household welcomes him in, asks him to sit down, but does not agree to the loan. Instead the host reminds his friend of the relative who now lives abroad, and suggests that he contacts this person and ask him to send some money via Western Union. The procedure is easy and a representative from Western Union will call when the money arrives. The call will most likely come though on the telephone located in the parlor where the two men are sitting. Although the host will not lend his friend money, he will presumably allow him to use his private telephone line.

According to the imagined world of these commercials, the parlor is a site linked to a global network of goods and finance, where Gambian cooking can become modern as long as it does not alter perceived gender relations or the taste of good food, and where information and banking technology do not defeat local systems of credit but serve to extend them out across the Atlantic (there's no suggestion of borrowing from a bank). The parlor is an anchor point – a place where you can feel welcomed, sit comfortably, and think about people who have gone away and where calls can come in. It is also a point of no departure, the last stop on the line, a trap. While Gambians can receive money from abroad, they cannot reciprocate – Western Union does not have the facilities to send money out of The Gambia.

Traces of the past bureaucratic encounters that established the present parlor aesthetic remain settled, like the dust that historically enters the household with the advent of modern furnishing (see Mumford 1961:383). A colonial residue laminates some of the feeling of belonging and being cherished that lies in the soul of the parlor. For example, it is common for people to write a "welcome" in the inside cover of a photograph album. The invitation to view a collection of snaps is usually administrative and legislative in tone, and written in upper case: "Attention! Attention! For your information, look at the card or picture to your satisfaction. But do not remove any card please. By Order. Thanks," "Please do not remove any picture from this album until you are told. By Order," and "Visit the pages but never pull out any card without permission. By Order." A signature always accompanies the instructions, lending the authority of ownership that belongs to the individuated and named resident.

Modern techniques of administrative individuation (i.e. fingerprinting, identification cards and photos, census reporting) appear in the parlor in recently emerged forms of courtship and romance, designed explicitly to make a loved-one feel cherished. Valentine's Day is a new feast in The Gambia and is not widely celebrated. Young people, however, wishing to stay hip and cutting-edge, buy locally produced Valentine cards, composed out of a montage of images and song lyrics (see Figure 2.3). A white rectangular space is always left open so that the sender can insert the name of the loved one. Valentine's Cards are always given to *specific* people even if the giver does not reveal his/her identity.

Valentines usually add their cards to the photo displays in their parlors, sliding them into the glass panes of a cupboard or an ornate bed. If the loved ones are not able to put their cards on display, they will often hide them in locked boxes under their beds. The cards themselves

Figure 2.3 Valentine card, purchased in Bakau, The Gambia, 2000

are often considered to be morally suspect in both their function and their content. For parents in The Gambia, the discovery of Valentine's cards and other photographs locked up under an adolescent's bed is a cause for great concern – in much the same way that the discovery of drugs, weapons, pornography, or contraception might disturb parents in the West. Fathers will look at the Valentine cards, shaking their heads, and disapprove of the design in terms of a specific model of sociality: "They must be made by Nigerians or Senegalese. The design is just there to catch people's attention." Mothers will look at the two people depicted in the card and say: "hmm these people, I don't know who they are. I don't think they don't know each other. Who would buy these cards anyway?" And finally: "I don't think these are people. The guy isn't human. He's more like a mannequin." To those outside this economy of love, Valentine's Cards suggest a dangerous form of sociality based on receiving of gifts from anonymous givers whose humanity is doubted even if they are surrounded by hearts.

Valentines Cards belong to a larger category of depiction known as the "love sign." According to popular imagination, these images function as the stuff of "love magic." In the city, people associate this form of sorcery with a breakdown in a model of family structure that generated relationships between men and women in the past without recourse to the idea of love and romance. The sorcery itself is associated with persons from the provinces who brought the magic with them when they migrated into the city during the 1970s and 1980s.

The actual content of the Valentine's Cards comes from television. The couple on the card are Marima and Sergio, who appeared in a Brazilian soap opera that was televised in The Gambia in 1998. The story involved a romantic relationship between a woman (Marima) from a poor family and a man (Sergio) from a wealthy family. Sergio's stepmother sends some hit men to kill Marima – they kill her grandmother instead. Marima is separated from her father who does not know that she is alive. Marima's father owns the hotel where she works. Marima and Sergio have a baby, and split up. Marima's father kills himself. She inherits his fortune...

The viewing demographic for this show consisted primarily of young women who followed the lives of the star-crossed lovers both on- and off-screen. (The actors who played Marima and Sergio were married in real life.) GRTS (Gambia Radio and Television Service) screened the soap opera at 7 p.m., and groups of women would meet in parlors to watch that night's episode. On the nights when there were electricity cuts (as there often were), the streets would be filled with women leaving their dark parlors and walking to visit a mutual friend with a television set who lived in a neighborhood that still had power. The fans collected episodes recorded onto videocassettes and wore t-shirts printed with the faces of Marima and Sergio. The show inspired a fashion style that season as young women wore dresses, earrings, watches, shoes, and handbags that all matched the outfits that Marima wore on screen. Presumably photographers must also have watched the show, for the images of Marima and Sergio on the Valentine's Card were snapped off the television.

Photographers tap into this market by assuming the persona of the Valentine lover. Many decorate their storefronts with hearts and with statements such as *Photographe, Photo'maah, Yamaacidoy*, meaning, "Photographer, photograph me – you're enough for me." (See Jamagen Photo and Video Studio in Serrekunda, and Saine Photo and Penda's Beauty Salon on the Bundung Highway, for example.) The final statement of anticipated satisfaction derives from a contemporary idiom of romance and would be the kind of sweet nuthin' that lovers would whisper to each other.

Young women fondly remember Marima and Sergio. They speak not only of the characters and the stories, but also of the importance of the camaraderie of watching the show and of shopping for the right outfit at the market. Around this soap, viewed in a parlor, emerged forms of prized knowledge and loyalty based on feminine consumption practices and styles of socializing, and most significantly, on the friendship that exists between young women. As a means of mobilizing a population to consider themselves part of an imagined community, the media in this case rallies an audience consisting of those persons – the adolescent and the female – who are usually left disenfranchised by the nation (see Sreberny 2000:75).

In their Western context, the rules of courtship were evidence of how the ways of the palace replicated themselves in the private domestic interiors of people's homes. Through their sensory engagement with the materiality of furnishings and decorations, people in Gambian parlors explore modern forms of authority and engage modern questions of allegiance – however, it is not clear as to what is sovereign over that authority or sense of duty. While the administrative ethos of the nation might inspire the way that people sense themselves – emotionally and physically – to be wanted and cherished, it does not control the reverie of the parlor, or the way that thoughts and conversation always drift back to questions of what looks elegant and why that is important. Portraiture makes people feel beautiful according to the capacity of persons to exist intimately with their material environments. The loyalties and loves that substantiate the intimacy of this relationship – like the feeling of skin touching as friends hold hands – are not finally subject to the concept of the state. The call of the state – much like a prop telephone held in a portrait that may or may not be real (see Figure 2.4) – might be sensed but it need not be answered.

Figure 2.4 Beach portrait by Muntaga Jallow (Hollywood Studio), Bakau, The Gambia, 2000

Acknowledgments

The Wenner-Gren Foundation for Anthropological Research funded the research for material treated in this chapter (grant no. 6465). Many people have helped me in the collection and analysis of the presented data. I am grateful to George Mentore, J. David Sapir, Adria LaViolette, Carroll Ann Friedmann, Malick Seck, Ousman Njie, Peter Kwesi Adjei, Lamin Sanyang, Bob McEwan, Saffiatou Baldeh, Ndey Adams, Abdoulie Kanteh, Muntaga Jallow, Modou Jeng, Sahr Ellie; to the people of Adamskunda who welcomed me into their compound; to Redmond Tobin for always looking out for me; and to Stephen Amat Bahoum and Pa Segga Gaye – my uncle and older brother, who made me feel at home.

Notes

1. All terms are in Wolof, unless otherwise noted.
2. Intelligence Reports 1933–1942 CRN1/4 Commissioner North Bank Province Correspondence. Document 31 January 1941.
3. The feast is also known as Eid al-Adha (Celebration of Sacrifice) and Eid al-Kabir (The Great Celebration).

References

Anderson, Benedict. 1991. *Imagined Communities: Reflections on the Origin and Spread of Nationalism*. London: Verso.

Aspen, Harald. 1986. "Ghost Corporations: The Gambian Aku's Responses to Dethronement." MA Thesis, Department of Social Anthropology, University of Trondheim.

Bachelard, Gaston. 1994. *The Poetics of Space*. Boston, MA: Beacon.

Benjamin, Walter. 1999. *The Arcades Project*. Cambridge, MA: Belknap.

Bourdier, Jean-Paul and Trinh T. Minh-Ha. 1996. *Drawn from African Dwellings*. Bloomington, IN: Indiana University Press.

Bourdieu, Pierre. 1990. *Photography: A Middlebrow Art*. Stanford, CA: Stanford University Press.

Buckley, Liam. 2001. "Self and Accessory in Gambian Studio Photography." *Visual Anthropology Review* 16(2): 71–91.

Cunningham, Clark E. 1973. "Order in the Atoni House." In *Right and Left: Essays on Dual Symbolic Classification*, ed. Rodney Needham. Chicago: University of Chicago Press.

De Mare, Heidi. 1999. "Domesticity in Dispute: A Reconsideration of Sources." In *At Home: Anthropology of Domestic Space*, ed. Irene Cieraad. Syracuse, NY: Syracuse University Press.

Douglas, Mary. 1972. "Symbolic Order in the Use of Domestic Space." In *Man, Settlement and Urbanism*, ed. Peter J. Ucko, Ruth Tringham and G.W. Dimbleby. London: Duckwork.

Fortes, Myer. 1949. *The Web of Kinship among the Tallensi*. London: Oxford University Press.

Foucault, Michel. 1977. "Nietzsche, Genealogy, History." In *Language, Counter-Memory, Practice*, ed. Donald Bouchard. Ithaca, NY: Cornell University Press.

Kent, Susan (ed.). 1990. *Domestic Architecture and the Use of Space: An Interdisciplinary Cross-Cultural Study*. London: Cambridge University Press.

Lévi-Strauss, Claude. 1988. *The Way of the Masks*. Seattle, WA: University of Washington Press.

Mumford, Lewis. 1961. *The City in History: Its Origins, its Transformations, and its Prospects*. New York: Harcourt, Brace.

Rosselin, Celine. 1999. "The Ins and Out of the Hall: A Parisian Example." In *At Home: Anthropology of Domestic Space*, ed. Irene Cieraad. Syracuse, NY: Syracuse University Press.

Sreberny, Annabelle. 2000. "Television, Gender, and Democratization in the Middle East." In *De-Westernizing Media Studies*, ed. James Curran and Myung-Jin Park. New York: Routledge.

three

Cooking Skill, the Senses, and Memory: The Fate of Practical Knowledge

David Sutton

How, after all, did my grandmother acquire her culinary magic? It required an elder not just willing but determined to share her powers with a neophyte. And it required an upstart who craved to follow the path treaded by forebears. Is it possible that as much as my grandmother's eighteen progeny revered her, that none of them wanted to be her?

Stephen Steinberg, "Bubbie's Challah"

How might we think of ordinary food preparation as a site that brings together skilled practice, the senses, and memory? In reflecting on his grandmother's *challah* bread, Steinberg suggests some of the larger identity issues embedded in the relationship between people and their socio-material environment, in this case a set of relatives and a set of kitchen tools, flavors, and ingredients. He evokes an image of "traditional" cooking, without recipes, cookbooks, cuisinarts, or bread machines, but with the implied hierarchy of gerontocratic authority passed in a female line. He further suggests that loss of tradition, which is, in fact, a loss of particular *skills*, is a necessary part of becoming the modern, individualistic Americans that his family members aspired to be. Is this image, then, a relic of grandmothers past? How do people face the task of everyday cooking under conditions of "modernity," and what might this mean for issues of skill, memory, and embodied sensory knowledge, particularly given modernity's uncomfortable relationship to the "lower senses" and devaluation of "practical knowledge," "tradition," and social embeddedness. How have recent times – modernization – changed people's relationship to the various kinds of cooking tools, ranging from their sense organs (the nose, the tongue) to pots and pans, knives, even bread machines, with which they structure their kitchen environment?

Recent debates within anthropology and the social sciences more broadly have taken opposing views on the question of cultural homogenization and de-skilling. While some support the "McDonaldization" thesis implicit in changing relations of production and distribution that have allowed Western hegemony to extend consumer capitalism to the far reaches of the globe, others argue for an endless proliferation of individual creativity and cultural meanings and reinterpretations of Western processes and products. In a sense, however, the two sides may be talking past each other, one focusing on production and distribution, the other tending to put more emphasis on the endless diversity of consumption practices. Cooking provides an interesting, transgressive object in this regard in that its products are in some sense both produced and consumed in the home and nearly simultaneously;[1] indeed consumption itself (through tasting) is part of the process of skilled food production. Yet there has been relatively little research on consumption as not simply a creative, but a *skilled* process, involving judgment and the reasoned use of the senses. Memory is also a key concept to be considered, as it connects the senses to skilled, embodied practices through the habits that Steinberg suggests require apprenticeship and repetition, and through the comparisons necessary to judge the successful dish.

In what follows, then, I will consider approaches to *skill* in the context of production and consumption under conditions of modernity. I will begin with a theoretical consideration of the way skill and practical knowledge can be harnessed to recent approaches to the senses and memory. I then develop these ideas in relation to my own research on everyday cooking in Greece and in Southern Illinois.

Habit Memory and the Social Nature of the Senses

The senses are once again matters of theoretical and ethnographic concern, after what David Howes (2003:xii) refers to as "a long, dry period in which the senses and sensuality were bypassed by most academics as antithetical to intellectual investigation." But what does this mean in the case of "taste," perhaps the most ethnographically neglected of the senses? Taste, of course, has a double meaning in English, and in one of its senses, it has been explored by a number of authors, most extensively Bourdieu, who examines the ways that "good taste" is turned into cultural capital in the pursuit of class distinction. While Bourdieu is dealing with taste in the "social" sense, with people's "taste" in home furnishings, clothing, and recreation, he does in this context touch on actual practices of eating. "Taste" he says "is class culture ... embodied" (1982:19). With echoes of Lévi-Strauss in the background, and perhaps because he focused on a thoroughly "modern Western" society, Bourdieu argues that the middle class perform their freedom from need, necessity, and nature by consuming small portions of light, less-filling food, chewed carefully. While working-class (men here) shun such eating practices "the whole body schema ... governs the selection of certain foods ... in the working classes fish tends to be regarded as an unsuitable food for men, not only because it is a light food, insufficiently 'filling', ... but above all, it is because fish has to be eaten in a way which totally contradicts the masculine way of eating, that is, with restraint, in small mouthfuls, chewed gently, with the front of the mouth..." (1982:190). Which is another way of saying that apparently real French men don't eat quiche either! Connerton develops Bourdieu's argument in elaborating a notion of skill as fluid performance. For the European nobility (here in contradistinction to the bourgeoisie), such performance is evidenced in skills which *take time* to acquire (in a sense, like Steinberg's grandmother's *challah*), and cannot be simply reproduced or copied:

> To own a chateau or manor house is not primarily to display disposal over money; one must appropriate also the skill of bottling and tasting fine wines, the secrets of fishing ... the knowledge of the hunt. All these competencies are ancient, they can be learned only slowly, they can be enjoyed only by those who take their time, they ... require that one occupy one's time not economically but ceremonially.

For Connerton, the key point about such practices is that they are not simply signs which everyone can recognize, but skills, which few can incorporate into their bodies (1989:87, 90). Thus Connerton makes the dimension of memory more explicit than Bourdieu, referring to these skills as habit memories, "acquired in such as way as not to require explicit reflection on their performance" (1989:102). In the case of a fluid piano performance, Connerton refers to such skills as "a remembrance in the hands" (1989:93). Thus Connerton directs us to questions of enculturation and enskillment, the process by which taste is learned, mobilized, and repeatedly practiced, so that it gains the aura of naturalization which makes it such a critical marker of class distinction.[2]

But there is the other meaning of taste, that of a sensory experience, which is neglected, or at least not ethnographically explored in the studies above. How are we to approach that? I think a consensus (no pun intended) has begun to develop in studies of the senses that we are not dealing with radical cultural difference, but with shifting emphases, with cultural elaborations on a continuum of experience. How and in what ways are sensory registers elaborated in different societies? The study of taste or smell might lead one to look at the realm of myth and the afterlife in one society (Bubant 1998), in another to issues of healing (Rasmussen 1999) and to the domain of advertising in a third (Classen et al. 1994). In some cases a specific sensory domain may be elaborated to the detriment of other domains, and in other cases the study of one domain may by necessity lead into others, the phenomenon of synesthesia that characterizes many aspects of nonhierarchized sensory perception that has not undergone the discipline of modernity. I have also argued (Sutton 2001) that this focus on intersensory connection is a potential facilitator of memory, that the cultural elaboration of taste and smell, and their interconnections, can lead food, for example, to be more memorable. These parameters form a set of ethnographic questions for exploration. In studying taste and other senses in the context of Greece I have been led to focus on Orthodox ritual on the one hand and cooking on the other. In looking at Greek sense-scapes one must be attentive to both linguistic and nonlinguistic elaborations. Nonlinguistic include such multisensory practices as the Orthodox liturgy. "An Orthodox Church service is a synesthetic experience: every sense is conveying the same message" (Kenna n.d.:5; see Sutton 2001).

Linguistic elaboration of the senses takes numerous forms. One particularly striking one is the expression "listen to that smell" which is used approvingly to refer to the odor of food cooking, and is often accompanied by a noisy intake of breath through the nose. The opposite, to indicate the failure to taste a dish, is "it is not hearable," a seemingly direct appreciation of the process of synesthesia, even if coded in everyday metaphor. Other metaphors tie one taste to another: A man tells his friend that he ate prickly pears the other day and they were tasteless, but today "they were honey!" A woman refers to fresh-caught tuna as "souvlaki!" and a man describes a batch of sweet oranges as "banana." In these cases we have some sense of the basis for the Proustian phenomenon of remembering through evocation of a powerful sensory image. The sweetness of a banana hardly seems similar to that of an orange, and yet, as an image of a food with a strikingly sweet flavor, "banana" does have a certain evocative power. In these cases and others the sensory *intensity* of the experience is stressed, and used as a sort of aid in the storage and retrieval of memory.

Against this background of everyday practices, we can begin to understand the role of sensory experiences and sensory images in more extended social memories of the type mentioned above. But implicit in these sensory distinctions is our other meaning of taste as well: taste as the ability to judge and compare. Just as wine tasting involves the cultivation of certain practices, as well as an elaborated metaphorical vocabulary, the sensory practices of food consumption on Kalymnos mean that Kalymnians have elaborated schemata by which they can compare foods present with meals past.

On Practical Knowledge or Skill

Connerton and Bourdieu pose the question of taste as embodied knowledge or incorporated skill. Thinking about it in these terms leads to a series of questions about *how* such skill is transmitted, deployed in daily practice and in our relationship to material objects in our environment. To think about these issues I suggest we develop the notion of skill or practical knowledge through looking at recent work by Ingold in anthropology and by others working in the field of "activity theory." Ingold's work fits well with that of Bourdieu and Connerton, in that all three take as their starting point a critique of lingering structuralist assumptions that practice can be seen as the execution of a preexistent code. But Ingold is useful in situating his critique within an attack on modernity as a key source of the notion of abstract knowledge and the devaluation of bodily practice which has gone with it.

For Ingold, as for Connerton, skilled practice involves not the mind telling the body what to do according to a preconceived plan, but rather a mobilization of the mind/body within an environment of "objects" which "afford" different possibilities for human use.[3] Skill, then, involves much more than the application of a sort of mechanical force to objects (which he sees as the model of technology), but an extension of the mind/body, often through the use of tools, requiring constant and shifting use of judgment and dexterity within a changing environment.[4] The environment is not objectified as a "problem" that humans must "adapt" to; it itself is part of the total field of activity, as in the example of a woodsman who in chopping wood, consults the world with his senses for guidance, not a picture in his head. "The world is its own best model" (Ingold 2001:12; see also Lave 1988). It is through such skilled practices, then, that forms are generated, rather than through the execution of a mental plan, though mental plans may provide guideposts for practices, i.e., they can allow you to assess your work at various moments. This approach has implications for the transmission of skill as well, which, as with Connerton, is seen as impossible to objectify into a set of rules. Skill must be learned through the sensuous and sensory engagement of a novice with the environment and/or with a skilled practitioner. What we tend to refer to as "enculturation" is seen by Ingold as an "education of attention," or, as he puts it, speaking of his father, "His manner of teaching was to show me things, literally to point them out. If I would but notice the things to which he directed my attention, and recognize the sights, smells and tastes that he wanted me to experience ... then I would discover for myself much of what he already knew" (Ingold 2000:20). I would call this not only an education of *attention*, but of *memory*, a training of the total person into practices that make certain things and events in the environment memorable, just as Kalymnians are trained to attend to the specific sensory qualities of certain foods. Learning from others involves copying, but it is the copying of Connerton's "incorporation" rather than a transcription of knowledge from one head to another, of "guided rediscovery" (2001:11) in a sensorily rich environment.[5] One can see here why Ingold's view of skilled practice might be compatible with an anthropology of the senses. As with recent studies in material culture, Ingold does not view objects or the "environment" as passive ciphers to which humans simply add symbolic meaning (see for example Myers 2001; Miller 2002). Rather objects, because of their sensual properties, "afford" certain possibilities for human use, the semiotic and the material constantly cross-cut and convert into each other (and this is not a neo- or paleo-functionalism, as here once again there is no distinction made between "practical" or "functional" and "symbolic" use). Hiking boots, for example, by their material nature "afford" certain possibilities in relation to nature by "expanding the range of possible actions available to the body" (Michael 2000:112).[6] This in no way limits the meaning or uses of hiking boots, any more than recognizing distinctions between the proximate senses (taste, smell, touch) and the distance senses (vision, hearing) limits the cultural elaborations of these different domains, as discussed above. Someone somewhere no doubt uses hiking boots as candleholders or wine-decanters. But hiking boots also make possible certain new relationships with the environment, and it is these materio-semiotic possibilities that such authors suggest need exploration.[7]

Ingold's approach has certain strong implications for his view of "modernity," which puts him on one side of a more general debate within anthropology. Ingold argues that the abstraction of knowledge and the senses characteristic of modernity is counter to our social natures, insofar as it subordinates skill and the senses to the rational paradigm of plans and mental operations. Similarly, modern technology is seen as very different from tool use. A traditional tool is "not a mere mechanical adjunction to the body, serving to deliver a set of commands issued to it by the mind, rather it extends the whole person [into the environment]" (Ingold 1993:440). Modern technology, by contrast, disembeds the tool from a social context and a context of skilled practice, and treats the workman as a mere operator. If the tool draws its power from and extends the human body, the logic of technology's operation lies outside human bodies (1993:434–5).

Technology involves an "objectification of productive forces" (Ingold 2000:319), a disembodying and disembedding. In the same way modern society disembeds time from the task (in the Evans-Pritchard sense) objectifying it both in technology (the clock, the punch card) and in social practices (division of time into labor time and leisure time). This is part of the general process of "abstraction" of production, consumption, and exchange characteristic of modernity that has been well described by Carrier (1990; 1996; 1998). Ingold suggests that this new type of abstract knowledge and disembedded practice does not fully replace traditional skill, which exists both at the margins of modern society (housewives) and in what Scott would call the "hidden transcripts" of working practices, as people learn to "cope with" machines by refusing to follow explicitly codified procedures and directives laid down from above, but adapting technology to their own "rules of thumb" (Ingold 2000:332), a process he illustrates for railroad conductors. Ingold seems to be hedging here to avoid accusations of an evolutionary perspective from tradition to modernity.[8] It is clear that the overall thrust of his argument suggests the loss of something inherently human, i.e. skill, and a struggle against this loss.

In this regard, his view fits with other writers on technology, such as Baudrillard and Borgman, and of course Marx's work is the acknowledged Ur-Text here. Baudrillard writes of modernity's disenchantment of objects even more pessimistically than Ingold, because he sees this disenchantment as taking place in the home just as much as the workplace, in household appliances which work "with the touch of a button" (Baudrillard 1993:68).[9]

An alternate perspective sees less of a great divide between tradition and modernity. Or as Latour (1993) famously puts it "we have never been modern," or perhaps better "we have always been modern, except, that is, when we're not." Such a view emphasizes the way that human-environment interactions have always already been technologically mediated, and draws a less sharp distinction between "tools" and "technology" in terms of embodied practice and sensory input. Indeed, a recent collection on the anthropology of technology (Schiffer 2001) does not include "tools" in the index, as the authors in the collection make no distinction akin to Ingold's between tools and technology. Ihde, for example, in his philosophical meditation *Technology and the Lifeworld* (1990), eschews what he calls the "Edenic" approach to technology. The oven, for example is a kind of externalized stomach, a disembodying and disembedding technology that few cooks would have any desire to abandon (but see my comments on microwave on p. 96). Ihde notes that technologies often lead to an increased embodiment of the environment:

> The modern high-technology boat, precisely in its capacity to allow oneself to be embodied through it, places one more closely in tune with wind and water than was so through the insulated and dampened result in the resistance-to-maneuvering of the older wooden vessel. (1990:164)

One can, no doubt, multiply such examples. Writing, itself, as we know from a long tradition of orality/literacy studies, is less embodied than speech, but opens up all sorts of new possibilities of embodiment which come to the fore when writing is "threatened" by word processing, and itself becomes the more embodied, sensory technology.[10] "Digital writing supplants the framework of the book: it replaces the craftsman's care for resistant materials with automated manipulation" (Heim 1987). But as Ihde points out, writing does not disappear, and computerization affords possibilities that writing, in a sense, superseded: "Computer graphics are concocted imagery, a clearly designed *hermeneutic* imagery. They are the analogues of returning writing back towards a kind of pictorial representationalism, a reverse evolution" (Ihde 1990:186).[11] One could argue with Ihde that most of his examples come from the realm of consumption rather than production, particularly that of his fiberglass boat. Similarly, recent technological developments in the field of stereophonics has allowed many to develop new skills of auditory discrimination that might be similar to that of Kalymnians distinguishing the taste of different olive oils. But once again, this is a matter of consumption, and the kind of cultural capital and distinction that Bourdieu has analyzed, rather than the skill connected to productive labor, the process of making rather than consuming.

Suchman, a leading proponent of "activity theory," provides an important example, then, because focused on productive relations. She explores these relations ethnographically in her study of civil engineering practices. She expected to see a replacement of paper drawings with Computer-Aided Design (CAD) workstations in which an engineering application is layered on top of a graphics application among younger engineers. Each certainly involved different embodiments: the CAD was used with "elbows close to the sides of [one's] body, hands constrained within the narrow terrain of the keyboard, eyes glued to the screen ... [as opposed to] standing over a large sheet of paper, arms outstretched or hands and arms engaged in a variety of actions of drawing, measuring, turning the paper to get another angle" (Suchman 2000:12). She found, however, no such evolution but more of a hybrid situation in which CAD was used at some points in the process and paper drawings at other points. The CAD station allowed for easy access to an array of different parts of the project, thus it was better for getting a synoptic view. While paper allows a larger "meatier" view of the design, which allows better access for collective work, as well as better "memory" as different calculations may be left on the paper copy which would be deleted on the screen version. Suchman concludes that "rather than a simple progression from paper to CAD, the maturing of electronically based engineering practice may emerge as the informed, selective use of both ... based on a deepening understanding of their particularities [read: sensory, embodied aspects] and of their effective interrelations" (2000:14).[12]

The reader perhaps can see in this contrast of approaches another iteration of the "McDonaldization" debate, which has been taking place in different guises throughout the social sciences. Does one see a basic, detrimental shift, or endlessly new creative possibilities in the processes of change that mark our current global condition? How much weight does one give to issues of production, exchange, or consumption? And what are the political implications of these different approaches? Certainly Ingold's work allows for a more large-scale political critique which seems to be blunted by the more "hybrid" approach of these latter authors, who focus their political interventions on the small scale (the "projects" of actor-network theory), and do not take into account the kind of "structural power" that Eric Wolf (1990) has been so eloquent in drawing our attention to.[13]

In the Kitchen

How do these issues and oppositions apply to food and cooking processes? As argued above, cooking is interesting in part because it seems to blur the line between production and consumption, allowing for no hard-and-fast distinction, and implicating the processes discussed both by Ingold and Baudrillard, and by Ihde and Suchman. I believe these issues have been too long mired in stereotypes, and a bombardment of newspaper articles about the "end of cooking" or the "end of the family meal."[14] The only way to advance these issues is through sustained ethnographic treatment, an ethnography of everyday cooking. A number of areas of investigation seem to be indicated.

Cooking Tools

Clearly the above debate can be and has been applied to the tools of the kitchen, the contrast between Ingold's knife, extending the body and requiring considerable manual dexterity, as contrasted with the bread machine, requiring assembly of ingredients and a touch of a few buttons. The measuring cup and spoon is a different sort of technological innovation which does not disembody as much as it standardizes, another specter of modernity that I will take up later. The microwave is another such device that seems to de-skill the cook in relation to the traditional oven. But as with all these cases, the other side comes from studies of the "use" of these technologies, the way the microwave, bread machine, etc., in fact, require many reasoned judgments, new skills to manipulate (think VCR remotes here). The microwave and the bread machine could also be found ethnographically to be supplemental, as Suchman argues, good for some things, but not replacing older skills.[15] Finally, one has to consider the potential social implications, including the freedoms afforded by such cooking technologies to the intensive labors that traditionally have fallen on women (see Sutton 2001; Adams 1994; but see Cowan 1983 for an extended critique of this view). As material possessions, kitchen tools themselves may carry family histories and multiple, layered stories, is this also the case for kitchen technologies? These are some of the questions that my research hopes to address (see Hernandez and Sutton 2003a, b).

Plans and Recipes (and Their Transmission)

Ingold himself contrasts his view and that of Sperber in relation to the question of recipes. Sperber's view of a recipe for mornay sauce is that it is a prototypical cultural representation or meme that can be transmitted to others containing all the information one needs to produce the sauce by simply converting the instructions into bodily behavior. But as Ingold (2001:10) argues, such conversion is not generally such a simple matter, unless the recipe speaks to skills already acquired from melting, stirring, handling different substances, to finding the relevant ingredients and utensils within the layout of the kitchen (no mean feat, those of you with children untrained in kitchen skills no doubt know). Thus cooking from a recipe assumes a certain amount of embodied memory and "taste," in Connerton's sense discussed earlier. This goes along with the sensory components, from the kinesthetics of various cooking procedures, chopping, mixing, etc. to the use of the tongue and nose as "tools" to mark the progress of the dish and make the constant judgments and adjustments that are part and parcel of skillful cooking. The recipe may provide certain "critical junctures" in the process, but "between these points ... the cook is expected to be able to find her way around, attentively and responsively, but without further recourse to explicit rules of procedure – or in a word, skillfully" (Ingold 2001:11; see also Schlanger 1990). Planning itself is a type of "situated action" and plans are simply one among a number of resources for actions, which still take place *in situ* (Leudar and Costall 1996). It will be of small surprise to those who cook that cooking is best learned through embodied experience, or even apprenticeship (as it is in most societies, a fully social apprenticeship of a younger generation to a set of female relatives, in which one learns much more than how to get dinner on). But what this "experience" consists of has had minimal ethnographic elaboration. In other words, how do people learn to cook in different societies, who teaches them, under what circumstances, and with how much stress on observation, participation, positive or negative reinforcement, "play-frames," challenges to elders (see for example Herzfeld 1995:137)? There is a substantial literature on apprenticeship in anthropology and archaeology which has developed concepts such as scaffolding, distributive competencies, etc. (see Lave and Wenger 1991; Lemmonier 1993). Surprisingly, none of this has been applied to the homely craft of cooking. Another set of questions is raised by the *lack of* cooking apprenticeship that seems to characterize modern, or even more postmodern society, where transmission of knowledge from experienced elders to juniors is explicitly and in practice often eschewed. Once again, cooking seems to be increasingly socially disembedded if not disembodied, though we mustn't neglect new sources of cooking apprenticeship such as the ubiquitous cooking shows, socially disembedded and commodified, but at least engaging the sense of sight in transmitting cooking knowledge, and perhaps evoking other senses as well. What kind of implications does all this have for an Ingold-type approach?

To conclude this section I once again want to pose the question of whether there are new narratives to tell this story, which avoid the opposition between loss of traditional knowledge or recuperation and invention, especially when these narratives seem to have salience to my ethnographic subjects. One of the goals of my research is to find such new narratives, or at least new metaphors that would push us beyond the stale antinomies of the past (as Fernandez (1973) put it). Before turning to my ethnographic research it will be helpful to present a short history of cooking's relationship to modernity and postmodernity in the United States, in order to give a sense of how we have come to some of the current predicaments in our thinking about cooking, and, one hopes, how we might emerge from them.

Cooking 101: The Not Very Tasty Culture of Scientific Feeding

An offshoot of first-wave feminism, though going in a direction which seems to lead more toward Martha Stewart than it does grrl power, the development of the "domestic science" movement at the turn of the twentieth century is richly chronicled in Laura Shapiro's book *Perfection Salad* (1986). Here I attempt to present some of the highlights of this history to suggest some of the tensions that led to the present. Shapiro chronicles the rise of the domestic science movement at a time when "science and technology were gaining the aura of divinity: such forces could do no wrong, and their very presence lent dignity to otherwise humble lives" (1986:4, following page-number references are to this source), while "the nation's eating habits underwent their most definitive turn toward modernity" (1986:48). The women reformers who founded this movement were committed to claiming the prestige of heretofore "male" science for housework and cooking, to move cooking, nutrition, and hygiene into the public sphere in its importance for the nation. Thus the interest of the domestic science movement in food was "because it offered the easiest and most immediate access to the homes of the nation" (5). And through this scientific cookery, women would be able to alleviate not just malnutrition, but the key social problems of the day: poverty, worker discontent, alcoholism, and criminality were all put down to improper diet and improper knowledge of scientific householding principles.

In order to making cooking scientific, the women in the movement, initially associated with the Boston Cooking School, attacked "tradition," which included all kinds of things from the kind of transmission from grandmother to mother to daughter discussed above, to ethnic differences in food habits, to the home as a center for productive activity (see Carrier 1998). All of these past practices were stamped as backwards: women who hewed to tradition were labeled as "drudges," "stuck in the past." While the cooking schools they established, some to train servants and aspiring working-class women, some for the middle classes, did not ignore issues of skill and manual dexterity, they held the occupations of the mind and "theory" as crucial to their goal,[16] not just how to make a cream sauce "but the abiding reasons why heat acts upon starch in such a way as to produce cream sauce" (Shapiro 1986:68). Thus cooking was a science of the transformation of food substances to create the optimal nutrition, digestion, and hygiene. Standardization and measurement were key components of such a project. Indeed, Fannie Farmer, a leading figure in this movement, was known as "the mother of level measure-ments." "Exact measurement was the foundation of everything else that happened in the scientific kitchen" (Shapiro 1986:115). In this she was aided by the development of measuring cups and spoons in the late nineteenth century, which added a new precision to previous vague recipes for "a teacupful of flour."[17] Farmer added more precision by calling for "level" measurements, and dispensing with imagery in her recipes and cookbooks, such as "butter the size of an egg." She encouraged cooks to use a knife to level the surface of their measured ingredients for additional precision. There should be no "margin for error" (or imagination for that matter) in recipes, and she was known to specify that strips of pimento be cut "three quarters of an inch long and half an inch wide" and to measure out spices by the grain (Shapiro 1986:116). In all this she was guided as much by a business model of standardization as by the scientific model, as will be discussed shortly.

What was left out of this course in scientific cookery, of course, was taste, or any of the lower senses for that matter. The food itself was uninteresting except as a route to nutrition and to a better society. While this movement was hardly the first to see good-tasting food as problematic in American society, this had a much longer history tied to Christianity and notions of sin (see for example Mintz 1996 on the threat of ice cream to public morals), they were certainly influenced by this tradition, as well as one that saw middle-class women as a key force in taming the "natural" and "primitive" instincts of middle-class men and the lower classes in general (Shapiro 1986:73, 139).[18] Appetite was too low a sense to fit with the "nobler purposes" to which these women aspired (71). Cooking schools saw eating as problematic, and rarely allowed their students to consume their finished products; these were sometimes disposed of, or sold to the poor at cost. Food itself, was, in pure Lévi-Straussian fashion, brought under control by science and careful hygiene. Appeal to the sense of sight was permitted, and considerable imagination was allowed in decorating and arranging the food: shaping it into various objects, color-coordinating it, miniaturizing it (102).[19] The key was to contain and *disguise* food, to control its "volatility," and thus to make highly nutritious food *visually* palatable, to wean Americans away from their unhealthy reliance on fried foods, cakes, and pies. Even touch was seen as problematic, partly for hygiene reasons, hence the popularity of the innovation at this time the chafing dish, which allowed meals to be prepared by women "who hardly seemed to be cooking, so distant [were they] from the intimation of raw food" (103).

Fannie Farmer was an important transition figure in this movement, as her reliance on business imperatives – standardization and novelty – was much stronger than that of other women in the movement. The fact that she published so many cookbooks through her constant search for diversity, new combinations of ingredients and preparations, of course within the bounds of scientific principles (although she did tend to pay somewhat more attention to taste than many of her colleagues), perhaps accounts for her enduring popularity. The rise of the food industry in the early twentieth century, however, found a strong ally in rhetoric and in practice, in the domestic science movement. Novelty itself, of course, always has had the ring of "progress," as many of us remember from childhood bombardments of products promising to be "new and improved." Processed foods seemed to offer possibilities for sterility unavailable in individual kitchens. They also promised standardization in the sense of invariability, each bottle of catsup the same as the previous one, which was later one of the key aspects of the rise of the fast-food industry. Indeed, machinery promised to remove human hands and, once again, the senses or simply messiness from the process of cooking. One innovator of the time, in a prelude to the modern-day bread machine, introduced a series of devices that would produce bread "'which no human hand has touched from the time the wheat was planted until it was taken from the pan in which the loaf was baked'" (Shapiro 1986:151), leading some movement women to hope that "'home cooking as we now know it' would soon be a thing of the past, at least for city dwellers" (210). While these predictions have not all been borne out, Shapiro suggests that they were successful insofar as the home cook came to measure her culinary success "in conviction, not skill" (215). Indeed, well into the 1970s the popularity of the notion of "the meal in a pill" as the promise of the future (see Belasco 2000) argues for the long-term appeal of these ideals. However, the food industry and the domestic science movement parted company in the 1950s, when increasingly cooking was portrayed popularly as drudgery to be combated with TV dinners and "convenience" foods, involving not only a bodily de-skilling in Ingold's sense, but a loss of even the kind of theoretical knowledge of nutrition and ingredients which the movement valued. The homemaker of the 1950s was told that femininity and coy sexuality were the key to their husband's faithfulness; in the kitchen, she became an assembler, not a cook: "Scientific cooks had anticipated the era of culinary regimentation but not the intellectual collapse that would accompany it" (Shapiro 1986:229).

But in another sense capitalism's need for innovation also no doubt led us away from these ideals and to a present where flavor, in ever diverse combinations and "authentic origins," is once again on the menu. Shapiro does not document this shift, but suggests that the liberation movements of the 1960s also liberated our appetites to appreciate the sensory again (and to distrust the food industry). The ethnic revival and the rise of multiculturalism have also no doubt played a role, and many have written on the politics of "tasting the other." Much less has been written about this period in American food history, though the recent growth of "Martha" studies suggests that this is soon to be rectified.[20] Zygmunt Baumann sees the shift in terms of a larger-scale societal shift from concern for the "producer body," the soldier, the worker, to the "consuming body," the seeker of new experiences or "sensations-gatherer" (Baumann 1996:115) so amicable to a flexible capitalism. Whether this shift in taste practices was a result of the demands of capitalism or simply a "happy" coincidence is an open question. But Baumann suggests that the postmodern politics of the "Other" has some advantages over the modern. No longer is the "Other" (in this case other foodways) something to be brought under control, ordered, and normalized, changed beyond recognition, as the domestic science movement hoped to do for all "traditional" and immigrant foodways. The sensations-gatherer demands that the other be preserved in its otherness. The sensations-gatherer would have to be skilled at consumption, to have "taste" as well as "taste," as I have been arguing throughout this chapter. But has the sensations-gatherer irrevocably undone the link between food production and consumption, transferring production, as in the rest of flexible capitalism, to the "third world" and to immigrants, who labor to create the objects of our skilled consumption?

It is important to note that this characterization of our postmodern food condition is meant to be in broad strokes, and that we need to be attentive to the many historical strands of experience that go into making the present moment, the domestic science movement, the food industry, and the multicultural/pleasure nexus being three prominent ones. In the final section I consider some of these issues ethnographically through a beginning ethnography of everyday cooking that I have been pursuing in Greece and Southern Illinois.[21]

Toward an Ethnography of Everyday Cooking

One way that we have been approaching such an ethnography is through intensive filming of a small number of subjects as they go about cooking "ordinary" and "special" dishes. This allows us to develop a profile and also a sort of culinary biography of some of the key experiences and values that have led people to their current cooking practices. Such biographies, we hope, will help avoid the problem of dichotomies discussed earlier, although given that "tradition" and "modernity" are very much part of our informants' discourse, we inevitably have to confront these categories. In this section I present some preliminary findings based on two of our subjects, one a Greek woman, Georgia Vourneli from the city of Thessaloniki, a middle-class housewife born and raised in a village in Northern Greece, whom we filmed while she was visiting her son in Southern Illinois; the other, Jane Adams, a Professor of Anthropology, native of Southern Illinois and longtime political activist. As this research is in its beginning stages, I choose Georgia and Jane because they are two of the most complete cases at this time (each was filmed and interviewed on three separate occasions, preparing different dishes). They also provide interesting comparisons and contrasts, as Georgia and Jane share similar gender and relative income levels, but very different cultural contexts and educational levels, Georgia having grown up in a village in northern Greece but living most of her adult life in urban Thessaloniki, while Jane has lived most of her life in semi-rural Southern Illinois. For reasons of space I will limit my discussion to a few of the issues raised in earlier sections of the chapter, specifically those of tool use and measurement, as well as judgment and taste. Other issues that I have examined in relation to these subjects include: shopping, structuring of the kitchen environment, recipe and cookbook use, and teaching and learning.

Georgia's relationship to Greek tradition is, like her relationship to Greek modernity, a hybrid one. She works out at a private gym twice a day, owns her own car (which for her is a potent symbol of personal independence), and has western-European-based sense of fashion and style, including permed, dyed-blond hair. According to her son Leo Vournelis, she has a large collection of "modern" kitchen utensils and appliances. Even though her kitchen is filled with shiny utensils and machines, when it comes to matters of food and food preparation, Georgia seems to spurn this technology. She embraces nativistic values of the superiority of things "Greek," in both tools and food, as well as the techniques of cooking she was taught by her mother and her grandmother.

Georgia prepared the dish leek pie (Prasopita). *During the time the leeks were cooking and reducing, Georgia began the process of making the Philo for the Prasopita. She began by pouring a large amount of bleached flour into a large bowl. At first we believed that Georgia was measuring the flour by sight, but rather she folded the bag and measured the amount of flour by the size and weight of the flour remaining in the bag. After the desired amount of flour was placed in the bowl, Georgia used the back of her hand to create a hole for future ingredients. She made several passes through the center to create the right depth, so that the liquid ingredients could be contained.*

At no point in the process does she employ measuring spoons or cups. In this case the ingredients themselves become "tools" and perform the role of "measuring" other ingredients. In a sense the use of ingredients as tool can be seen as part of the structuring of the cooking environment itself as a mnemonic, or memory-jog, which we have documented in other cooking practices (cf. De Leon 2003; Kirsch 1996). For example, cooking implements in much of Greece are hung on the wall, in plain sight, rather than in a cupboard or under a counter, reminding the cook of their potential for use. This would fit well with Ingold's view of using the environment as a form of memory storage – "the world is its own best model" (see also Norman 1998).

Georgia placed the following ingredients within the hole in the flour: olive oil, vinegar, salt, egg yolk, and water. In this recipe all but two ingredients were measured by sight. The two excluded from this were vinegar and an egg. Drawing her fingers together and pulling up slightly to create a cup of her right hand with her thumb forming the outer edge of the bowl by being crooked against her first finger, she poured the vinegar into her left hand to measure

Figure 3.1 Georgia Vourneli

Figure 3.2 Pouring oil into the flour hole

Figure 3.3 "Measuring" the vinegar

Figure 3.4 Rolling the Philo

the correct amount. She allowed the vinegar to drizzle over the ingredient holding area as well as the rest of the bowl. When it came to adding the egg yolk, Georgia used her left hand, formed as a shallow bowl, as a strainer separating the white from the yolk. The egg white was strained into another bowl and discarded. The yolk remaining in her hand was then added to the hole in the center of the bowl of flour.

In this case it is not the environment, but the body that becomes a measuring tool, much more directly than in the metaphoric gauge "three fingers." It is interesting that Georgia's embrace of middle-class values (health club, Walmarts) does not extend to this embodied aspect of the cooking she had learned from her grandmother. As she puts it when asked about her preference for hand kneading of the dough: "The tools are not good. The traditional way is the right way ... before tools." She complains about the limited tools at her son's house. In response to the question "where do you get your tools," she doesn't mention the fancy store-purchased machines, but instead "I got my tools from my mother's home place. In the village where she had a carpenter make for her a rolling pin and table that was low. Mother would sit with her legs under the table and roll Philo."

Georgia complains that she does not have her own rolling pin. And yet the rolling pin she uses is the same "traditional" type as the one she has at home. A conventional, "modern" rolling pin (i.e., the ultra-smooth model with low-friction ball bearings, and a larger, heavier dowel) is eschewed in this case for a smooth stick, which allows one to feel every nuance of the rolling action and its effect on the elasticity of the dough. In contrast the "modern" rolling pin construction disconnects the cook from the dough by being designed to produce uniform strokes and dimensionality to the dough. The standard Greek rolling pin is also different from its American "tapered" equivalent, designed for rolling out pie crust, and thus for creating an unevenness in the dough (thinner toward the middle). The Greek rolling pin is both thinner, and all the same width, creating an even dough, and allowing for "closer" contact with the dough than the American thicker equivalent. The Greek type of rolling pin allows Georgia to "feel" when the dough is right (without being able to verbalize the process), since this type of roller is once again a simple extension of the hands, not a tool meant to achieve the rolling process with minimal human effort. At one point she cast her eyes around her son's apartment, and her gaze fell on his wooden-handled broom. Deciding that this was the right width for the task, she asked her son to cut up the broom to create for her a proper rolling pin. Once again improvisation, the importance of responding to the problem of the moment rather than executing a preestablished plan, seems to be a thread running through Georgia's cooking practices and her explicit philosophy where "tradition" isn't static, but is infinitely adaptable.[22] Clearly Georgia illustrates many aspects of the relationship to tool use described by Ingold, in which tools of production simply extend the body and the senses into the environment. Georgia's case also shows that such practices can exist alongside a self-conscious "modernity" that characterizes Georgia's relationship to other aspects of her life, such as home decoration and female body image. In part this may reflect the

Figure 3.5 Jane Adams

Figure 3.6 Kneading the dough

Figure 3.7 Applying the rub to the port loin

fact that contemporary Greek discourse on food, reflecting perhaps global trends, places a high value on the "authentic" (see, for example Gefou-Madianou 1999; Sutton 2001).

Jane Adams also learned to cook from her mother. But, unlike Georgia, who did not encounter any of the modernizing discourses discussed above, Jane's mother encouraged her to use recipes and standard measurements. Jane also learned to cook in 4-H club, where they would learn to follow recipes and create menus. Jane notes: "My mother was very modern and I learned from her the use of measurements. She would convert recipes she did by 'feel' into measurements: 1/4 tsp. thyme, 1/2 tsp. oregano, etc. And she was a stickler about using level measurements for cakes and other similar baked goods." Jane also notes that since her mother was working outside of the home, she would often leave written instructions for Jane to follow, giving her early on a textualized mediation of cooking. "I used cookbooks from the time I could read. Mother got me one for children and I made things from it." Jane's mother also taught Jane to can vegetables, an embodied apprenticeship. "I was a pair of hands," Jane notes. Canning is a practice that Jane continues to this day, producing a hot pepper sauce from ingredients bought at the local farmers' market. Jane defines "authentic" food as having a connection to the ingredients or to the place where the dish came from. But she also believes in eating globally, suggesting that the environmental movement is mistaken to limit their eating to what is available locally, indeed that the availability of foods from around the world is one of the benefits of globalization that we should appreciate. Georgia is, of course, also a global consumer, as reflected in her idolization of Walmart. Her embrace of global commodities, however, does not by and large extend to food items, but rather to those items oriented toward display; thus the global is not "internalized" in the same way for Georgia as it is for Jane.

In one session Jane was preparing several loaves of French bread to accompany a meal of pork loin. She was assisted in cooking by her husband D. Gorton. Jane eschews bread makers, saying that they only used one when they lived far from a grocery store, but otherwise "if you're going to use a bread maker you might as well buy it from the store, the only advantage is that you get to eat it hot." For French bread she used a set of aluminum mold pans, which she had found when she moved into a house, as well as the recipe that accompanies the pans, suggesting a serendipitous approach to cooking that seemed to characterize a number of our American subjects. She noted that with other breads she experiments but with this one she follows the recipe exactly, measuring out the ingredients using standard cups and spoons, though carelessly measuring the flour, since this, she said, is added till it feels right. As she prepared the dough she reminisced about women in the community who used to make their own yeast out of hops, noting that she always wanted to make a sourdough starter, but felt the climate would not be right for it in Southern Illinois. She kneaded the dough by pulling from the back and folding over in a motion that quickly became automatic. As she kneaded she noted that the recipe calls for using four pans but she only used three because she liked the loaves to be larger. She also noted that the recipe called for letting it rise on a towel and then sliding it into the pans, but she found that too cumbersome and didn't know the reason for it. Her husband interjected that the pans cooled the dough and thus would affect the yeast, but she shrugged and said that she hadn't seen any difference.

David: Can the dough be underkneaded or overkneaded?
Jane: Certainly underkneaded, but overkneaded? I don't think so.
D.:   Overkneaded would get the glutens too worked up, make the bread stringy.
Jane: I don't know. The recipe says to knead for ten minutes, but I just use a trick: you put your hand on the dough and count to 10 and if it doesn't stick then the dough is done.
David: Where did you learn that?
Jane: I don't remember. I think in 4-H club.

Jane then prepared a rub for the pork loin, using a number of different spices. The rub was a family recipe that her uncle had taught her mother. First she chopped garlic, then mixed herbs and spices with it in a mortar. While she used a measuring spoon to put the paprika in the mortar, it was used more as a scoop than a measurer. She measured the herbs by hand, grinding them between her palms. Once ground, she added water and used her finger to mix it and to distribute it on the pork. She chopped the garlic rather than using a press, noting that she could never find a press that gets the garlic the way she wants it, that produces the right flavor. This leads D. to raise the question of why Jane won't use sage in her rub.

Jane: I'm not crazy about the taste of sage. I like growing it.
D.:   To me sage and pork go together. But not to Jane. This is the way she grew up making it.
Jane: This is the way it's supposed to taste. This is the way it should taste. This is the moral way (laughing).

In the interview that accompanied this session, Jane and D. spoke of the relationship of food, morality, and politics, which they see as having been basically altered in the 1960s. They identify this period as marking a shift from the Boston Cooking School approach (of which they were knowledgeable) to a valorization of "pleasure" in cooking and eating, as well as in other spheres of life. While Jane clearly valued the sensory and pleasureful aspects of the food she prepared, in an interview session a year later Jane and D. had gone on a no-carb diet, and thus homemade bread was, at least for a time, off the menu.

Like Georgia, Jane is a hybrid of practices, judgments, and values in relation to cooking. Georgia's hybridity, as noted, seems to lie less in her cooking practices than in her outfitting of the kitchen with expensive, but unused, marks of distinction. Jane's hybridity lies more in a combination of influences in her learning to cook: her mother, 4-H club and cookbooks, as well as in the values she sees expressed in her practice: cosmopolitanism, local history, pleasure, and moderation. Standardized measurements and writing (recipes) play somewhat more of a role in Jane's cooking. Recipes and cookbooks form a backup reference for things that she can't remember (e.g., the correct temperature to cook the pork loin). But at the same time there are also many "rules of thumb" (Ingold 2000:332) (for judging the bread dough) and sensory memories – the automaticity of kneading as a kind of memory in the hands, the tastes of childhood which form the tastescape of the present, the set of unarticulated taste memories which allow for comparison and judgment, and which can determine the choice of tools (knife vs. garlic press), or of spices. Furthermore, cooking technologies like the bread machine are explicitly rejected.

The connection of all these small gestures to Jane's goals and values is encapsulated in her joking reference to "the moral way of preparing the dish," that is, by duplicating past tastes she is preserving something of her mother's commitment to good food (and social justice: her mother is a leading community social activist).[23] Thus both Georgia and Jane refer back to childhood as a key touchstone for their cooking. But while Georgia frames all her cooking in terms of being true to her mother, her grandmother, and to Greece, Jane's explicit discourse speaks of innovation as well, learning new tastes as part of her life course. (Time spent in Mexico began a long-term passion for Mexican food, for example.) In spite of this more "globalized" influence, certain dishes for Jane can be a source of stories about the local past, family, and community as well. Both express hybrid desires and feelings, as Georgia's "traditional" cooking sits side by side with her fancy, unused gadgets, and Jane's "moral cooking" has room for a cosmopolitan tasting of what the world has to offer, as well as for dietary fads. Both preserve the gestures and judgments of the past, even if Jane in some cases defers to measuring spoons and recipes (at least as memory jogs), part, perhaps, of the legacy of 4-H and other normalizing discourses as described by Shapiro. Much of their similarities, no doubt, can be traced to the fact that both learned the basics of cooking largely in a social context, from their mothers and other relatives. But neither of them has passed on this tradition: Georgia because she had no daughters. Jane has a daughter, who has continued Jane's political activism, but rejected this type of embodied knowledge: "My greatest disappointment was not teaching my daughter how to cook, but she never took an interest and I never made her." Thus the fact that there are fewer milieus for cultural transmission of cooking knowledge through families raises questions which can only be answered by studying the next generation: Jane and Georgia's children.

This short ethnography is meant to be suggestive rather than con-clusive. It provides a taste of how we might operationalize the different concepts discussed in this chapter. While it does not resolve the many issues raised, I hope it begins to suggest the fruitfulness of wedding a concern with "taste" to one with "taste." That is, in each case I have tried to suggest that such cooking "biographies" need to be attentive to both the "technical" skills and sensory aspects of cooking, and its more explicitly social dimensions. The latter is reflected in my discussion of Georgia and Jane's individual goals and values, as well as the ways in which these goals and values interact with the larger totalities (culturally inflected notions of authenticity, morality, globality, and locality) in which they are enmeshed. This chapter, then, is also meant as a critique of food studies that have focused on symbols rather than on processes ("food as a symbol of identity"), suggesting here that meaning, like cooking, is very much "in the making."[24]

Acknowledgments

I am grateful to Richard Fox and the Wenner-Gren Foundation for hosting the symposium for which the material in this chapter was written, as well as the organizers of the symposium, Elizabeth Edwards, Chris Gosden, and Ruth Phillips, and the other participants, for a most stimulating week. Thanks to Michael Hernandez for his superlative filming and general collaboration on the research for this chapter. Thanks also to a number of people who read and commented on various drafts of this chapter: Janet Dixon Keller, Linda Smith, Constance Sutton, Amy Trubek, Leo Vournelis, and Peter Wogan.

Notes

1. Of course this is not true of food itself, nor of cooking tools and technologies, but only of the products of cooking, which makes things a bit more complicated.

2. Howes and Lalonde (1991) make a similar argument in showing the development of the concept of taste in eighteenth-century England. They trace the shift from the visual to taste as a class marker to a change from feudal times, when class distinction was stable and apparent from one's dress, to times of more fluid class relations, when the "proximate senses" became more important for judging people's supposed "true character."

3. Ingold draws here on the notion of "affordances" from the work of ecological psychologist James Gibson (1979).

4. As *New York Times* food writer Amanda Hesser puts it: "When I am cooking, a fork becomes an extension of my own hand, a set of fine claws to deftly manipulate things I cannot touch. And whatever the task, the bone handle stays cool" (2003:17–18).

5. Or as James Scott (1998:329) notes, "Any experienced practitioner of a skill or craft will develop a large repertoire of moves, visual judgments, a sense of touch, or a discriminating gestalt for assessing the work as well as a range of accurate intuitions born of experience that defy being communicated apart from practice." See also Keller and Dixon-Keller 1999; Keller 2001.

6. Michael suggests that we think of objects in terms of a "cascade of affordances," "for example, socks afford the easier wearing of boots which afford the attachment of crampons which afford the climbing of snow-covered slopes which themselves become 'affordable', that is to say, climbable" (2000:112).

7. The work of Latour, Law, Callon and others in "Actor Network Theory" is also relevant here in arguing for an approach that uses the same vocabulary to describe technical, natural, and social "actors" (see e.g., Callon 1986). Coming from a somewhat different angle, the *chaîne opératoire* approach to technology, Schlanger (1994:148) makes a similar point: "Techniques are indeed ... a dialogue: the lithic medium is, to all intents and purposes, an interlocutor whose physical reactions cannot be ignored, and the human "partner" needs to monitor permanently, and critically, all undertaken or projected actions,

to consider the given results in view of the expected, to assess anew the possibility and desirability of the guiding design, to rectify plans according to imagined future eventualities, and to undertake new material actions in view of the above." While written with flint-knapping in view, what a wonderful description this is of processes of cooking as well!

8. Similarly Dobres sees all humans engaged with technology, but there is a clear moral judgment implied in the following: "It is on the basis of this sensuous and cultured engagement that producers and consumers create their bodies of technical know how and skill – whether through the cavalier act of flicking on a light switch (little knowing or caring about principles of electricity or the complex knowledge, labor, machinery, and economic network making this possible), or whether one executes on their own the entire sequence for making and firing a hand-thrown pot (in this case, being intimately familiar with the performance characteristics of each material encountered)" (2001:50).

9. Borgman (1992) describes the same phenomenon as a "receding of reality" from everyday experience, which he tracks in domain of politics, art, and scholarship, as well as labor processes, in which receding reality refers to the loss of sensory input when computer calculations replace trained judgments. He cites a pulp mill operator as follows: "With computerization I am further away from my job than I have ever been before. I used to listen to the sounds the boiler makes and know just how it was running. I could look at the fire in the furnace and tell by its color how it was burning. I knew what kinds of adjustments were needed by the shades of color I saw. A lot of the men also said that there were smells that told you different things about how it was running. I feel uncomfortable being away from these sights and smells. Now I only have numbers to go by" (cited in Borgman 1992:165).

10. The pencil, for example, becomes an extension of the finger as it is used for pointing and highlighting when explaining some process (Suchman 2000:12).

11. For a similar argument in relation to video cameras, see Ginsburg (1997), Turner (1997). For an opposing viewpoint see Weiner (1997).

12. Star, a proponent of science and technology studies (sts), seems more agnostic in suggesting that technology does hide certain kinds of socio-material relations, which the analyst must then rediscover and unpack: "Technology freezes inscriptions, knowledge, information, alliances, and actions inside black boxes, where they become invisible, transportable, and powerful in hitherto unknown ways as part of socio-technical networks" (Star 1991:32). She recounts the struggles of someone trying to eat at McDonald's, but allergic to onions. Thus Star is concerned with the effects of power and of the standardization associated with modernity, but suggests that we explore the

heterogeneity "which is permanently escaping, subverting, but nevertheless in relationship with the standardized" (39).

13. Wolf defines structural power as "power that operates not only within settings or domains but that also organizes and orchestrates the settings themselves, and that specifies the distribution and direction of energy flows... [It] is intended to emphasize power to deploy and allocate social labor. These governing relations do not come into view when you think of power primarily in interactional terms" (1990:586–7).

14. See, for example, Murcott's (1997) discussion of "golden age" nostalgia and the lack of actual data on food practices to sustain media pronouncements.

15. As Gottdiener notes, because of the microwave "members of the household are no longer dependent on one parent – traditionally, almost exclusively the mother – to make meals. Use of the microwave liberates individuals from this dependency and hyperdifferentiates both meal choices and meal eating times ... Increased flexibility of meal preparation may aid and may be a concomitant effect of flexible or extended work schedules" (1995:50–1). But see also Ormrod 1994 on some of the ways that microwaves may reinscribe traditional gender roles in their manufacture and marketing, a general point made in feminist studies of domestic technology (see Cowan 1983; Wajcman 1991).

16. Indeed, as Shapiro documents, they established Domestic Science as part of many university curricula based on persuading universities that theirs was a theoretical discipline.

17. This development and spread of measuring cups and spoons seems ripe for a historical treatment written from the Actor-Network Theory approach.

18. Middle-class women were generally thought to have a minimal appetite for food, among other things.

19. It would be interesting to compare these aesthetic principles to those that guide Japanese cooking, as discussed by Allison (1991).

20. See the special issue of *American Studies* devoted to Martha Stewart (Mechling 2001). McFeely (2000) documents some of the shifts in the 1960s, in particular the influence of Betty Friedan and Julia Child, who in different ways set the tone for promoting "self-fulfillment," which for some took the form of seeing cooking as an art, rather than a science. McFeely further suggests that Child's influence made cooking seem like a challenging and complicated task requiring skill, rather than simply domestic drudgery. The role of travel and immigration in exposing "mainstream America" to new tastes is also discussed. Since the initial writing of this article, Laura Shapiro has published an important new book documenting changes in cooking in the 1950s, which I do not consider here (see Shapiro 2004).

21. I have been pursuing this project in conjunction with Michael Hernandez. See Hernandez and Sutton 2003a, b. Thus I use the first-person plural to discuss this research in the next section.

22. Note that this "trick" may be a rediscovery of a common technique used by Greek migrants in the United States, as described by Papanikolas (1987:7).

23. On reading a version of this chapter, Jane commented "I think the link between food and social justice is complicated: My mother was very much into good nutrition, and in that sense (and many others) fully in line with scientific housekeeping, but it was also inflected with an aesthetic sensibility that was more connected to the socialist movement, of arts and crafts (which has now moved to Martha Stewart – the ironies of history). So menus were in fact 'moral' – a 'balanced diet.' But appropriate herbs hearkened more to a sense of good eating which was probably Jewish – it certainly wasn't local. So there was a degree of snobbery, of 'taste' in Bourdieu's sense in there as well."

24. Quote from Dobres 2001. See also Pfaffenberger 2001.

References

Adams, J. 1994. *The Transformation of Rural Life: Southern Illinois 1890–1990*. Chapel Hill, NC: University of North Carolina Press.

Allison, A. 1991. "Japanese Mothers and Obentos: The Lunch Box as Ideological State Apparatus." *Anthropological Quarterly* 64: 195–208.

Baudrillard, J. 1993. *The System of Objects*. Trans. James Benedict. London: Verso.

Baumann, Z. 1996. *Life in Fragments: Essays in Postmodern Morality*. Oxford: Blackwell.

Belasco, W. 2000. "Future Notes: The Meal-in-a-Pill." *Food and Foodways* 8: 253–71.

Borgmann, A. 1992. "The Artificial and the Real: Reflections on Baudrillard's America." In *Jean Baudrillard: The Disappearance of Art and Politics*, ed. W. Stearns and W. Chaloupka, New York: St. Martin's Press.

Bourdieu, P. 1982. *Distinction: A Social Critique of the Judgement of Taste*. Trans. Richard Nice. Cambridge MA: Harvard University Press.

Bubant, N. 1998. "The Odour of Things: Smell and the Cultural Elaboration of Disgust in Eastern Indonesia." *Ethnos* 63: 48–80.

Callon, M. 1986. "Some Elements of a Sociology of Translation: Domestication of the Scallops and the Fishermen of St. Brieuc Bay." In *Power, Action and Belief: A New Sociology of Knowledge*, ed. J. Law. London: Routledge.

Carrier, J. 1990. "Gifts in a World of Commodities: The Ideology of the Perfect Gift in American Society." *Social Analysis* 29: 19–37.

——. 1996. "Emerging Alienation in Production: A Maussian History." *Man* 27: 539–58.

——. 1998. "Abstraction in Western Economic Practice." In *Virtualism: A New Political Economy*, ed. J. Carrier and D. Miller. Oxford: Berg.

Classen, C., D. Howes, and A. Synnott. 1994. *Aroma: The Cultural History of Smell*. London: Routledge.

Connerton, P. 1989. *How Societies Remember*. Cambridge: Cambridge University Press.

Cowan, R. 1983. *More Work for Mother: The Ironies of Household Technology from the Open Hearth to the Microwave*. New York: Basic Books.

De Leon, D. 2003. *Artifactual Intelligence: The Development and Use of Cognitively Congenial Artifacts*. Lund, Sweden: Lund University Cognitive Studies #105.

Dobres, M. A. 2001. "Meaning in the Making: Agency and the Social Embodiment of Technology and Art." In *Anthropological Perspectives on Technology*, ed. M.B. Schiffer. Albuquerque: University of New Mexico Press.

Fernandez, J. 1973. "Analysis of Ritual: Metaphoric Correspondences as the Elementary Forms." *Science* 182: 1366–67.

Gefou-Madianou, D. 1999. "Cultural Polyphony and Identity Formation: Negotiating Tradition in Attica." *American Ethnologist* 26: 412–39.

Gibson, J. 1979. *The Ecological Approach to Visual Perception*. Boston: Houghton Mifflin.

Ginsburg, F. 1997. "Response to Weiner." *Current Anthropology* 38: 213–16.

Gottdiener, M. 1995. *Postmodern Semiotics: Material Culture and the Forms of Postmodern Life*. Oxford: Basil Blackwell.

Heim, M. 1987. *Electric Language: A Philosophical Study of Word Processing*. New Haven, CT: Yale University Press.

Hernandez, M., and D. Sutton. 2003a. "Hands that Remember: An Ethnography of Everyday Cooking." *Expedition: Journal of the University of Pennsylvania Museum* 45: 30–7.

——. 2003b. "Voices in the Kitchen: Tools that Remember." Paper presented at the AAA meetings, Chicago, November 20.

Herzfeld, M. 1995. "It Takes One to Know One: Collective Resentment and Mutual Recognition among Greeks in Local and Global Contexts." In *Counterworks: Managing the Diversity of Knowledge*, ed. R. Fardon. London: Routledge.

Hesser, A. 2003. "The Torch is Passed, Handle First." In *Best Food Writing 2003*, ed. H. Hughes. New York: Marlow.

Howes, D. 2003. *Sensual Relations: Engaging the Senses in Culture and Social Theory*. Ann Arbor: University of Michigan Press.

—— and M. Lalonde. 1991. "The History of Sensibilities." *Dialectical Anthropology* 16: 125–35.

Ihde, D. 1990. *Technology and the Lifeworld: From Garden to Earth*. Bloomington: Indiana University Press.

Ingold, T. 1993. "Tool-Use, Sociality and Intelligence." In *Tools, Language and Cognition in Human Evolution*. ed. K. Gibson and T. Ingold. Cambridge: Cambridge University Press.

——. 2000. *The Perception of the Environment: Essays on Livelihood, Dwelling and Skill*. London: Routledge.

——. 2001."From the Transmission of Representations to the Education of Attention." Paper Archive. *Mind, Culture and Activity,* http://lchc.ucsd.edu/MCA

Keller, C. 2001. "Thought and Production: Insights of the Practitioner." In *Anthropological Perspectives on Technology*, ed. M.B. Schiffer. Albuquerque: University of New Mexico Press.

——. and J.D. Keller. 1999. "Imagery in Cultural Tradition and Innovation." *Mind, Culture and Activity* 6: 3–32.

Kenna, M. n.d. "Why Does Incense Smell Religious? The Anthropology of Smell Meets Greek Orthodoxy." Manuscript. Department of Anthropology, University of Wales, Swansea.

Kirsch, D. 1996. "The Intelligent Use of Space." *Artificial Intelligence* 73: 31–68.

Latour, B. 1993. *We Have Never Been Modern*. Cambridge MA: Harvard University Press.

Lave, J. 1988. *Cognition in Practice: Mind, Mathematics and Culture in Everyday Life*. Cambridge: Cambridge University Press.

——. and E. Wenger. (eds). 1991. *Situated Learning: Legitimate Peripheral Participation*. Cambridge: Cambridge University Press.

Lemmonier, P. (ed.). 1993. *Technological Choices: Transformation in Material Cultures since the Neolithic*. London: Routledge.

Leudar, I., and A. Costall. 1996. "Situating Action IV: Planning as Situated Action." *Ecological Psychology* 8: 153–70.

McFeely, M. 2000. *Can She Bake a Cherry Pie? American Women and the Kitchen in the Twentieth Century*. Amherst, MA: University of Massachusetts Press.

Mechling, J. (ed.). 2001. "Martha Stewart Roundtable." *American Studies* 42: 67–125.

Michael, M. 2000. "'These Boots are made for Walking...' Mundane Technology, the Body and Human-Environment Relations." *Body and Society* 6: 107–26.

Miller, D. 2002. "Should Objects be termed Agents?" Paper Delivered at the American Anthropological Association Meetings, New Orleans, November 21.

Mintz, S. 1996. *Tasting Food, Tasting Freedom.* Boston: Beacon Press.

Murcott, A. 1997. "Family Meals – A Thing of the Past?" In *Food, Health and Identity,* ed. P. Caplan. London: Routledge.

Myers, F. (ed.). 2001. *The Empire of Things: Regimes of Value and Material Culture.* Santa Fe, NM: School of American Research Press.

Norman, D. 1998. *The Design of Everyday Things.* London: MIT Press.

Ormrod, S. 1994. "'Let's nuke the dinner': Discursive Practices of Gender in the Creation of a New Cooking Process." In *Bringing Technology Home: Gender and Technology in a Changing Europe,* ed. C. Cockburn and R. Furst-Dilic. Buckingham, UK: Open University Press.

Papanikolas, H. 1987. *Amilia-Yeiorgos.* Salt Lake City, UT: University of Utah Press.

Pfaffenberger, B. 2001. "Symbols Do Not Creat Meanings – Activities Do: Or, Why Symbolic Anthropology Needs the Anthropology of Technology." In *Anthropological Perspectives on Technology,* ed. M.B. Schiffer. Albuquerque: University of New Mexico Press.

Rasmussen, S. 1999. "Making Better 'Scents' in Anthropology: Aroma in Tuareg Sociocultural Systems and the Shaping of Ethnography." *Anthropological Quarterly* 72: 55–73.

Schiffer, M. (ed.). 2001. *Anthropological Perspectives on Technology.* Albuquerque: University of New Mexico Press.

Schlanger, N. 1990. "The Making of a Soufflé: Practical Knowledge and Social Senses." *Techniques et Culture* 15: 29–52.

——. 1994. "Mindful Technology: Unleashing the *Chaîne Opératoire* for an Archaeology of Mind." In *The Ancient Mind: Elements of a Cognitive Archaeology,* ed. C. Renfrew and E. Zubrow. Cambridge: Cambridge University Press.

Scott, J. 1998. *Seeing Like a State: How Certain Schemes to Improve the Human Condition Have Failed.* New Haven, CT: Yale University Press.

Shapiro, L. 1986. *Perfection Salad: Women and Cooking at the Turn of the Century.* New York: Farrar, Straus & Giroux.

——. 2004. *Something From the Oven: Reinventing Dinner in 1950s America.* New York: Viking.

Star, S.L. 1991. "Power, Technology and the Phenomenology of Conventions: On Being Allergic to Onions." In *A Sociology of Monsters:*

Essays on Power, Technology and Domination, ed. J. Law. London: Routledge.

Steinberg, S. 1998. "Bubbie's Challah." In *Eating Culture,* ed. R. Scapp and B. Seitz. Albany, NY: SUNY Press.

Suchman, L. 2000. "Embodied Practices of Engineering Work." *Mind, Culture and Activity,* 7: 4–18.

Sutton, D. 2001. *Remembrance of Repasts: An Anthropology of Food and Memory.* Oxford: Berg.

Turner, T. 1997. "Response to Weiner." *Current Anthropology* 38: 226–29.

Wajcman, J. 1991. *Feminism Confronts Technology.* University Park, PA: Pennsylvania State University Press.

Weiner, J. 1997. "Televisualist Anthropology: Representation, Aesthetics, Politics." *Current Anthropology* 38: 197–235.

Wolf, E. 1990. "Facing Power: Old Questions, New Insights." *American Anthropologist* 92: 586–96.

Part 2

Colonialism

four

Mata Ora: Chiseling the Living Face – Dimensions of Maori Tattoo

Ngahuia Te Awekotuku

Origins: The Beginnings

Tukua mai kia au
Kia whakangaoa
Ki te uhi a Mataora.
Taria, e tuku atu
Ki to wahine
To kiri korito
Komae kowhara
Naku koe i whakanako . . .

Release yourself to me
To be gouged
By the chisel of Mataora.
Incised, you give yourself
To your lover
Your skin glistens
Joyful, gleaming
For I adorned you . . .

Excerpt from a chant performed
during the procedure.[1]

Ta moko is the process; *moko* is the outcome. *Ta moko* is the art of decorative scarification, unique to the Maori people of Aotearoa/New Zealand. It involves the chiseling of human skin and the insertion of pigment, and is related to *tatau*, the Pacific tradition of puncturing and staining the flesh. From this technique, *tatau*, comes the English word "tattoo" and its Western practice. As one mode of transforming oneself forever, the origins of *moko* are found in myth.

Mataora was a jealous mortal chief who won the heart of Niwareka, a woman from the Underworld. Unsure of her love, he abused her, and she fled home to her father, the patriarch Uetonga. Her husband followed her, guilty and griefstricken. His tears ruined his face paint. Seeing him, her family, whose adornment was permanently incised, mocked him as a vain and arrogant fool. Ashamed of his behavior, ashamed of his smeared and muddy features, he begged their forgiveness and promised to look after Niwareka and never abuse her again. And from Uetonga, he requested the knowledge of their skin art. The immortal artist obliged him, and Mataora was marked, thus learning the art; his name reflected his new look – *Mata Ora* – the Living Face. The couple reconciled, and returned to humankind with the awesome bounty of *taniko* weaving, and *ta moko* adornment. And from strife and pain came one of the Maori world's most distinctive and enduring treasures.

> I remember my breathing. Catching it – the rhythm. Every chisel strike, biting my skin. Tasting it. Breaking through. I remember smelling the color of blood, my blood. Chanting. Breathing. Each strike, my breath. In, out. Every cut a heart beat, every cut, a breath. In, out. Beyond the chanting; beyond the pain, just the smell, the taste, the rhythm. My blood. My heart beat. I fell asleep, lulled away, breathing my hearbeat, the rhythm. Far away. When I came back, I looked in the mirror. And I saw someone else. Mako, project participant 2003.[2]

Ta moko as an art form engages all the senses, every single one, on a number of levels, and in a number of ways. Over the last 200 years, it has been the subject of awed fascination, vigorous collection and commodification, missionary contempt and abolition, active resurgence, painterly and photographic documentation and recording, a perceived but not complete decline and, finally, Western appropriation, and the passionate revival of the last two decades.

Yet Maori have always marked their bodies, and there has never been a time, in the history of these islands, that there has not been at least one ornamented face, challenging, smiling, chanting, on the ceremonial courtyard of the Maori world. Despite colonial incursion, the legacy of Mataora and Niwareka has always been there for the people to see, covet, and admire.

Certainly, the first newcomers to Aotearoa did exactly that, as Banks remarks on those early faces:

Their faces are the most remarkable, on them they by some art unknown to me dig furrows in their faces a line deep at least and as broad, the edges of which are often indented and most perfectly black. (Banks 1962 [1768–71])

And Augustus Earle, the traveling English artist, records with interest,

The art of tattooing has been brought to such perfection here, that whenever we have seen a New Zealander whose skin is thus ornamented, we have admired him. It is looked upon as answering the same purposes as clothes. When a chief throws off his mats, he seems as proud of displaying the beautiful ornaments figured on his skin as a first rate exquisite is in exhibiting himself in his last fashionable attire. (Earle 1966 [1832])

The Technique

Unlike the other *tatau* traditions of the Pacific, *Ta moko* actually gouged and chiseled the skin, on the face and on the buttocks. A raised texture with the skin ridged and the color inserted was desirable, as the pattern was well defined and enhanced the contours of the face and body. Each *moko* was as unique as its wearer. A competent artist would consider the musculature and conformation beneath the surface, and design accordingly. This ensured that no two people ever had the same pattern and that each facial *moko* was different. The design was applied with fine chisels between 3mm and 10mm wide, wrought from albatross or human bone, and lashed to a carefully balanced haft. During the procedure, the chisels would be repeatedly dipped into a small container of *ngarahu*, a deep black dye made from diluted fish or human oil mixed with the soot of burned organic material, usually *kauri* tree resin or dried *aweto* caterpillars.

The *tohunga ta moko*, or practitioner, chiseled into the skin with a steady, chanted rhythm; this often had a soporific effect on the recipient, who merged into a trance state also caused by the acute pain. Because of the latter, to effect a full coverage of the face, a number of sessions were required. Blood was staunched with special woven fiber wipes, and various plant remedies treated the swelling and assisted the healing process. To distract the recipient of facial work, or intensify her/his psychological state, water or a nourishing broth would be dripped into the mouth via an elegantly carved, visually suggestive *korere*, or funnel-like wooden beaker.

Thigh designs and larger body work involved wider instruments which punctured and stamped in the pigment, rather than gouging into the flesh. This puncture technique, comparably rhythmic, visual, and tactile, is still practiced in Samoa and the Hawaiian Islands today.

These differences were observed in the first years of encounter:

> There is a remarkable difference in the tattoo of the New Zealanders, and that of the Navigators', Fiigee or Friendly Islands. In the latter, the skin is just perforated with a small pointed instrument, and the staining matter introduced; so that, in passing the hand over the part that has been tattooed the skin feels smooth, and the surface is fair; whilst in the former, the incision is very deep, and leaves furrows and ridges so uneven, that in some places, when long enough, it would be possible to lay a pin, which would be nearly buried in them. (Yate 1835)

Yate's mentor, Samuel Marsden, also observed,

> The chisel seemed to pass through the skin at every stroke and cut it as a carver cuts a piece of wood. The chisel was constantly dipped in a liquid made of soot ... I observed proud flesh rising in some part of the breech which had been cut almost one month before. (Marsden 1932 [1765–1838])

This account was echoed some generations later, by a contemporary *ta moko* artist, who declared most emphatically that "we never stopped doing Ta Moko. We were just hitting our chisels into wood instead of skin. So the tradition never stopped."[3] Such rich images – the furrows and ridges, the proud flesh rising – intrigued and excited the newcomers from the northern hemisphere. They were initially astonished by the sensuality and aesthetic sensibility, the industriousness and martial vigor, the theater and prosperity of the Maori people. They wanted to collect, to explore, to consume, to own, to categorize. And possibly, in a few rare cases, to understand.

Upoko tuhi: the Colonial Macabre

Maori society was essentially a warrior society, made up of regional clans or *iwi*, each descended from named crew members of the great migrant voyaging canoes. These purposefully left Eastern Polynesia between 1000 and 1500 CE. For this reason, many Maori of today's 400,000 prefer to be identified primarily as "Tuhoe", "Te Arawa," or

"Waikato", rather than by the generic term, "Maori". This means "clear or natural" as in spring water, and came into popular use only after the missionary incursion and for colonial administrative convenience. (Te Awekotuku 1996). Settled within distinct geographic boundaries, the various clans were often at war with each other for fishing and forest resources, arable land, and frequently vengeance and matters of pride. The God of War, Tumatauenga, was honored by the tattooed face, and this honor was also a forceful memento mori.

The inscribed visage was often more than transient, more than the passing artwork of one man's lifetime. The beauty of a chief's facial adornment could outlast him, beyond death. Sight, smell, touch, taste, were all engaged. Only the voice of the chief was absent, was unfelt, but his words may endure, too, in chant, in recalling his orations, in *pepeha*, his familiar sayings. Preservation of heads, by steam drying and herbal treatment, demonstrated the genius of the Maori mortician's art. This was done to comfort the bereaved, and sustain the presence of the deceased. Handsomely tattooed heads were also taken from those fallen in battle, to be mocked and violated, shown off as special gifts of victory, or exchanged in the rituals of peacemaking. These are known as *upoko tuhi* – inscribed heads – or *moko mokai*, which refers to their origins as prisoners of war or war trophies.

Marsden the missionary details his own visual impression in this clearly affected and poignant account:

> I observed in the stern the head of a chief, the features of the face as natural as life, and one of the finest countenances I ever saw. The chief must have been previous to his death about thirty years old. The hair was long, and every lock combed straight, and the whole brought up to the crown and tied in a knot and ornamented with feathers according to the custom of the chiefs when in full dress, the hair and countenance both shining with oil with which they had been lately dressed. From the beautiful tattooing on the face, the chief must have been a person of high rank. (Marsden 1932 [1765–1838])

Such items inevitably aroused a predictable European reaction. As another clergyman records,

> As from a collector's point of view a preserved head formed a very desirable item in an assortment of foreign curios, attempts to secure specimens were made from the very earliest period of our intercourse with the Maoris. (Walsh 1894)

And how did this macabre colonial intercourse begin?

Banks, the naturalist and gentleman explorer, acquired the original, with some difficulty, from an elderly Maori on Cook's first voyage:

> He was very jealous of shewing them. One I bought tho much against the inclinations of its owner, for tho he likd the price I offerd he hesitated much to send it up, yet having taken the price I insisted either to have that returnd or the head given, but could not prevail until I enforc'd my threats by shewing Him a musquet on which he chose to part with the head rather than the price he had got, which was a pair of old Drawers of very white linen. (Banks 1962 [1770])

The currency changed over the next forty years. Firearms and gunpowder replaced cast-off underwear, and those tribes with access to the lethal new weaponry expanded their borders, settled ancient disputes, agitated new ones, and harvested a ghastly wealth of trade, as Manning recalls,

> All the heads on the hill were the heads of enemies, and several of them are now in museums in Europe ... the skippers of many of the colonial trading schooners were always ready to deal with a man who had a "real good head", and used to commission such men as my companion of the morning to "pick up heads" for them. It is a positive fact that sometime after this the head of a live man was sold and paid for beforehand, and afterwards honestly delivered "as per agreement". (Manning 1906)

This need for *pakeha* weaponry consumed almost the entire northern island, and traffic in *upoko tuhi* had reached a point which prompted Marsden to ask Ralph Darling, the Governor of New South Wales, to intervene. He petitioned the Governor expressing his own outrage, and also the grief of those visionary chiefs who wished to develop trading contacts in agricultural produce and timber with the colony of New South Wales. On 16 April 1831, the "disgusting traffic" was outlawed by a Declaration which emphasized

> The scandal and prejudice which it cannot fail to raise against the name and character of British traders in a country with which it has now become highly important to cultivate feelings of natural goodwill. (NSW Government Order, 16 April 1831)[4]

The trade was effectively terminated, possibly also because the two principal chiefs engaged in the commerce, Hongi Hika and Pomare, both of Ngapuhi, had died in 1828 and 1826 respectively, and the Christian missionaries were bringing in far more distracting and bountiful treasures and diversions – literacy, big exotic animals, machinery, fresh crops, metal tools, and new knowledge. With such opportunity offered to a pragmatic, omnivorous, and adaptable people, change was inevitable.

Upoko Tuhi: Diverting to the Present Time

What became of the *upoko tuhi* of the trading period? Nearly 300 were sold. Of these, according to the Mokomokai Education Trust, which is engaged in their repatriation, 127 are in foreign museums and 70 in private collections. There are more than 50 in the metropolitan museums of Aotearoa/New Zealand – some Maori say almost, but not quite, home. Of these, 37 were repatriated by the inimitable, charismatic Maui Pomare in his brief and extraordinary lifetime. Repatriation remains an intensely loaded and contentious issue. So does identification of the people themselves in this era of DNA sampling and forensic science. For to Maori, to me, they are people. They sang, loved, smelled, looked, tasted, listened, fought, laughed, touched, perished. And people heard them, tasted them, scented them, viewed them, caressed them, even after death. Now, two centuries later, how do the senses engage these chiefs? With grief for we must bring them home.[5]

The Nineteenth Century: Viewing, Venerating, Vilifying

'A hurihurihia to tupu hauroa, to tupu haunui, e I
'A kite iho au to kiri I ahua ki te wai ngarahu
To mata I haea ki te uhi matarau,
Waiho nei nga iwi, huhe kau ake!

Your body, grown so tall, so magnificent
I gently turn over; I gaze
At your finely patterned skin,
At your face incised exquisitely;
Ah, losing you will devastate the people.

This lament was composed by Te Heuheu III Iwikau in 1846, for the loss of his son Te Heuheu Tukino (II) in a catastrophic landslide.[6] Describing the youth's beauty and his significance to the people, the chant reveals how the Maori aesthetic, the sensuality and immediacy of *moko*, endured. *Moko* not only was perceived as a form of artistry and individual self-presentation; it also embodied the self. Patterns identified the wearer to others, and were unique to that person, though they could also be recognized as derived from the traditional repertoire of design forms unique to his or her tribe or clan.

Such designs could also become his or her own personal text, a form of marker or signifier, most commonly presented in the nineteenth century as an actual signature. Te Peehi Kupe, a famous war leader, traveled to England in the 1820s to purchase guns. He had a face of astonishing beauty, and charmed his new aristocratic English friends by drawing copies for them: "'Europee man write with pen his name,' he would say. 'Te Pehi's name is here,' and he would point to his forehead."[7] Such signings occur on a number of land deeds of sale or lease, the most notable being that of Jack Tuhawaiki of Otakau (Jones 2000). Similarly, the Treaty of Waitangi, the constitutional basis of contemporary Aotearoa New Zealand, was signed in 1840 between representative chiefs and the viceregal delegate. This document has scores of *moko* signatures – delicately meaningful designs that exactly record the spiral on a nostril, the curl above an eyebrow, the gouge beneath the lip. In this context particularly, *moko* was about *mana*, about authority and prestige, about making things matter. It is about power and empowerment, authority, and having the right to authorize. It is an extension of the self.

This was also acknowledged and explored by one of the few eccentric and courageous *pakeha* who underwent the ordeal. The flax trader Barnet Burns recounts how the marking which he had on his lower body, buttocks, thighs, and face seems very much in the nature of a canny commercial investment:

> I might as well have it done completely, particularly as it would be of service to me – and so it was. In the first place, I could travel to any part of the country... I was made and considered chief of a tribe of upwards of six hundred persons... I could purchase flax when others could not. (Burns 1844:14–15)

Another *pakeha*, Jack Rutherford, who returned to England and worked in a circus after sixteen years of living as a "fighting chief" with the well-armed clans of Ngapuhi, made a comparably colorful figure indeed, with body work from Hawaii, Samoa, and the Marquesas as well (Rutherford 1908). His dermagraphic extravagance anticipated the cross-cultural explorations of today's "modern primitives."

Such enthusiasm was, however, exceptional. Most settlers and new-comers shared the view expressed by Nicholas, "It is hoped that this barbarous practice will be abolished in time among the New Zealanders, and that the missionaries will exert all the influence they are possessed of to dissuade them from it" (1817). Missionary accounts record an exuberant and impassioned campaign to vilify the practice. The settlers also supposedly set an example: "Tattooing is going out of fashion, partly from the influence of the missionaries, who described it as the Devil's art, but chiefly from the example of the settlers" (Thomson 1859).Yet it was settler greed that caused a conflagration of hostility and armed resistance throughout the northern island, in wars which occurred in the 1840s and then in a second wave between 1860 and 1880. By 1895, there were 600,000 settlers, more than the number of Maori today. And they needed land, for they had been promised it by canny colonial developers. The last fatal confrontation between Maori seeking self-determination and armed agents of the Crown was in 1916.

Millions of acres of land were unjustly confiscated in these decades of brazen and outrageous breaches of the Treaty. Some land has been returned, and much reconciliation and apology have occurred, while the Waitangi Tribunal, established in 1975 to resolve these breaches, continues to hear claims from wronged tribal authorities, cheated tribes and subtribes, and aggrieved family groups.

Tumatauenga – the God of War – was close to the consciousness of Maori during these turbulent years. Serving him, and inspired by such leaders as the utterly singular Tawhiao Matutaera, the Second Maori King, many warriors submitted to the *uhi*, the chisel of the *tohunga ta moko*. Some instruments from this period have survived. They are metal chisels, revealing that the technology itself was changing. But by the turn of the century, there were very few ornamented male faces to be seen, in contrast to the consistently high numbers of women. With the seeming decline of the male full-face marking, a new technique, and a considerable number of roving practitioners, sustained the *moko kauae*, or chin tattoo, of traditional Maori femininity.

As one contemporary writer observes,

a full moko was more obtrusively Maori and less easily reconciled with the pervasive process of Europeanization and newly acquired aesthetic tastes. Women, however, were less vulnerable to these pressures, and fe-male tattooing continued for another century. There was no association of their moko with fighting. Female moko had connotations of beauty,

sex appeal and marriageability, and they became very much an assertion
of minority group identity. (King 1975)

The decline of the full facial *moko* became a metaphor for the alleged
decline of the "Maori race." In 1895, after the land wars, introduced
disease, and Christianity, the Maori population was at its nadir; 42,000
remained, and they became the subject of intensive ethnographic and
pictorial scrutiny. Having collected the grisly three-dimensional trophies
of the organic tattooed head, the settlers' interests turned to making
and acquiring images, of "the Maori As He Was" – and, one assumed,
never ever would be again.

From the earliest encounters, and Sydney Parkinson's exquisite pen-
and-wash drawings from Cook's first voyage, the Maori face and body
featured in the work of artists from the northern hemisphere. There is a
large canon of material which includes William Hodges, George French
Angas and Augustus Earle, the last one notable for his friendship with
Rangi, a *tohunga ta moko* whom he considered an accomplished artist
and "great natural genius."

The Land Wars period coincided with the arrival of the colony's first
photographers, according to a photographic historian:

> The hostilities created a demand for Maori portraits which was unpreced-
> ented ... a new innovation, the carte de visite, enabled him to produce
> his wares cheaply ... the public wanted cheap pictures of Maoris and
> this they got in abundance. (Main 1975:2–3)

Samuel Carnell produced dozens of chiefly portraits for popular consumption, as did George Henry Swan, and John McGarrigle's Auckland
Photographic Company was actively patronized by Maori who eagerly
sought his images of them. John Nichol Crombie even advertised
his "Portraits of the Native Chiefs" as early as 1856. His sitters were
flattered and intrigued by his attention, and by the process. They also
enjoyed having copies of the outcome, images of themselves for their
families.

For all of these cameramen, the adorned skin had an almost fetishistic
appeal, even to their deliberately touching up or exaggerating the
skin's inscribed effect, thus feeding on the comparable fascination of
their buying public. The extensive collection of 10x8 inch plates by
Pulman and Company illustrate this most graphically, as the sitters'
moko were dramatically retouched and even crudely redesigned.
Moko – the adorned face – was graphically commodified. Of the early

photographers, Alfred Henry Burton of Dunedin was the most sensitive, and the most responsible. He documented much of Maori experience in those final, transitional years of the nineteenth century. Though many of his images are of *moko* people, they are framed within a particular cultural and economic environment. They are not offered for colonial or tourist consumption. This gives his work a poignant and particular significance for Maori today, as he documented so much of that troubled period (see Knight 1980).

At that same time, the portraitists Charles Frederick Goldie and Gottfried Lindauer were also recording the *fin de siècle* Maori face, reflecting on the supposed prediction:

Kei muri I te awe kapara, he tangata ke.
Mana e noho te ao nei, he ma.

After the tatooed face someone,
with unmarked skin,
may claim this world.

Goldie (1870–1947) painted sitters whom he paid fairly, and with whom he enjoyed warm friendships. His Maori portraiture extended over the first four decades of the last century. In 1935, his work drew the comment that "His great pictures of Maori men and women will be 'Old Masters' – and connoisseurs will fight for them at Christie's and elsewhere, perhaps when none of the race he perpetuates are here" (Blackley 1997:50). His approach is perhaps most evident in the titles of his portraits – *A Hero of Many Fights*, *The Memory of What has been, and Never more will be*, *The Calm Close of Valour's Valorious Day*, *A Noble Relic of a Noble Race*, *Treasured Dreams of Times Long Past*, *The Last of the Tohunga or Priests*, and *Life's Long Day Closes* exemplify a few. For their specific *moko* designs and visual impact, they remain an awesome pictorial record. They are greatly revered by the descendants of the sitters, who weep over them to this very day and treasure the carefully framed and lovingly enshrined reproductions, which hold pride of place in private homes and in ceremonial buildings.

Gottfried Lindauer (1839–1926) left Bohemia in 1873, intending to paint the Maori of these islands. His approach was certainly in contrast to Goldie's. With the assistance of Henry Partridge, an Auckland entrepreneur, he secured portrait sittings with many influential chiefly families. Many of these native aristocrats also privately commissioned him, and the fine originals still grace their descendants' houses. He also worked closely from photographs, painting his sitters with fastidious accuracy. For Maori, Lindauer's portraits have iconic value, as images of people admired and long gone. One writer comments,

> Over the years hundreds of old-time Maoris have studied these pictures intently ... communed so closely with the subjects that they have burst into impassioned speeches as if they were speaking to live people. (Graham 1975)

The images made of the nineteenth-century Maori presented a narrative of fascination and nostalgia, modifying the notion of the threatening other, the fighting chief, the vengeful cunning native. Because it was thought likely that the native was fated to extinction, the romance of the languishing, lost exotic was permissible; the tattooed male face was fading indeed.

Coming into the Twentieth Century

Maori women continued to sustain the practice, even after the passing of the various tattoo practitioners who traveled from one community to the next, inscribing the chins and arms with a new technique. Metal chisels were still used in some areas, but the use of metal needle clusters became popular. Similar to the Japanese *irezumi*, the needle clusters punched in the pigment in a series of rythmic strikes to the upper layers of skin. In contrast to the *uhi*, which effectively carved, this method pricked and stained the flesh, which healed to a flat, colored surface. The tactile effect was minimal, without the high-relief three-dimensionality of *uhi* work. Similarly, the pain factor was reduced, and for many, this distinction became a matter of prestige. Perceived as a mark of pain, a *kauae moko* inscribed with chisels, with its high texture and keloid ridges, was initially considered superior to the flat but very black needle-cluster version. Chisel work proved a woman's ability to endure extreme pain, and it felt, and looked, different. Yet both were worn with pride.

> The moko was seen ... as a visible embodiment of Maori culture, as an assertion of Maori separateness in a world that was becoming increasingly European in orientation. Wiremu Poutapu, master carver of Ngaruawahia, remembers the situation this way. "In those days (the early days of this century), a Maori lady was not a Maori lady unless she had a moko. The other people had them and you just had to fit in with that kind of thing..." Some women were conscious of this need for moko as a deep instinct within them. (King and Friedlander 1972)

Just as the male face was captured on canvas by the portraitists of a century earlier, in the latter years of the twentieth century these aged matriarchs became the subject of scrutiny and visual documentation, and these images are similarly treasured, as they recall *kuia* from living memory, grandmothers and grand aunts, mothers and sisters, whom we knew, and loved, and learned so much from. Yet there is a difference, for their beauty has remained with us in the faces of their *mokopuna*, their granddaughters, and their *tamahine*, their daughters. As the very last survivor of that generation passed away in the 1970s, women of the next generation were choosing, deliberately and consciously, to take the *moko*, wear the mantle, and honor the tradition. And these courageous souls approached *pakeha* – white male Western – tattoo artists, working in the parlors of the metropolitan cities, inking the skins of sailors, soldiers, and social outcasts.

> Those involved in this first wave of revival were active in women's rituals and performance, famous as composers and chanters, weavers and oral historians. Motivated by an assertion of identity, they reclaimed the art form and reinforced their mana whenua in highly visual, indelible, terms. Soon after this, the first male, a colorful and passionate orator, began work on his face. (Te Awekotuku 1997:114)

Within another generation, there were Maori practitioners, men and a couple of women, offering *moko* – traditional Maori design for Maori skin, applied within a Maori context. Electric machines were engaged, simple handmade rotary "guns" fashioned from electric razors and home appliances, as well as the more sophisticated equipment advertised in tattoo magazines. In the first flush of this exciting revival, most had trained as traditional woodcarvers, and were exploring a new and challenging medium. The earliest to cut Maori design into modern skin was Laurie Te Rangikaihoro Nicholas. A graduate of the New Zealand School of Maori Arts & Crafts, he was mentored by the great classical master Hone Taiapa. With the enthusiasm of brother carvers and admirers (including the writer), and tutored eagerly by European tattoo experts Jurgen Christiansen of Denmark and Henk Schiffmaker of the Netherlands, the movement flourished. Maori dermagraphic artists were emerging from the prisons, and Maori gang culture, so forcefully portrayed in the 1994 film *Once were Warriors*, consciously manipulated Maori imagery as part of their own distinctive visual expression (Cairns 2001). In the rural communities, particularly in the Eastern Bay of Plenty, Te Urewera Ranges, and the Tai Rawhiti

(East) Coast, local activists and community leaders claimed the *moko* as a powerful and permanent affirmation of being Maori, as a potent symbol of Maori identity.

Such dynamic assertion reflects other developments in the Maori world over the last three decades. One example is the Maori-language movement, now subsidized by the Taura Whiri I te Reo Maori/Maori Language Commission, which works on retaining the Maori language as a living, growing, everyday feature of these islands, for everyone. One significant achievement after many decades has been the successful establishment of preschool-, elementary-, secondary-, and tertiary-education providers in which Maori is the language of instruction. Others are the Waitangi Tribunal, a claims process referred to earlier in this chapter, and the setting up of efficiently sustained and independent tribal economies based, for example, in agriculture, tourism, aquaculture, and resource management. Nevertheless, such critical indicators as health, justice, and housing reveal that we still have a long way to go, and the struggle certainly continues as more and more Maori – 80 percent of a population of 400,000 – live in the urban environment. One of the most courageous of the first wave of men, Herbie King, took up his facial work in the late 1980s, on arriving in the city. He told the world who he was in this way:

> I looked for my people and I couldn't find them, I couldn't identify them. I felt a need to have something show I am Maori, and the idea came to me that I should get the moko. (see Johansson 1994:16)

For almost everyone, *moko* says it all – it celebrates the successes, confronts the challenges, and reminds Maori of the recent past. As a collective proclaims in its editorial,

> The resurgence of ta moko among Maori is a direct means of asserting our tino rangatiratanga (absolute sovereignty). It is in defiance of past and present political agendas, laws and regulations that continually deny access to our lands, language, customs and beliefs... Wearers of the art of ta moko ensure that this tradition continues into the new millennium. (Neleman et al. 1999:9)

It is a political act, an exercise of will, and a declaration of resistance. It is an active defiance of mainstream middle-class white New Zealand's aesthetic sensibility so often agitated by media distortion. It is also an elegant reclaiming and celebration, as another wearer confides: "What started as an expression of identity and a political statement of autonomy and freedom, now represents inner mana" (Sam Utatao in ibid.:133).

Although the most decisive and dramatic form of *moko* is the full facial work on men, and the chin patterns and midbrow designs, with occasional marking on the nostrils, upper lip, and throat, other parts of the body are also being enhanced. Over the last fifteen years, many men and a few women have affected the lower body coverage – thighs, buttocks, hips, lower backs – and also extensive work on the upper back, shoulders, and neck. Some women have assumed the *tara whakairo* and *kopu whakairo*: lower abdomen and genital designs described in traditional accounts, though this is comparatively rare. The most commonly seen work occurs on the arms, or one shoulder. Often selection, size, and placement are determined by cost, and by access to a preferred artist. At the time of writing, there are two formally trained chisel artists, a male tutored by the late great Paulo Sulu'ape of Samoa, and the other, the exceptional sister of the pioneer Te Rangikaihoro. She received instruction in Hawaiian chisel work from Keone Nunes of Wai'anae, Oahu.

Taia I te Ahi Manuka: Here and Now

Ta Moko – taking *moko* – is a serious commitment. It inscribes your soul, it uplifts your senses, and it changes you forever. It is the ultimate engagement of oneself with one's body, because it cannot be removed. You cannot take it off, you forfeit that choice, commitment is irrevocable. One elderly gentleman, Netana Whakaari Rakuraku of the Waimana Valley, had this to say of his finely inscribed face in 1921:

> Taia o moko, hai hoa matenga mou. You may lose your most valuable property through misfortune in various ways. You may lose your house, your patupounamu, your wife, and other treasures – you may be robbed of all your most prized possessions, but of your moko you cannot be deprived. Except by death. It will be your ornament and your companion until your last day. (Cowan 1921)

Many decades later, one of his *mokopuna*, a young woman with a proud *moko kauae* on her chin, shared these thoughts:

> Moko is a lifelong commitment, I believe and trust my moko will take me to the places I need to be. I couldn't imagine myself or my life without the presence of my moko. It has become more significant to me than

I have ever predicted. It teaches me self discipline, self tolerance, self acceptance, and more. (Hine Te Wai in Neleman et al. 1999:131)

Though part of the body, it is as if the *moko* also has its own life, its own unique individuality, as a companion, as an extension of the body and the senses, as a dramatic emphasis, as another woman remarks of her elaborately incised arm, back, and full shoulder patterns:

Moko has added emphasis to one's character and personality and one's visual appearance – because that's what's different on my body. Moko creates an awareness of such exquisite beauty, reverence and integrity ... that's the art ... the patterns, the creation, the colours.[8]

This commitment is declared not just in the visual impact of the outcome, a modified body, a body that is different and perceived as such by the viewer and sensed as such by one's self. It is also demonstrated by the often intense, even extreme, physical pain of the process. Everyone I have ever discussed this with concurs – it is necessary, the suffering, the endurance, the screaming of the senses and the nerve endings, for with it comes an appreciation of what our forebears went through. "Enduring this pain ... is definitely relevant; it is part of what the moko is all about" (Hare Wikaira in Hatfield and Steur 2002).

Some artists, however, sometimes also test the limits of their clients, as one survivor with a splendidly ornamented face reports:

Man he's got a heavy hand ... trying to torture me. I think he was trying to see how much pain I could endure. Especially under that kauae. It was like the old dentist was getting in there with his pliers and drilling holes in your teeth. Meanest pain I've ever felt. Under the kauae. Everywhere else. Oh the bones, you feel it all right. (on the skin) ... Burns like dozens of bees. (Poniania in Rua 2003:69)

Meeting the pain threshold, many clients drift into the sound of voices chanting and lilting, focus on the texture and strength of the many hands caressing and massaging them, apart from the latex-gloved incursions of the artist. They inhale the blood and sweat and tears and fragrant oils or burning native herbs, and they endure, often accepting lines being recut, and reopened, as a pattern is perfected, and completed.

It became medicinal, the moko itself like a healing inside me. The pain vanished before it began, really. At first we didn't know things like how

deep to make it. Some lines would look good but then heal up completely, so we"d go back and do it again. Some lines took four or five
attempts. (Hepa Poutini in Neleman et al. 1999:134)

And for those whose senses are attuned, and who often undergo months
of preparation, with fasting, special food, and spiritual discipline, there
may be another experience, an uplifting, and engagement with the
ancestors, as described in this account:

I couldn't feel the pain because I had put myself in another level where
you don't feel pain. When I did feel the pain was when it hit the bone
over here. That's all. Nowhere else. I was in a different dimension in
a different realm at the time, as I was being done. (Putaringa in Rua
2003:58)

Ta moko is about pain, firing the five senses, resolving them, moving through that passage, and emerging reconciled, complete, and
beautified.

Celebrated so passionately in the contemporary Maori world, *moko* has
inevitably attracted global attention over many decades. At first, this was
naively manifested by the imprinting of Lindauer and Goldie portraits
on European skin. Now *moko* design occurs in the complex blackwork
favored by urban modern primitives, and fashionably accessorized by
glamorous pop icons like Robbie Williams and Ben Harper. Inked in by
Maori artists Te Rangitu Netana and Toi Gordon Hatfield respectively,
the two musicians' body work raises questions of appropriateness and
appropriation, particularly within the Maori and Pacific community,
and is the subject of volatile ongoing debate.[9]

Moko and *ta moko* – the outcome from the process – are essentially
about engaging, and exciting, all the senses. From the earliest colonial
encounters, it has been appreciated, fetishized, vilified, admired,
demonized. Most of all, it has been recorded. In its many forms, as an
artifactual and tangible object, and also as a living, organic medium, it
has been collected and commodified. And it continues to grow, beyond
the colonial notions of containment and categorization, beyond the
strictures of Western academic inquiry and scholarly reflection. *Moko*
is still for, and about, its people, its lovers, its wearers. And admirers,
too. As a narrative art form, as an engagement of all five senses, *moko*
remains a compelling visceral, visible, textual, and textured reality for
Maori in this millennium.

One young woman rejoices in its meaning for her:

Now I have moko and I will continue to take on more moko because it fills me with ihi – it excites me. It affects me in many ways. It affects who I am. It is one of the ways I share how I feel about being Maori … to celebrate the beauty of what it is to belong to a race of people so rich in culture, so rich in history. (Aneta Morgan in Hatfield and Steur 2002:22)

And so the present is predicted by the past, as one of her ancestors recalls the sensual vanities of his own vigorous youth:

Tu te takitaki, e ha!
Oti te hopehope ra!
No mua ra, e Pa ma, I taia ai aku reherehe
Ka pai au te haere I te one I Te Piu, e ha!

My thigh designs were strengthened, thus!
And my hips completely patterned, so!
For long ago, oh friends,
with my buttocks engraved, exquisite,
I strode with pride across Te Piu's sands. (Te Ikatere 1932)

Moko is about living, the Living Face, *Mata Ora*. It is about life. *Pai marire*: blessed be.

Notes

1. This is a *whakawai*, a traditional chant performed by the *tohunga ta moko* – practitioner – during the procedure. A version of this chant is in the manuscript number 89 of Wiremu te Rangikaheke, held in the Grey Collection at the Auckland Public Library, Auckland, New Zealand.

2. Mako was a participant in the research project "Ta Moko, Culture, Body Modification and the Psychology of Identity" supported by the Marsden Fund at the Maori & Psychology Research Unit, Waikato University, concluded in December 2004.

3. Toi Gordon Hatfield, personal communication, September 2000.

4. Records of the Colony of New South Wales. Government Order, 16 April 1831, Colonial Secretary's Office Sydney, signed by Alexander MccLeay for Governor Darling. Held in NSW State Library, Sydney.

5. This issue is addressed in Te Awekotuku 2004.

6. "He Tangi Mo Te Heuheu Tukino (II) i Horoa e te Whenua," Song 60 in Part One, lines 14–17 (Te Heuheu 1932).

7. *Te Ao Hou the Maori Magazine* no. 43, June 1963.

8. Comments by Kiwi, a participant in the Marsden project (see Note 2), in 2003.

9. One lively current example: www.aotearoa.maori.nz

References

Banks, J. 1962 [1768–1771]. *The Endeavour Journal of Joseph Banks*, 2 vols. ed. J.C. Beagehole. Sydney: Public Library of New South Wales.

Blackley, Roger (ed.). 1997. *Goldie*. Auckland: David Bateman.

Burns, Barnet. 1844. *A Brief Narrative of a New Zealand Chief*. Belfast: R & D Read, Crown-Entry.

Cairns, Puawai. 2001. "He Taonga te Moko – Reimaging/Reimagining the Moko: Examining Current Representations of Ta Moko." Unpublished Master's thesis, University of Waikato, Hamilton, New Zealand.

Cowan, James. 1921. "Maori Tattooing Survivals: Some Notes on Moko." *Journal of the Polynesian Society* 30: 241–5.

Earle, A. 1966 [1832]. *Augustus Earle: Narrative of a Residence in New Zealand. Journal of a Residence in Tristan da Cunha*, ed. E.H. McCormick. Oxford: Clarendon.

Graham, J.C. 1975. *Maori Paintings by Gottfried Lindauer*. Honolulu: East West Center Press.

Hatfield, Gordon Toi and Patricia Steur. 2002. *Dedicated by Blood Whakautu ki te toto Renaissance of Ta Moko*. The Hague: Hunter Media.

Johansson, D. 1994. *Wearing Ink: The Art of Tattoo in New Zealand*. Auckland: David Bateman.

Jones, Sarah. 2000. "A Curious Document." Paper presented to the BSANZ Conference, Expanding Horizons, Print Cultures across the South Pacific, September 2000.

King, Michael. 1975. *Face Value: A Study in Maori Portraiture*. Dunedin: Dunedin Public Art Gallery. Unpaginated exhibition catalogue.

—— and Marti Friedlander. 1972. *Moku Maori Tattooing in the 20th Century*. Unpaginated. Wellington: Alister Taylor.

Knight, Hardwicke. 1980. *Burton Brothers: Photographers*. Dunedin: John McIndoe Press.

Main, William. 1976. *Maori in Focus: A Selection of Photographs of the Maori 1850–1914*. Wellington: Millwood.

Manning, F.E. 1906. *Old New Zealand: A Tale of the Good Old Times*. Christchurch: Whitcombe and Tombs.

Marsden, S. 1932 [1765–1838]. *The Letters and Journals of Samuel Marsden*, ed. John Rawson Elder. Dunedin: Coulls Somerville Wilkie/A.H. Reed for the Otago University Council.

Mokomokai Education Trust. Information website. www.digitalus.co.nz/mokomokai/index1.html

Neleman, Hans, Tame Wairere Iti, Pita Turei, and Nicole McDonald. 1999. *Moku Maori Tattoo: Photographs by Hans Neleman*. Zurich: Edition Stemmle.

Nicholas, J.L. 1817. *Narrative of a Voyage to New Zealand Performed in the Years 1814 and 1815 in Company with the Rev. Samuel Marsden, Principal Chaplain of New South Wales*, 2 vols. London: James Black.

Rua, Mohi. 2003. "Moko: Maori Facial Tattoos – the Experiences of Contemporary Wearers." Unpublished Master's thesis. University of Waikato, Hamilton, New Zealand.

Rutherford, J. 1908. *John Rutherford the White Chief: A Story of Adventure in New Zealand*, ed. James Drummond. Wellington: Whitcombe and Tombs.

Te Awekotuku, Ngahuia. 1996. "Maori People and Culture." In *Maori Art and Culture*, ed. D. Starzecka. London: British Museum Press.

——. 1997. "Ta Moko: Maori Tattoo." In *Goldie*, ed. Roger Blackley. 1997. Auckland: David Bateman.

——. 2004. "He Maimai Aroha: A Disgusting Traffic for Collectors: The Trade in Preserved Human Heads in Aotearoa, New Zealand." In *Obsession, Compulsion, Collection: On Objects, Display Culture and Interpretation*, ed. Anthony Kiendl. Banff, Canada: Banff Centre Press.

Te Heuheu III Iwikau. 1932. *Nga Moteatea – He Maramara rere no nga waka maha: The Songs – Scattered Pieces from Many Canoe Areas* [trans. present author], 3 vols., ed. Apirana Ngata. Wellington: Reed for the Polynesian Society.

Te Ikatere. 1932. *Nga Moteatea – He Maramara rere no nga waka maha: The Songs – Scattered Pieces from Many Canoe Areas* [trans. present author], 3 vols., ed. Apirana Ngata. Wellington: Reed for the Polynesian Society.

Thomson, A.S. 1859. *The Story of New Zealand*, 2 vols. London: John Murray.

Walsh, Revd Philip. 1894. "Maori Preserved Heads." Transactions and Proceedings of the New Zealand Institute 27: 610–61.

Yate, W. 1835. *An Account of New Zealand and of the Formation of the Church Missionary Society's Mission in New Zealand*. London: Church Missionary Society.

five

Smoked Fish and Fermented Oil: Taste and Smell among the Kwakwaka'wakw

Aldona Jonaitis

I find them best when cooked in Indian stile which is by roasting a number of them together on a wooden spit without any previous prep-eration whatever. They are so fat they require no additional sauce, and I think them superior to any fish I ever tasted, even more delicate and lussious than the white fish of the [Great] lakes which have heretofore formed my standart of excellence among the fishes. The natives do not appear to be very scrupelous about eating them when a little feated [fetid]. (Merriweather Lewis, on the eulachon fish he encountered at Fort Clatsop, 1806)

James Sewid, a high-ranking Kwakwaka'wakw born in Alert Bay, British Columbia in 1910, describes these fish, when "feated," in strikingly different terms. Of special importance to his culture is *t'lina*, grease rendered from eulachon, the "lussious" fish to which Lewis referred. Sewid describes how his relatives, who had spent time in Knight Inlet where they harvested the abundant run of this anadromous fish and rendered its oil, returned with "quite a bit [of oil] ... especially for me. They asked me to go and give it out to some of the people in Alert Bay, so I gave it out and everybody had one or two gallons. It used to be quite an honor to receive olachen [sic] oil at a feast in the old days because that was a very precious food to all the Indians" (Sewid 1969:235). That grease, so delectable to the Kwakwaka'wakw (as well as other Northwest Coast First Nations people), was processed from fish that had been allowed to partially putrefy – to the distaste of Merriweather Lewis. Used as a condiment by the Kwakwaka'wakw to make food more flavorful, eulachon grease has rarely found favor among non-Natives. The contrasting value of *t'lina* for First Nations and non-Natives represents an especially striking example of how food, by means of its taste, smell, and social significance, transcends its sustenance function and becomes a player in colonial and postcolonial dynamics.

Boas and Hunt's "Recipes"

The title of James Sewid's biography from which the above is quoted, *Guests Never Leave Hungry* (Sewid 1969), addresses two significant features of Kwakwaka'wakw culture that revolve around food: hosting feasts and ensuring satiated guests. He reflects proudly on the abundance and variety of food among his people: "we could cook halibut or salmon in many more ways than the white people even knew… I used to live on fish that had been barbequed or boiled in oil and it would be different for every meal" (Sewid 1969:235). Franz Boas recognized the importance of food to the Kwakwaka'wakw and assigned George Hunt, his half-Native collaborator, to collect information among them on food acquisition, preparation, and eating.[1] Hunt also recorded from his wife over 300 pages of "recipes" that include 33 ways to prepare salmon, 15 to serve halibut, and 17 to process various berries.[2] These provide vivid evidence of Sewid's proud claim for the diversity of Kwakwaka'wakw food (Boas 1921:305–601). While halibut and salmon reside within both the Kwakwaka'wakw and the Canadian culinary repertoires, the Kwakwaka'wakw prepare those fish in ways unimaginable by whites. Thus, embedded in Sewid's comments is another significant point – that food in some way *distinguishes* the Kwakwaka'wakw from their colonizers and thus serves as a marker of difference.

The literature on the anthropology of food demonstrates how food, in addition to being essential for survival, functions within a culture by solidifying social and political alliances, defining gender roles, and reinforcing or even shaping attitudes toward the self, others, and relationships (Meigs 1997:103). But food also works on the senses. Its taste, smell, feel, and color contribute to what Carole Counihan and Penny Van Esterik term "a rich symbolic alphabet … to be elaborated and combined in infinite ways" (Counihan and Van Esterik 1997:2). With its sensuous appeal, the abundant and varied Kwakwaka'wakw cuisine becomes, in its own way, a form of art.

Not everyone has recognized the value of Hunt's recipes. For example, Victor Barnouw uses the recipes to criticize Boasian historical particularism: "This fascination for details may lead to a lack of focus. For example, Boas recorded page after page of blueberry-pie recipes in the Kwakiutl language, with the English translation on facing pages. We still do not know to what use they may ultimately be put" (Barnouw 1975:32).[3] These recipes, without which this chapter could not have been written, describe Kwakwaka'wakw food at a critical moment in history, after a century of interactions with settlers, and before a period of intense cultural repression by the Canadian authorities, and constitute a baseline upon which twentieth-century culinary developments can be evaluated. Food today, although not so varied as in Sewid's time, remains important to the Kwakwaka'wakw and continues to serve as an expression of distinction within the contemporary and globalized world.

Barnouw is not alone in his dismissal of Kwakwaka'wakw recipes. Of the numerous books and articles based largely on the Hunt and Boas materials, few dwell on the social and artistic aspects of food. For example, the vividly painted bowls for serving feast foods and carefully carved ladles for pouring precious fish oil onto foods are usually treated as works of sculpture, analyzed stylistically and symbolically. Although occasionally information is provided on their culinary usage, most books and museum exhibits ignore smell and taste, touch and hearing while concentrating on the dramatic and dynamic visual expressions of Kwakwaka'wakw culture. As a result, the representation of a potlatch, in virtually all media, ignores what for the people themselves is a central component.

In large measure this is inevitable, for most non-Kwakwaka'wakw learn about Kwakwaka'wakw culture through reading ethnographic accounts, looking at illustrations in books, and visiting museum exhibits of carvings and paintings. Films of Kwakwaka'wakw ceremonies enhance these sources with sound and movement, but cannot convey the smells, tastes, and feelings of the potlatch. Limitations of such representations become clear during contemporary potlatches at Alert Bay, Fort Rupert, or Campbell River. During the impressive display of masks and regalia, dancers snap the articulated beaks of cannibal bird masks and issue forth high-pitched raven cries. The building reverberates with drumming. Chiefs sing. Women swirl by in vivid robes that swish and create breezes. The house is pungent with smells of the salmon. And the abundant food tastes delicious. As Marcell Mauss contends in his classic work, *The Gift*, potlatches are "banquets themselves in which everyone participates; everything, food, objects and services ... is the cause of aesthetic emotion" (Mauss 1990 {1950}:79). Mere descriptions or images of artifacts fail to convey the complete sensual experience of the potlatch.

The recipes, documents about production and consumption of food, and objects used for serving and eating reinforce the social role of food among the Kwakwaka'wakw. Analysis of these data along with historical documents and contemporary information produces further insights into Kwakwaka'wakw culture, including their response to colonialism, gender roles, and the significance of the taste of certain foods in the postcolonial era. In a recent essay on visual culture, W.J.T. Mitchell argues that culture constructs vision which is in turn influenced by factors such as history, politics, economics, and philosophy. But the objects of visual culture are not merely vehicles that express cultural concepts, but instead are themselves players in a dynamic process. Mitchell turns the tables on conventional perspectives on objects, claiming:

> Works of art, media, figures and metaphors have "lives of their own," and cannot be explained simply as rhetorical, communicative instruments or epistemological windows onto reality ... Vision is never a one-way street, but a multiple intersection teeming with dialectical images ... It makes it clear why the questions to ask about images are not just "what do they mean?" or "what do they do?" but "what is the secret of their vitality?" and "what do they want?" (Mitchell 2002:97)

What is true for objects is also true for food, and in this chapter, after describing what food "means" and "does," I hope to speculate on what its "secret vitality" may be, and what it "wants."

The Kwakwaka'wakw Potlatch

The Kwakwaka'wakw, who live on northern Vancouver Island and the mainland opposite, have been subjected to extensive ethnographic study. In the words of Gloria Cranmer Webster, retired director of the U'mista Cultural Center , and great-granddaughter of George Hunt, "we are the most anthropologized people in the world" (personal conversation, 2003). Whether or not that is actually true, Franz Boas concentrated on this group, whom he judged to be the least acculturated on the coast. His goal, to assemble a complete representation of their culture, could be attained by acquiring as much data on them as possible. Sometimes he provided first-hand accounts of events, such as a 60-page detailed chronicle of a potlatch he attended in Fort Rupert from November 15 to December 3, 1895 (Boas 1966:179–241). But, more often, Boas relied for information on George Hunt who provided thousands of pages on rituals, social organization, technology, economics, material culture, art, myths, and histories. Hunt also collected hundreds of Kwakwaka'wakw artifacts for the American Museum of Natural History where Boas was a curator between 1895 and 1905 (Jonaitis 1988).

Probably the best known and most exhaustively analyzed feature of Kwakwaka'wakw culture is the potlatch, an elaborate ceremony of feasting, oration, masquerade, dancing, singing, and, finally, distribution of goods. Mauss represents it as a "total" cultural phenomenon, with religious, shamanistic, mythological, economic, social, juridical, and aesthetic elements (Mauss 1990:38).[4] The vast majority of interpretations of this event draw information from Boas's copious materials on the Kwakwaka'wakw potlatch, and many share Boas's opinion that the primary motivation for this elaborate ceremony is acquisition of prestige.[5] Kwakwaka'wakw potlatches could be hosted for a variety of reasons, including marriages, memorials, or assumptions of new names, and always include feasting, distribution of goods, and demonstrations of privileges such as songs, dances, and masquerades, that embody the host family's status. Acceptance of the goods by guests validates the host's claim to his family's social position within the hierarchy (Jonaitis 1991).

The potlatches Boas described in his publications were to become the canonical events upon which were based most subsequent analyses. In reality, those late nineteenth-century potlatches differed from ones hosted earlier in that century and in precontact times, having been influenced by 100 years of visitors and settlers. By the time Boas visited Vancouver Island, hosts at these highly competitive and sometimes categorically hostile events, distributed – or even destroyed – abundant amounts of goods. In contrast, earlier potlatches had been relatively small affairs, with moderate amounts of food eaten and limited numbers of gifts distributed. During the nineteenth century, as warfare declined among the Kwakwaka'wakw in response to Canadian pressure, potlatches are thought to have become substitutes for battles, and incorporated the antagonisms, hostilities, and belligerent actions characteristic of warriors (Codere 1950).

Demographic and economic developments inspired other modifications. Epidemics had decimated the Kwakwaka'wakw population, causing extinction of certain chiefly families and vacancies in some of the 700 traditional chiefly positions. Meanwhile, some lower-ranking families were accruing great wealth by participating in the cash economy. By the late nineteenth century, men traveled to the Bering Sea to hunt fur seals, and both men and women worked in the British Columbia lumber camps, hops fields, fish salteries, and canneries, and some women became prostitutes. As a consequence, some families of lesser rank became rich, and appropriated empty chiefly positions, often through the agency of a potlatch. What had earlier been dignified, low-key affairs intended to maintain a certain social order were now arenas for hostile contests between new and old wealth. Potlatches became flamboyant displays of wealth as well as sites of ever-escalating competitiveness. Missionaries and officials found the excesses of potlatches appalling, and encouraged the passage of legislation in 1885 that criminalized the potlatches as well as the related *hamatsa* or cannibal dances.

Boas's account of the nine sequential potlatches, which represent "the way to be walked by true chiefs" during which a chief settles his marriage debt with his in-laws, lists goods given away, such as boxes, button blankets, gold, silver and copper bracelets, small coppers, box covers, chief's hats, abalone shell, masks, and spoons, as well as the food eaten. Food, too, had a role. For example, at the second of the nine potlatches, hosts serve dried salmon, clover roots, and "all kinds of food." The fourth feast centers on oil of the eulachon, the so-called candlefish whose rendered grease is a great delicacy along the entire Northwest Coast. For the eighth potlatch, called "the last eating of the food for paying the marriage debt" the host invites the guests into his house:

> Then they have the last eating of the food paying for the marriage debt. When all the tribes are inside they are given much dry salmon to eat. And after they have done so all different kinds of foods are taken and given to all the men. And when it is gone then they take many mats and give them away and the spoons. Now the payment for the marriage debt is done. (Boas 1966:102)

The most common visual image of the lavish Kwakwaka'wakw gift-payments illustrates impressive stacks of Hudson's Bay Company blankets. But, as this quote reveals, food stood alongside such material signifiers of wealth as appropriate, and sometimes even required, pot-latch payments.[6] It might even be that the anti-potlatch legislation was in part inspired by the feasting that Victorians would have judged unfittingly sybaritic.

Food and Culture

Hunt's recipes contain considerable amounts of information on culinary traditions. It is impossible in a discussion such as this to deal with them comprehensively, so I will briefly mention some themes contained therein. In earlier times, the Kwakwaka'wakw adhered to many now-inactive prescriptions concerning food. For example, breakfast has to consist of less fatty food that does not make one sleepy, so fresh dog salmon and halibut heads, both of which have too much fat, are excluded. Dried salmon, in contrast, is an excellent Kwakwaka'wakw breakfast food which the wife scorches, breaks into pieces in a dish, and serves alongside another dish of eulachon oil.

Water has its own prescriptions. Although water consumption is essential before and after all meals to prevent people from "rot[ting] inside," it is especially obligatory at breakfast for ridding the throat of "sleepiness" (Boas 1921:377). But drinking during a meal is highly inappropriate. One type of food, roasted salmon-backs, can irritate the throat and induce a fit of coughing, checked only by water. Because coughing and drinking during a meal are embarrassing and require a face-saving potlatch, chiefs shun roasted salmon-backs:

> Those who have a man's mind would not do this in this manner when they get choked, for they would be ashamed to show that they are choking, for, if they should get choked, they would have to drink water in the middle (of the meal) before they finish eating. Then they would at once promise a potlatch. Therefore they would rather choke to death [than drink water]. (Boas 1909:427–8)

Or even better, avoid the cough-inducing food altogether.

The recipes not only detail how to make food, they also describe the social contexts of meals and feasts. Breakfast is usually a family meal, but other meals can involve more people. Meals for up to six guests are handled like a casual family meal, while meals served to greater numbers become more formal and include special invitations, singing, drumming, and hand clapping. For example, a man might decide to feed eight friends soaked salmon. After he cleans the house, he sends a house member to invite the friends, who enter and sing feast songs while the host boils soaked roasted salmon in water. Once done, the host's wife breaks the fish into bite-size pieces, and ladles them into wooden dishes, each of which contains enough food for two men. She also pours oil into small bowls for dipping the salmon. Once the food is placed before them, and the singing stops, the guests take water to rinse their mouths and drink. As is the case with the serving of virtually all meals, the highest ranking man receives his water first. Then everyone can eat. Afterward, they drink more water and finally wash their hands in a cleaned bowl (Boas 1921:319–22).

Utensils contribute to the aesthetics of a meal. Normally, dry food is served on a food mat and eaten with one's hands, while wet food requires dishes and spoons. Simple, undecorated, yet well-crafted bowls are used for everyday meals and small feasts, while elaborately carved and painted ones appear at great potlatches. Spoons, gracefully crafted in one of three different materials – alder, hemlock, or yew wood, mountain goat horn, and shell – must be rinsed after eating, to prevent witches from performing magic on any remaining saliva (Boas 1909:427).[7]

Many undecorated bowls assume the shape of a canoe. In addition to being essential for transportation, canoes are one of numerous Kwakwaka'wakw signifiers of wealth and abundance, the quintessential image of richness being a canoe laden with expensive goods. Canoe-shaped dishes, according to Boas, represent a miniaturized wealth-bringer, now fully loaded with abundant food (Boas 1896:101–2). Small canoe-shaped dishes feed one person, while larger ones can hold sufficient food for three. Eulachon oil is poured into even smaller yet somewhat wider canoe-shaped bowls. Canoes sometimes actually function as large mixing-bowls. For example, the Kwakwaka'wakw prepare an especially high-ranking dish by soaking dried salal-berries with water inside a small canoe, and mixing them with crab apples and eulachon oil. They serve this preparation directly out of the canoe. They also render eulachon oil inside a full-size canoe (see this chapter, pp. 155–7).

Kwakwaka'wakw society is highly stratified, and so is their food. Not all food is of equal significance, with some appropriate for feasts and some correct only for everyday meals. The difference between ordinary and special, however, does not always reside in the food itself, but in its method of preparation. For example, steamed clover can be given at great feasts, but boiled clover is eaten only by the family (Boas 1921:531–3). Roast halibut edges are restricted to family eating, whereas boiling transforms the edges into "valuable food for feasts, for this kind is very costly" (Boas 1921:368–70). Fresh codfish is also prepared differently for home consumption and for feasts (ibid.:378–9), but only the family can enjoy the very favorite form of this fish, tainted boiled codfish (ibid.:386). To prepare this pungent food, codfish is placed in the corner of the house until well-rotted. Then the wife soaks it in water, scrapes off the scales, beats it to loosen the flesh from the bones, cuts it into steaks and boils it. The family happily consume this delicacy with spoons, saving the choicest edible part, the head, for the husband.

Kwakwaka'wakw food contributes to maintaining social stratification. Highest-ranking chiefs are always served first, and only they can dine on highly valued fern roots served with oil and boiled seal offal (ibid.:457, 523). Food challenges become one expression of intense rivalry between chiefs at potlatches. A chief wishing to insult a nobleman can host a great seal feast and, before 80 to 100 guests, serve his victim the portion of meat from the body that commoners would normally receive (ibid.:751).

Sometimes food-related artifacts function in the maintenance of hierarchies and expressions of hostility. The 6-foot-long Dzunukwa dish is actually an array of different-sized dishes. The mythic being lies face-up on very short arms and legs, her body a large cavity, her face one bowl, her breasts, navel, and kneecaps five more. Guests are served out of different bowls depending on rank: highest-ranking chiefs from the head, and descending from second-ranking to sixth-ranking chiefs, from the right breast, the left breast, the navel, the right kneecap, and the left kneecap. Everyone else gets food held within the body (Mochon 1966:88–90).[7] To communicate his respect for his guests, and express his evaluation that they have the resources to reciprocate this potlatch, the host directs his men to position the bowl with its head facing away from the door, toward the guests. But, to insult his guests with a gesture indicating his disdain for their weakness and poverty, the chief has the dish situated with its back facing the guests. In response to this grievous affront, the injured party might attempt to cast the dish into the fire. Host and guest alike wrestle each other, attempting an act of utter humiliation: throwing a rival into the dish itself.

This very brief summary of some salient features of the Hunt-Boas food documents provides some indication of the wealth of information available. In addition to descriptions of how to actually prepare food, there are details on the social aspects of food among the Kwakwaka'wakw. The preparation, presentation, and consumption of food can indicate the nature of a meal – private or public, everyday or feastly.[9] All-important social rankings find expressions in the menu, the service, the cuts of meat and parts of fish, the elaboration or simplicity of dishes. One can even glean insights into the changing roles of food among the Kwakwaka'wakw, for, when late nineteenth-century potlatches became competitive, food began serving as a vehicle for expressions of aggression and hostility.[10]

Changes in Food

The potlatch – and the food hosts serve at the event – changed over the period from precontact times to the late nineteenth-century, and continues to change today. In 1885, the Canadian government, horrified at what they viewed as the flagrant excess of giving away vast quantities of goods as well as the appearance of cannibalism, passed a law criminalizing the potlatch and the *hamatsa*. The Kwakwaka'wakw, characterized by some as "incorrigible," resisted the law, and continued potlatching until the 1920s when the government arrested and jailed some who had been at a potlatch. Nevertheless, some continued hosting potlatches covertly and, when the law was dropped in 1951, the Kwakaka'wakw began potlatching actively.

The intrusion of the capitalist economy during the nineteenth century had affected Kwakwaka'wakw subsistence activities. Some groups, like the Kwagiul who had moved from older village sites to Fort Rupert, adjacent to a Hudson's Bay Company station, purchased some dried salmon from other people like the Nimpkish, instead of acquiring and processing their own (Ford 1941). The Nakwoktak and Newitti sold halibut to other tribes, and whoever had *t'lina* sold it to other groups, also for cash (Galolis 1994:59) In mixed villages such as Alert Bay, and large towns such as Nanaimo and Victoria, Kwakwaka'wakw spent their cash at white-run stores, which supplied staples, such as rice, previously not part of the Native diet.

Potlatch hosts incorporated both traditional and new cuisine into their menus. In addition to detailing the complex events of an 18-day Fort Rupert potlatch he attended in 1895, Boas described the food served. On November 16, the day after Boas arrived in Fort Rupert, he attended a feast which had as its first course soapberries, a traditional fruit that whips up into a froth, and as its second, rice from the store (Boas 1966:179–80). Other food over the days included seal, salmon and berries with oil, crab apples mixed with oil, dried salmon and oil.

In keeping with Boas's instructions to obtain "traditional" information, Hunt's recipes are meant to represent culinary customs from precontact times. By comparing these with actual food-related practices at historic potlatches, changes in Kwakwaka'wakw food culture become evident. According to Hunt, etiquette demands that nobles, especially women, eat limited quantities of food. The rule that the elite eat limited amounts of food may perhaps have been operative in the past when potlatches were quieter, smaller, noncompetitive affairs. But by the late nineteenth century, excess had become the rule, and vast quantities of food the norm. High-status food such as crab apples and oil still remained on potlatch menus, but were now accompanied by the everyday yet abundantly available salmon. Equally ample amounts of store-bought food like rice was also readily obtained. As a result, celebratory cuisine had become a postcontact mixture of traditional feast foods, common foods, and introduced foods, parallelling the changing nature of the entire Kwakwaka'wakw potlatch. Everyday food also reflected changes. Charley Nowell, a Kwakwaka'wakw chief whose biography, *Smoke From Their Fires* (Ford 1941), like that of James Sewid, describes the importance of food, comments that breakfast could be boiled dried salmon and oil, followed by what is called "after-food," which could be hemlock bark sap, but might be the rice, bread, or molasses from the Fort Rupert store that were convenient to purchase and easy to use.

The Kwakwaka'wakw responded creatively to the anti-potlatch law. Sometimes, they held potlatches around Christmas time, arguing that they were following the Christian tradition of distributing presents. At other times they gave away sacks of flour and sugar as well as boxes of pilot biscuits, arguing that they were giving their hungry relatives food. Photographs of such potlatches show stacks of these commodities, piled high in a manner reminiscent of Hudson's Bay blankets. A container holding a commercially-produced foodstuff, although ostensibly a source of nutrition for hungry relatives, was now an ingenious indicator of resistance.

Food still remains central to the potlatch. What struck me at the first potlatch I ever attended, in 1989 at Alert Bay, was the careful preparation of large quantities of delicious food such as venison stew, grilled salmon, fish soup, home-baked bread and cookies. As Webster notes, making these foods constitutes a significant part of the potlatch:

> Women prepare huge quantities of food, including fish and venison stews, clam chowder, salmon cooked in a variety of ways, smoked and salted eulachons, seaweed, salads, and baked goods ... Herring roe on kelp or hemlock boughs is a special treat, as it is difficult to obtain these days. Early in the morning [of the potlatch], as many as twenty women gather to make about twelve hundred sandwiches ... The work goes quickly, with a lot of joking and gossiping. (Webster 1991:229)

At the end of the potlatch today, unapologetically non-Native goods such as acrylic blankets and tupperware bowls loaded into plastic laundry baskets represent the payments to potlatch witnesses who accept the host's claims to prestige, serving the functions of skins in precontact times, and Hudson's Bay blankets during the late nineteenth century. The potlatch cooking that includes some Native and some Canadian fare similarly represents an accommodation to contemporary life, a new version of the mixed cuisine described by Boas, and a vivid indication of the significance food still plays in the potlatch.

Women and Food

Typical accounts of potlatches focus on masquerades, singing, dancing and oration, and pay short shrift to gustatory elements. But, as Webster demonstrates, food activities, particularly those involving women, constitute a significant part of the event. In his book investigating power in several different cultures including the Kwakwaka'wakw, Eric Wolf comments that Boas's texts fail to offer insights into women's lives, informal roles, potlatch dances, and personal experiences: "what women did and thought was not explored in their own terms, and their informal roles received no attention" (Wolf 1999:73). As has so often been the case in historical and anthropological representations, such omissions have led to misunderstandings of Kwakwaka'wakw women's roles. For example, in his structuralist analysis of Kwakwaka'wakw culture, Irving Goldman argues not only that ranking among men is distinctly different from women's rankings, but also that it has far greater importance:

> As an order of relative strengths, rank falls naturally within the sphere of masculine aggressiveness and predatory acquisitiveness on the analogy of the eagle who eats first. By contrast, the nongraded status of noble women is associated with the concept of brides as passive. The bride is the source of great powers, but it is the groom as a member of a ranked order who demonstrates the capability of taking her. As the most highly esteemed masculine trait, aggressiveness is a most admired trait in general among the Kwakiutl. (Goldman 1975:52)

This could not be more wrong. Webster assures us that women, in both past and present, wield considerable power and bear responsibility for many major decisions affecting the community (Webster 1995:196). Margaret Seguin's comments about Tsimshian women could apply equally to the Kwakwaka'wakw: "It is clear from early accounts and from the poise and potency of many Tsimshian women today that it would be a mistake to extend tired Western notions about active/passive, "nuturance"/aggressiveness uncritically to the Tsimshian; the most obvious data must be mutilated to make it fit" (Seguin 1985:60).

When I was beginning to work on *Chiefly Feasts: The Enduring Kwakiutl Potlatch*, an exhibition designed and first displayed at the American Museum of Natural History in 1991, and later traveled to British Columbia, I met numerous impressively strong and knowledgeable women. My experience was so at odds with Goldman's assessment of women that, with the consent of Gloria Cranmer Webster and our Native consultants, the exhibit included a section on women in the potlatch, which focused on female privileges such as the *Tuxw'id*. This is a special female privilege demonstrated during the winter ceremony, often with dramatic displays of legerdemain. In one performance, the dancer conjures up out of the floor a large double-headed serpent or *sisiuytl* which seems to move, accordion-like, through the air. In another, she insists someone kill her by decapitation, and indeed, when her head is cut off, massive blood flowed from her neck; in reality she had a lifelike human head atop her own which was covered with robes, and broke a bladder full of seal blood at the appropriate time. Other *tuxw'id* performances include directing crabs (actually, puppets pulled by strings invisible in the dark house) to scamper across the floor and puppets to fly through the air, or even giving birth to a frog.

Women play important roles during *hamatsa*, or cannibal dance ceremonies. A frenzied *hamatsa* is a threat, for, if unpacified, he would so disrupt normal life that people would "not be able to eat in [their] houses on account of him" (Boas 1966:207). Women's services become critical at this point, for only they can calm a wildman, by dancing before the *hamatsa*, singing:

> I am the real tamer of Baxbakualanuxsiwe
> I pull the cedar bark from Baxbakualanuxsiwe's back.
> It is my power to pacify you when you are in a state of ecstasy.
> (Boas 1897:527)

Thus, it is the woman who can control the *hamatsa* and lead him back to the human, orderly world. Although Goldman argues this is a lesser power, one could argue equally that power to ensure a functioning society is greater.

In daily life, women gather large amounts of food such as shellfish, berries, and edible roots, and do most of the food processing and cooking. In their introduction to *Food and Culture: A Reader*, Carole Counihan and Penny Van Esterik point to the importance of women as wielders of power during food acquisition and preparation: "Control of food across history and cultures has often been a key source of power for women. Several authors have noted that women's ability to prepare and serve food gives them direct influence over others, both material and magical" (Counihan and Van Esterik 1997:3). The association of Kwakwaka'wakw women, power, and food becomes most vivid in the context of the special food dishes that accompany a bride to her husband's home.

When a woman marries, her husband's family pays a bride price, and receives both material and immaterial privileges such as food bowls, names, and the rights to be initiated into sodalities such as the *hamatsa*. After a period of time, the bride's family hosts a lavish potlatch, which serves to repay the bride price and thus terminate the marriage. To keep this wife, the husband must pay a new bride price which, after some time, her family repays, and she is once again liberated from that marriage. Another man can also marry this woman if he can afford the price. Such serial marriages and annulments – the ideal number is four – that bestow immense prestige upon women and their offspring so scandalized the Canadian officials that they included them as further justification to illegalize the potlatch.

A bride brings into her new home treasured hierlooms from her family called "house dishes" – also ideally four – which her husband's family can use. These esteemed carvings, which represent a variety of beings including the killer whale, hair seal, whale, sea lion, bear, grizzly bear, wolf, Dzonokwa, and Sisiutl appear only at large feasts. At her husband's potlatch, the four house dishes appear laden with prestigious food, bestowing the power and significance of his wife and her family.[11]

These treasured bowls often carried the foods identified by Hunt as high-ranking, such as cinquefoil roots, viburnum berries, crab apples, and dried salal-berry cakes. Boas never attempted to explain the principles behind food rankings, nor why vegetal cuisine would be so esteemed. Today, we tend to place flesh high in our own food hierarchy and green things lower; except for vegetarians, most dinners center on fish and meat, with appetizers, salads, and deserts secondary or even sometimes excluded. Although certain foods, such as half-dried halibut skin mixed with half-dried halibut meat, are limited to men of the highest rank (Boas 1921:361–3), many foods that enjoy immensely high rank in the Kwakwaka'wakw food hierarchy challenge the outsider's notions of the primacy of flesh. Steamed cinquefoil roots, for example, served with oil at great feasts, "are counted when chiefs count their feasts in rivalry." Normally, chiefs receive the long roots, commoners the short ones, but a host can insult a guest chief by serving him short roots (ibid.:542). Another high-ranking food is the viburnum berry; a feast of these fruits is said to be "next in greatness to the oil feast, which is the greatest feast given to many tribes" (ibid.:755).

At a potlatch, elite food is presented in the decorated house dishes that signify the wife's heritage and the host's acquired prestige. But what is it that makes vegetal foods like roots and berries enjoy such a high status? Some are time-consuming to prepare, but so is the tainted boiled codfish limited to family consumption (see this chapter, pp. 148–9). Perhaps the answer lies in gender: men hunt and fish, but women gather berries, dig roots, and process them into edible delicacies. The exceptional value of food acquired and made by women may draw upon and also contribute to women's power. At a potlatch, a woman's bowls take center stage at her husband's feast, filled to the brim with food closely associated with her gender. Webster explains that such actions are taken in the spirit of support, as the wife buttresses her husband's potlatch claims, and thus contributes to the ultimate outcome of enhanced family prestige (personal communication 1996).

In her intriguingly titled study "'I'm Not the Great Hunter, My Wife Is:' Iñupiat and Anthropological Models of Gender," (1990) Barbara Bodenhorn argues that Eskimo hunting is much more than men going out and killing game, but incorporates significant activities and actions by women which have largely been overlooked in the literature. Similarly, Kwakwaka'wakw women cannot be considered passive bystanders but, instead, active participants with considerable agency, who contribute to the potlatch prestigious foods and family heirlooms which only they control. These expressions of female power, in turn, function within the competitions of the nineteenth-century potlatches during which are manifested a complex web of family connections, social status, and responses to colonialism. And, returning to Mauss's ideas, these foods, their bowls, the setting, and the actual activity of feasting contribute to the potlatch as an aesthetic event.

T'lina

The relationship of the potlatch and colonial history has thus far concentrated on the event's changes since first contact. Now I would like to focus on one particular food that has been affected by colonial history. As Gosden and Knowles point out, the "reaction" of the colonial encounter brings about changes which are not "convergence or acculturation, but ... new forms of difference"; difference is thus maintained, but the nature of that difference has changed (Gosden and Knowles 2001:6).

This is apparent among the Kwakwaka'wakw who, despite a diet in most ways no different from that of other Canadians, still use food to maintain the distinction between themselves and their neighbors.

In the summer of 1990, anthropologist Peter Macnair of the Royal British Columbia Museum took a group of visitors to the remote village of Hopetown, accessible only by boat or floatplane. As we approached the village, the small community, led by Chief Tom Willie, greeted us with singing, accompanied by drumming, and welcomed us warmly. But the central focus of the visit was a feast that had been prepared for us by the chief's wife Elsie Williams – sun-dried halibut, stew of various seabirds, the inevitable (and quite delicious) salmon. Williams also served *t'lina*, the precious oil that serves as a condiment to accompany both ordinary and feast food. Today, smoked salmon, dried halibut, potatoes, and even lettuce are dipped into this intensely flavored oil.

Thus far I have said little about taste, partially because boiled, roasted, and dried fish are relatively familiar tastes. In contrast, eulachon oil represents one very important food that few non-Natives have ever tried, and among those, still fewer like. To prepare this oil, a family travels to their fish camps along the rivers, such as Knight Inlet, where eulachon migrate in the spring. They catch the smelt-like anadromous fish, which they place into a large pit dug in the ground and cover with logs. The fish "ripens" for ten days to three weeks, during which time it acquires a certain pungency. When judged sufficiently ripe, it is rendered. In the past, the fish was placed into a canoe with boiling water and cooked, the family skimming off the fat that floated to the top and placing it into kelp "bottles." Today metal pots and glass containers are used. The taste of this oil is quite indescribable, but is something like exceedingly strong fish with a slightly rancid undercurrent and an oily texture that coats the mouth. Although a delicacy for the Kwakwaka'wakw, non-Natives tend to react very negatively to *t'lina*; Boas, for example, could not stomach the mixture of dried berries and grease he was offered at a potlatch.

T'lina plays a major role in great potlatches, as it appears in many dishes. The greatest potlatch as well as a highly aggressive challenge to a rival is the "grease feast," during which the host intentionally throws oil onto the fire (Boas 1921:755). One remarkable type of art is the "vomiter beam" which includes an anthropomorphic carving out of whose mouth oil flows. Grease also appears in abundance when, at viburnum-berry feasts, the host belligerently attempts to to sicken the rival guests:

Now my feast! Go to him, the poor one who wants to be fed from the son of the chief whose name is "Full of Smoke," and "Greatest Smoke." Never mind; give him plenty to eat, make him drink [oil] until he will be qualmish and vomits. My feast steps over the fire right up to the [rival] chief. (Boas 1966:97–8)

Often reluctant to accept an invitation to such an event, guests cannot decline for fear of being judged cowardly by the host's entire family. So, as is proper, these reluctant guests willingly consume whatever grease they are given.

Another aggressive feast centers on a "stew" of dried and soaked salal-berry cakes, crab apples and oil that can "make one feel squeamish" (Boas 1921:770). In preparation for the event, the host, the four men who carry his ladles, and his speakers blacken their faces, an intimidating expression of hostility. After the guests are seated and have drunk water, men serve the oily mixture in the house-dishes and smaller dishes. But more oil is needed to make this a successful event, and four men dip their ladles into oil and offer some to the chiefs in ranking order. Each chief either drinks from the ladle or pretends to do so, letting the excess drip back into his dish of fruit and berries. But the host treats his rival differently, directing his men to pour oil aggressively *onto* the chief, a serious insult. The rival's family responds with its own acts of hostility, and tries to smother the fire with blankets they bring into the house. The host's men pour more oil over the fire, which then sets the blankets on fire, the flames leaping to the roof, sometimes even burning the roof-boards. As Boas notes, "This is the worst thing that chiefs do when they really get angry, and at such a time the house dishes are scorched by the fire" (ibid.:775). Etiquette demands that the guests act as if nothing is happening (Boas 1966:96). The dramatic gesture of intentionally burning so precious a substance communicates the host's abundant wealth, but doubtless represents a late modification to the potlatch.

Eulachon oil is not the only greasy substance esteemed by the Kwakwaka'wakw. Seal blubber, too, is eaten during the "feast of long strips of blubber." As in the butchering of seal meat, rank determines what part of the body the blubber given to an individual comes from – head chiefs receive chest blubber, second-ranking chiefs from the fore flippers, youngest chiefs from the hind flippers, and commoners long strips from the seal's body. This presents another opportunity for expressing hostility through an act of eating:

Two chiefs of one tribe do this; and the long strip is given to the speaker of the rival chief. A whole length of blubber is coiled into the feast-dish. Then they pour olachen-oil on it, and place it in front of the speaker. Then he arises, takes one end of the blubber, and puts it around his neck. He bites off the blubber from the singed skin and swallows it. If he is an expert at bolting it, he eats almost three fathoms (18 feet) of blubber ... Then the speaker of the chief just promises a seal-feast. (Boas 1921:460–1)

After this demonstration of skill by the rival's speaker, the host gives other guests strips of blubber which they too wrap around their necks and bolt. However, these are far shorter and not accompanied by oil. Afterwards, everyone goes outside to vomit, "for it really makes one feel squeamish," and to wash with hot water and urine.

After the 1920s, when persecution of Kwakwaka'wakw for potlatching became most intense, the potlatches that were hosted became quieter and more discreet. In 1963, twelve years afer the potlatch ban was dropped from Canadian Indian Act, the Alert Bay big house opened. The community decided that potlatches held in this structure must not demonstrate the intense and hostile rivalry exhibited at earlier events, so hosts of contemporary potlatches display none of the aggression Boas observed. Nonetheless, these potlatches remain vivid, with dramatic, and even, at times, bombastic oration. Feast foods like viburnum berry cakes and cinquefoil roots are no longer served at potlatches, but grease is sometimes offered to honored guests, and "grease feasts" hosted. At one such potlatch I attended in 1996, the hosts placed on the floor rows of gallon and half-gallon bottles filled with eulachon oil, and poured ladles full of oil onto the fire which, as expected, flamed up almost to the roof.

After this demonstration of wealth, the hosts distributed the jars to guests; the highest chiefs received the largest bottles, those of lower rank the smaller ones. There was by no means enough to give to everyone, but I noticed none was given to any of the non-Kwakwaka'wakw at the event. When I asked one of the family members why that was, she disdainfully responded, "oil is for us." And then, almost as an aside, "white people don't appreciate it." The latter comment is quite true, as I am the only white person I know who actually *likes* eulachon oil. But it also suggests that grease expresses difference within a changing world. Whereas non-Natives share with the Kwakwaka'wakw an appreciation for fish, most find eulachon oil highly unpalatable. Thus, this one food that colonizers cannot share, appropriate, and, certainly, enjoy, becomes something that differentiates the Kwakwaka'wakw from them. Part of this distinctiveness resides in how different groups experience the unique taste of grease. The pleasure evident among a group of Kwakwaka'wakw having grease with their meal contrasts vividly with the reaction of most whites to what they judge a repulsive substance.

During the process of making grease today, Kwakwaka'wakw engage in a subsistence activity associated with pre-modern times. As Webster asserts,

> *T'lina* [grease] is the strongest connection people have to the old ways. When we go to Knight Inlet to make it, it's like it used to be. People help each other out in ways they don't in Alert Bay. And you go to a beautiful remote place with mountains. You work really hard, and then you end up with wonderful stuff. It tastes so good. Fish without *t'lina*? You might as well be eating in a restaurant. (interview 2003)

Eulachon oil, a condiment which for centuries was a part of everyday eating as well as an indication of wealth, has become a mark of distinction for the Kwakwaka'wakw, clearly differentiating them from non-Native settlers on their land and reconnecting them to their past. That mark of distinction plays itself out both in the processing of grease and, perhaps most significantly, in its taste.

In the past, grease was one of many indications of wealth, status, and prestige. It was not, at that time, a signifier of difference, for colonization had not yet intruded as deeply into Kwakwaka'wakw cultural life as it would later. After the 1885 law was enacted, the potlatch itself became not only an event for demonstrating status, but also an expression of resistance. Today, the potlatch still reinforces status claims, but it is also a political activity, an expression of their sovereignty within the contemporary and globalized world. During the preparations for *Chiefly Feasts*, the Kwakwaka'wakw kept on repeating that they wanted the exhibit's visitors to learn that they were still living, and that their potlatch represented their strength. Embodying those sentiments and buttressing those messages, the flavorful oil of the candlefish continues to flow.

The Artistry of Grease

Taste and smell are perhaps the most difficult senses to represent in the museum. One can look at something unusual and attain a certain level of visual understanding. But one cannot, obviously, *see* taste or smell – those must be immediately experienced. Unlike light waves which travel from the object observed to the eyes, taste and smell are contained in the actual molecules that enter the nose and mouth. The immediacy, the subjectivity of the experience distinguishes these senses from the more objectified sight. Moreover, visual representations can sanitize the sensory experiences one would have if immersed in another culture; for example, a diorama of an Inuit family deprives the observer of the smells about which so many explorers commented. Indeed, the colonial record is replete with expressions of disgust and repulsion at the taste of food and smells of unfamiliar substances. In the case of *t'lina*, such negative responses to a sensory experience continue into the postcolonial era.

Several Northwest Coast artists and museum professionals have endeavored to make the non-Native public more aware of the value of eulachon oil. *Chiefly Feasts* included a section on food and feasting that displayed plain and decorated spoons, dishes, ladles, and bowls, with wall labels of Hunt's "recipes." To overcome the limitation of this fully non-sensual account of cuisine, Gloria Cranmer Webster prepared a public talk at the American Museum of Natural History on Kwakwaka'wakw food in which she intended to offer the audience tastes of delights like seaweed, soapberries, and, of course, *t'lina*. This would be an excellent way to transcend the monopoly of the visual, and offer the public taste and smell first hand. Unfortunately this proved impossible, for we discovered that the New York City Health Department's rules prevented distribution of such food at a lecture. Once again, legislation regulated the senses, and the full representation of the richness of Kwakwaka'wakw experience was denied.

Gitksan artist Eric Robertson installed an aluminum, stainless steel, copper sculpture entitled *The Hub* at the Kelowna Art Gallery from April to May 2001. The installation consisted of three large discs from which hung small metal fish. According to Robertson:

> This work is in celebration of Eulachon. Eulachon are small fish that reproduce in the major river systems on the West Coast. Their use has maintained a substantial role in cultural exchange, trade and commerce. This cultural exchange continues above the old intersecting travel routes known as "Grease Trails," which are today, the foundations of the province's major transportation highways. (see at www.galleries.bc.ca/kelowna/2001/eric_robertson_the_hub.htm)

The delicate small glittering fish do convey the visual experience of the eulachon fish runs, but, as was the case in *Chiefly Feasts*, the taste and pungent fragrance so delicious to the Northwest Coast First Nations peoples remains inaccessible.

Barb Cranmer, a Kwakwaka'wakw filmmaker, made another attempt to express the importance of this fish in *T'lina: The Rendering of Wealth*, awarded the Best Short Documentary prize at the 1999 American Indian Film Festival in San Francisco. Cranmer addresses some of the environmental issues connected to eulachon. This fish, of no commercial use, has become endangered, having been discarded as useless "bycatch" in the rapacious overharvesting of coastal fish resources. Logging creates problems as well, as the habitat destruction that accompanies clear-cutting destroys the small fish's spawning grounds. Then the filmmaker turns to the cultural aspects of *t'lina*. According to Cranmer,

> I have wanted to do this film for at least six years. It became urgent because many of our old people were dying and important knowledge and history were close to disappearing with them. When I made a research trip with my family to Dzawadi [Knight Inlet] in 1996, we witnessed a sharp decline in the eulachon run. It was important to do the story right now. In ten years we might not be going up there. The eulachon may be extinct. The families who travel annually to Dzawadi are strengthened by the experience. Each year brings something new. It is amazing that in these modern times our people are fortunate enough to be able to go to a place where we can still practice a traditional way of life. It is like traveling back in time as we reaffirm our connection to our traditional territory. We have discovered old houseposts, which supported many bighouses in the Dzawadi area. We can only imagine what it must have been like to live two hundred years ago in this same area.

In this award-winning film, Cranmer, like her aunt Gloria Cranmer Webster, associates the eulachon fishing experience with tradition and identity, but she also links it to issues of resource management and sovereignty.

Conclusion

Why might the sense of taste and the experience of actual eating be so neglected in the abundant literature on the Kwakwaka'wakw in contrast to their recognizably outstanding art? Certainly, one can more easily see a photograph or artifact than imagine a taste, especially one so unimaginable as grease. But taste is arguably one of the most sensuous of the senses. Compare, for example, the rather intellectual pleasure of seeing a beautiful painting with the utter delight in an exquisite flavor, the deep satisfaction after dining when hungry, the appeal of an intensely flavored delicacy. Brian Hayden, in his introduction to *Feasting: Archaeological and Ethnographic Perspectives on Food, Politics, and Power*, suggests that:

> Perhaps occidental researchers have been biased in their views of the importance of feasting, attributing such behavior to a sybaritic self-indulgent aspect of human nature that is unworthy of serious attention. Perhaps archeologists have simply written the study of feasting off as a frivolous type of psychological self-gratification that pleasure-loving individuals engage in, but which is not particularly important. (Hayden 2001:24)

To go even further, because the sense of taste could be considered too close to erotic pleasure, puritanical elements of Anglo-North American culture might have unconsciously censored this carnal – but nonetheless important – facet of the Kwakwaka'wakw experience.[12] Approaching food without considering taste is like studying a mask without referring to its dance, or analyzing a drum without hearing the music it plays.

Earlier I referred to the questions Mitchell poses to visual objects; questions which are equally applicable to food. The first – what does food mean? – is the most straightforward, and can be understood historically. Among the Kwakwaka'wakw from precontact times until the twentieth century, cuisine served the hierarchy by maintaining social distinctions. In the late nineteenth century, it functioned within competitions that occurred during times of significant social and cultural stress, but which ensured the maintenance of a hierarchy. While elements of earlier potlatches remained, major differences from precontact or early postcontact potlatches developed. And in today's globalized world, the food served at the potlatch distinguishes the Kwakwaka'wakw in a compelling and unique fashion.

The two other questions – What is the secret of food's vitality? What does food want? – are somewhat more difficult to answer. Among the Kwakwaka'wakw, food's energy seems embedded in its physical and symbolic qualities. The grease that has enhanced a wide variety of foods throughout time today maintains a connection to the past and expresses identity. The high-status vegetal foods draw much of their life from associations with female power. Throughout potlatch history, food has functioned as an object guests accept and consume, and a subject the host family treasures, thus both contributing vitality to and drawing vitality from the potlatch.

And the answer to what food wants perhaps lies squarely in its sensuous appeal. A partial source of power for *t'lina*, for example, lies in its distinctive taste that the Kwakwaka'wakw so enjoy and non-Natives detest. The pleasure inherent in eating something considered especially tasty could also serve a social function, especially in terms of commoners. Among the Kwakwaka'wakw, food sometimes functions to distinguish classes, as for example when rank determines which part of an animal is served to which people. When carving a hair-seal, the highest chiefs get the chest, next chiefs the limbs, commoners the body, and very low-ranking guests the tail. This distribution of hair-seal meat is said to "teach the common people their place" (Boas 1921:750–51). These commoners may learn that "lesson" through food, which, nevertheless, still tastes good; so, regardless of where you sit in the hierarchy, you can delight in the grease accompanying your food. The chief may be served one kind of food prohibited to the commoner, but what the commoner does receive is gratifying. It is not only the cultural meaning of food that supports its social functions, it is its very appeal to the senses. What food "wants," then, is to be eaten, tasted, and enjoyed – and through the resultant pleasure, it can do and mean and be many different things.

When a delegation of Kwakwaka'wakw elders came to New York City in 1990 to consult with staff at the American Museum of Natural History on the preparation of *Chiefly Feasts: the Enduring Kwakiutl Potlatch,* it was of utmost importance that we feed them abundantly and properly. So, in addition to numerous meals at the Museum, we brought the group to Chinatown where they had a 10–course Chinese banquet, a food-centered example of postmodern globalization. A special moment occurred when I hosted a lunch of salmon salad in my apartment. Elsie Williams commented that the food was nice, but could have used some grease. Delighted to accommodate her, I opened my cupboard and pulled out a jar of eulachon oil I had received the summer before, and distributed it to my honored guests. During the opening ceremonies of the exhibition, the chiefs bestowed upon me the name *Putlas*, which translates as "place from which one does not leave hungry." This, I hope, indicates that we treated our guests properly, that is, fed them correctly.

Notes

1. Hunt was the son of a Hudson's Bay Company official and his wife, a noble Tlingit woman from Alaska. Hunt was born in Fort Rupert, and grew up immersed in Kwakwaka'wakw culture, marrying two Kwakwaka'wakw women and siring an extensive family whose descendants are still very active in Kwakwaka'wakw affairs.

2. In her analysis of 80 texts transcribed by Hunt, Helen Codere identifies 60 dealing with food acquisition, preparation, and food-related industries such as halibut-hook manufacture (Codere 1950:16).

3. Barnouw is not entirely accurate here, for the Boas/Hunt materials do not offer recipes for blueberry pie, but rather numerous ways of preparing the variety of berries that grow in the region.

4. See Suttles and Jonaitis (1990:84–6) for a thorough discussion of the interpretations of the potlatch.

5. He also identified the potlatch as a form of "interest-bearing investment." See ibid., p. 85 for a discussion of this.

6. Not only is actual food important for potlatching, there are sometimes metaphoric references to eating, as well as vomiting. For example, during a potlatch Boas attended in 1895, dancers asserted that they had in their stomachs all the tribes, for "swallowing the tribes" signified giving away blankets. Another dancer mimicked vomiting, which meant he was vomiting the property to be given away (Boas 1966:192–3).

7. For examples of Kwakwaka'wakw spoons, ladles, and bowls, see Jonaitis (1991).

8. Hunt sent the model along with the note that it demonstrated the way "all the small ones [dishes] Belong to it" (Ostrowitz 1991:200).

9. Walens interprets the "recipes" collected by Hunt not so much as instructions on food preparation as descriptions of social events that occur during the preparation and consumption of food. Taking orality as a metaphor of proper behavior reflecting larger cosmic organization, Walens states that meals themselves are "sacred occasions" (Walens 1981:35), and that "For the Kwakiutl, food is not merely the inanimate edible remains of food-animals and plants, but is instead the substantial manifestation of the numinous nature of the universe … The eating of food, even when one is hungry and the food one is eating is delicious, is not a selfish act of personal gratification, but rather a stage in the complexly structured interrelationships of humans with each other and with the world around them" (1981:69). This is an impressively creative interpretation of the Boas/Hunt data.

10. Any consideration of eating at the potlatch, as well as of food in Kwakwaka'wakw culture, must include reference to the ceremonial eating

of human flesh. During the *tseka*, or winter ceremonial season, initiates into the *hamatsa* are said to be possessed of cannibalistic urges, at times lunging around the house, biting people, eating flesh of killed slaves, chewing pieces from mummified corpses.

11. Mauss also identifies the "productive power" of serving and eating utensils used during Kwakwaka'wakw feasts and potlatches in that they embody wealth, rank, and connection to ancestors, food sources, and the supernatural (Mauss 1990 [1950]:44).

12. For example, one of my cake recipes is described as "better than sex."

References

Barnouw, Victor. 1975. *An Introduction to Anthropology: Ethnology*. Homewood, IL: Dorsey.

Boas, Franz. 1896. "The Decorative Art of the Indians of the North Pacific Coast." *Science* 4: 101–3.

——. 1897. "The Social Organization and the Secret Societies of the Kwakiutl Indians." *Report for the U.S. National Museum for 1895*.

——. 1909. "The Kwakiutl of Vancouver Island." *Publications of the Jesup North Pacific Expedition* 5: 301–522.

——. 1921. "Ethnology of the Kwakiutl." *Bureau of American Ethnology Thirty-fifth Annual Report*, parts 1 and 2.

——. 1966. *Kwakiutl Ethnography*, ed. H. Codere. Chicago: University of Chicago Press.

Bodenhorn, Barbara. 1990. "'I'm Not the Great Hunter, My Wife Is'; Iñupiat and Anthropological Models of Gender." *Etudes Inuit Studies* 14(1–2).

Codere, Helen. 1950. *Fighting With Property: A Study of Kwakiutl Potlatching and Warfare, 1792–1930*. Seattle: University of Washington Press.

Counihan, Carole and Penny Van Esterik. 1997. *Food and Culture: A Reader*. New York: Routledge.

Ford, Clellan (ed.). 1941. *Smoke from Their Fires: The Life of a Kwakiutl Chief*. New Haven: Yale University Press.

Galois, Robert. 1994. *Kwakwaka'wakw Settlements, 1775–1920: A Geographical Analysis and Gazetteer*. Seattle: University of Washington Press.

Goldman, Irving. 1975. *Mouth of Heaven: An Introduction to Kwakiutl Religious Thought*. New York: John Wiley & Sons.

Gosden, Chris and Chantal Knowles. 2001. *Collecting Colonialism: Material Culture and Colonial Change*. Oxford: Berg.

Hayden, Brian. 2001. "Fabulous Feasts: A Prolegomenon to the Importance of Feasting." In *Feasting: Archaeological and Ethnographic Perspectives on Food, Politics, and Power*, ed. Michael Dietler and Brian Hayden. Washington D.C.: Smithsonian Institution Press.

Jonaitis, Aldona. 1988. *From the Land of the Totem Poles: The Northwest Coast Art Collection at the American Museum of Natural History*. New York and Seattle: American Museum of Natural History and University of Washington Press.

——. (ed.). 1991. *Chiefly Feasts: The Enduring Kwakiutl Potlatch*. New York and Seattle: American Museum of Natural History and University of Washington Press.

Mauss, Marcel. 1990 [1950]. *The Gift: The Form and Reason for Exchange in Archaic Societies*, trans. W.D. Halls. New York: Norton.

Meigs, Anna. 1997. "Food as Cultural Construction." In *Food and Culture: A Reader*, ed. C. Counihan and P. Van Esterik. New York: Routledge.

Miller, Daniel. 1998. "Why Some Things Matter." In *Material Cultures: Why Some Things Matter*, ed. D. Miller. Chicago: University of Chicago Press.

Mitchell, W.J.T. 2002. "Showing Seeing: A Critique of Visual Culture." In *The Visual Culture Reader*, ed. N. Mirzoeff. New York: Routledge.

Mochon, Marion. 1966. *Masks of the Northwest Coast*. Milwaukee: Milwaukee Public Museum.

Ostrowitz, Judith. 1991. *Notes on Objects in Chiefly Feasts: The Enduring Kwakiutl Potlatch*, ed. A. Jonaitis. New York and Seattle: American Museum of Natural History and University of Washington Press.

Seguin, Margaret. 1985. "Interpretive Contexts for Traditional and Current Coast Tsimshian Feasts." Mercury Series, Canadian Ethnology Service Paper No. 98. Gatineau, Quebec: Canadian Museum of Civilization.

Sewid, James. 1969. *Guests Never Leave Hungry: The Autobiography of James Sewid, A Kwakiutl Indian*, ed. James P. Spradley. New Haven: Yale University Press.

Suttles, Wayne and Aldona Jonaitis. 1990. "History of Research in Ethnology." In *Handbook of North American Indians*, vol. 7, *Northwest Coast*, ed. W. Suttles. Washington, DC: Smithsonian Institution.

Walens, Stanley. 1981. *Feasting with Cannibals: An Essay on Kwakiutl Cosmology*. Princeton: Princeton University Press.

Webster, Gloria Cranmer. 1991. "The Contemporary Potlatch." In *Chiefly Feasts: The Enduring Kwakiutl Potlatch*, ed. A. Jonaitis. New York and Seattle: American Museum of Natural History and University of Washington Press.

——. 1995. "Contemporary Kwakwaka'wakw Potlatches." In *The Spirit Within: Northwest Coast Native Art from the John H. Hauberg Collection.* Seattle: Seattle Art Museum.

Wolf, Eric. 1999. *Envisioning Power: Ideologies of Dominance and Crisis.* Berkeley: University of California Press.

Sonic Spectacles of Empire: The Audio-Visual Nexus, Delhi–London, 1911–12

Tim Barringer

This volume aims to refocus attention on the senses, acknowledging the variety and significance of sensory experience in our understanding and interpretation of culture. The so-called "linguistic turn," and its less ubiquitous successor, the "visual turn," have seen historians and anthropologists take a renewed, critical interest in the structure and fabric of texts and images. To reincorporate questions of sensory experience, however – to include hearing and smell alongside sight, and to reposition the enquiry to take account of the response of the perceiving individual – requires a rethinking of cultural history in general, and the cultural history of empire in particular. This chapter will consider the significance of the combination of hearing and sight in the historical experience of imperial pageantry, in India and in London. The production and manipulation of spectacle, both visual and aural, by the colonial authorities, I shall suggest, provided some of the most powerful and viscerally affective sensory and cultural events of empire.

While some work has been done on visual cultures of empire, the aural dimensions of imperial culture have been neglected, and the appeal to the ears, as well as the eyes, in imperial pageantry remains an unexplored problem. Yet as Steven Feld has pointed out, while musical sounds "overtly communicate through and about acoustic patterns, they are socially organised to do far more, by modulating special categories of sentiment and action when brought forth and properly contexted by features of staging and performance" (Feld 1991:79). The case for reintegrating music into a general, cultural history of empire is a pressing one. Such concerns are particularly apposite to the period from 1900 to 1914, when the connections between music and ethnic identity became a matter of intense creative and intellectual interest. Through the collection and arrangement of folksong, British composers and musicologists examined the local oral tradition for the survival of a pure emanation of British ethnicity, national identity in song (Hughes and Stradling 2001:194). This, too, was a crucial moment in the history of sound: the emergence of techniques for recording sound emerged in time to capture Queen Victoria's voice before her death in 1901. Sound recording would become a key anthropological research technique as well as a powerful medium of popular culture (Brady 1999), and British corporations began both to record music across the imperial territories and to distribute music recorded in Britain in India and throughout the British Empire, while also originating recordings in India (Kinnear 1994).

The evidential and interpretative challenges involved in writing an experiential history incorporating both hearing and sight, a history of sensory affect and response, are considerable. Among the data of cultural history, sound is more fugitive than the image or the word. Unlike those art forms which produce a unique material object – such as painting or sculpture – musical performance is ephemeral and leaves no physical trace. To write the history of empire as it was perceived visually, likewise, is not merely a question of examining representation and mimesis – the "images of empire" which have been a major concern of art historians and visual anthroplogists. Beyond the field of representation and imagery lies the much broader question of the visual culture of environment and landscape, the visual impact of ritual and performance, the ways in which empire was staged. Insoluble evidential problems surround the assessment of the affectivity of a musical or performed event: the response of the spectator is rarely recorded. In a colonial context, the primary sources tend to represent the colonizer's view, and the reconstruction of a "subaltern" view of imperial pageantry – an important, even an urgent historical task – would require massive archival research. What is offered here, more provisionally, is a reading, against the grain, of the official records; an attempt at a critical history of the British Empire's paradoxical attempts to manipulate the senses of sight and hearing to political ends.

A case study is provided by the events surrounding George V's coronation in Delhi on December 12, 1911 and the theatrical masque *The Crown of India* produced in London the following spring. These events, I argue, should be seen in the context of the British Empire's longstanding deployment of a self-legitimating myth which I call "colonial Gothic" (Barringer 2005). This complex formulation – as effective in music as in painting, in public spectacle, architecture, theatrical design or in a literary text – based the legitimacy of the British presence in India on supposed parallels between the social and aesthetic character of contemporary India with that of medieval England. Reactionary proponents of "colonial Gothic" found in "village India" a simulacrum of the untroubled society of medieval Britain, maintaining the hierarchical social structure (the caste system replicating feudal class distinctions), the "vertical friendships," and the visual splendor of the Middle Ages. In this account, modern India displayed, moreover, an absolute absence of the cultural forms of modernity – industrialization, urbanization, democratization – so prominent in the Britain of 1911. This almost entirely spurious account of Indian culture and history was concocted in order to assert that the British Empire held an immemorial inheritance on the subcontinent (though the Raj proper was only half a century old), at a historical moment when Indian nationalism was a burgeoning political force. Colonial Gothic also attempted to buttress the constitutional and political legitimacy of royal dominion in Britain, which in 1911 was also bitterly contested.

The proponents of colonial discourse theory have argued that "colonial cultures" may be taken to include the imperial capital, and that colonizer and colonized are bound together into a single dynamic whatever the inequalities of power and authority within it. This is a significant step, revealing that "British history" and "imperial history," so often conceived of as separate narratives, are intimately, inseparably linked. This chapter therefore discusses performances and pageants by which empire was represented both in Delhi and in London. These ephemeral, though profoundly influential, events have left historical traces through programs and descriptions, surviving texts, musical scores, and photographs. They spoke, like all forms of organized mass ritual, to the senses of both sight and hearing.

The Durbar as Colonial Gothic Spectacle

There existed by 1911 a well-developed iconography of imperial spectacle in British India. The visit of the Prince of Wales in 1875–76 and the Durbar of January 1, 1903, masterminded by Lord Curzon to celebrate the Coronation of Edward VII, were impressively choreographed. The very fact that far greater resources were expended on colonial extravaganzas of this kind than on ceremonial in the imperial center called for some explanation (Curzon 1906:305–9). Lord Lytton, Viceroy of India in 1877, felt it necessary to explain to Disraeli that the sensual impact of the Durbar had very real political and cultural value:

> I am afraid I may have seemed fussy or frivolous about the decorative details of the Delhi Assemblage … The decorative details of an Indian pageant are like those parts of an animal which are no use at all for butcher's meat, and are even unfit for scientific dissection, but from which augurs draw the omens that move armies and influence princes.
> (quoted in *India and the Durbar*, 1911:36)

The impact of durbars on the senses demonstrated the permanence and grandeur of empire far more effectively than other, textual, forms of proclamation. Yet there is also a coded language of gender in this passage. Lytton addresses a concern that the "fussy and frivolous," and thus inherently feminizing, impact of "decorative details" which "influence princes" might undermine the rugged masculinity of the imperial project. In 1902, Curzon would express the union between Britain and India in quasi-sexual terms:

> We are ordained to walk here in the same track together for many a long day to come. You cannot do without us. We should be impotent without you. Let the Englishman and the Indian accept the consecration of a union so mysterious as to have in it something of the divine. (Curzon 1906, title page)

Although the allure of India stimulated British imperial potency – according to Curzon's imagery – the danger of the perceived sensuality and passivity of Indian culture, its feminizing interest in "decorative details" was ever present. From Curzon's point of view, control of the senses provided the key to Britain's performance of masculine-imperial dominance over the potentially unruly colonial body politic. But it was through the senses, too, that the East could exercise its seductive and enervating magic over the colonist. The strangeness and excess of bodily sensations experienced by British colonists have only recently emerged as a significant presence in histories of empire (Collingham 2001).

Precisely because of the multisensory nature of its appeal as a form, the task of representing the Durbar to those who had not been present posed a significant problem for artists. The painter Valentine Cameron Prinsep created a massive, if ultimately static and lifeless, tableau of the 1877 Durbar or Imperial Assemblage (Millar 1992), whereas the draughtsman and etcher Mortimer Menpes, a friend and disciple of James McNeill Whistler, who attended the 1903 Durbar in Delhi, created a series of small, color-saturated watercolors whose atmospheric texture and dappled lighting alluded directly to the experience of being present at the Durbar (Menpes 1903). An emphasis on the vibrant tonalities of Indian clothing and an exaggerated chiaroscuro of skin color were central tropes of Victorian journalism and fiction of empire familiar from wood-engravings in the *Illustrated London News*. But it was not until the turn of the century, through the advent of cheap color reproduction, for which Menpes's illustrations were perfectly calibrated, that the perceived exoticism of India, in particular, could be reported to a wide public in vivid facsimile. As so often, the technologies of industrial modernity faciliatated the promotion of "colonial Gothic" myths. Where representations of British ceremonial had tended – as in the case of Andrew Carrick Gow's painting *Queen Victoria's Diamond Jubilee Service, June 22 1897* (London, Guildhall Art Gallery, 1897–99) – to focus literally on the uniformity of the participants, in Menpes's watercolors of the Durbar, the riotous variety of colors in the clothing of the Indian participants, notably the "native princes," client landowners of the British Raj, was emphasized (*Indian Princes* 1911). But while his main focus was the exotic, and to the British eye feminized, costume of the Indian princes and their retinues, it was in representations of *The State Entry as seen from the Jumma Masjid* and *Burmese Elephants at the State Entry* that Menpes established a newly vivid visual vocabulary of empire (Menpes 1903 opposite pp. 28 and 46), which used the visual in a way to extend the affective sensory qualities of that vision.

Despite its grandiose pretensions as "a chapter in the ritual of the State" (*India and the Durbar* 1911:40), and its massive number of participants, the 1903 Durbar was ultimately a paradoxical affair, as had been its predecessor in 1877. Curzon had expressed the hope in 1903 that "the great assemblage might be long remembered by the peoples of India, as having brought them into contact at a moment of great solemnity, with the personality and sentiments of their Sovereign" (quoted *Coronation Durbar*, 134). Yet the ceremony was compromised by the absence of the very body it fetishized, that of the monarch, in this case the wheezing King-Emperor Edward VII, whose health was too precarious to risk a colonial adventure. It was only the arrival, eight years later, of George V, the first reigning British monarch to visit the subcontinent, which would allow for the fulfilment of Curzon's vision. As a journalist for the *Allahabad Pioneer* noted in 1911, "deep as was the feeling on that occasion [1903], it cannot compare with that which has now been called

Figure 6.1 Mortimer and Dorothy Menpes, "Burmese Elephants at the State Entry," from M. Menpes, *The Durbar* (London: A & C Black, 1902), opposite p. 46

into being here, for that contact with personality which was symbolic in 1903 has been real and actual today" (*Coronation Durbar* 1912:134).

This ceremony conforms to the hybrid aesthetic of "colonial Gothic," which produced a hybrid style in architecture and the decorative arts. The visual parallels between Mughal and Gothic styles were compelling: the pointed arch of Mughal architecture seemed to echo the fanciful tapering of medieval windows, and the bright colors of Indian textiles echoed the heraldic hues admired and emulated by Gothic revival architects such as A.W.N. Pugin, and also found in the jewel-like tones of Edward Burne-Jones and William Morris's designs for stained glass and tapestry. The King-Emperor and Queen-Empress entered India at Bombay through a specially created "Gateway to India," a plaster confection built over wooden scaffolding which alluded to the Mughal style of the Taj Mahal (Volwahsen 2004:206–7). In 1914, it was decided to make this gateway a permanent fixture of the city's urban fabric. The final masonry Gateway, completed only in 1924, was a hybrid structure whose architect, George Wittet, self-consciously alluded not only to

Gujerati architecture of the sixteenth century, but also to the classical tradition of the triumphal arch, and further to Gothic and neo-Gothic buildings in Britain, such as Wilkins's gatehouse for King's College, Cambridge (Davies 1985:182). Wittet imagined it as the centerpiece of a grandiose architectural ensemble, a kind of durbar in stone, but the Gateway alone was completed. As if to confirm its status as an emanation of imperial hubris, resonant more of empire's fragility than of its permanence, it was through this Gateway that the last British troops left India in February 1948.

Another "colonial Gothic" move in 1911 was the reversion of the capital city from Calcutta, the trading center of the East India Company, to New Delhi. It was a brilliant gambit to hold the durbar on the plains outside the old city of Delhi, avoiding the problems of security and control inherent in the crowded and socially volatile urban area. The Durbar was chosen as the moment for laying a foundation stone for a great imperial capital – New Delhi. While Edwin Lutyens and Herbert Baker's designs for the new capital eschewed Gothic – the chosen style of Bombay's colonial governors – it would combine aspects of classical design with an eclectic selection of motifs from Buddhist, Hindu, and Islamic traditions. The new city, with its long vistas and massive parade grounds, as Hosagrahar Jyoti suggests, formed a permanent durbar, a stage-set for a performance piece of colonial domination through daily ritual and through the control of space, the segregation of ethnic groups, and the manipulation of sensory experience (Jyoti 1992:84). One of the delicious ironies of British imperialism is that the only truly grandiose city ever erected by the British Empire (for there is nothing to compare with New Delhi in London or Edinburgh, Toronto, Sydney, or Cape Town) was completed only at the very moment of the extinction of British world power, and became fully operational only as the administrative center of the newly independent India.

From Mughal to Imperial Durbar

While it vaguely echoed the medieval and Tudor practice of the royal progress, the durbar was essentially a Mughal form, self-consciously adapted to add luster to British rule after Disraeli's creation of the new title of Empress of India for Queen Victoria in 1876. Parallels with the glory days of the Mughal empire were constantly emphasized, and became something of an obsession during Lord Curzon's period as Viceroy. The durbar had served in Mughal culture as a means of reaffirming and enhancing the ties between the emperor and his administrators of *mansabdars* or office holders, and to provide a performative spectacle linking the ruler and his court with the people (Cohn 1983; Jyoti 1992:84).The pageantry and festivities of 1911–12 were portrayed as the solemn and necessary continuation of an immemorial Indian tradition, whose effects were both visual and aural, as the Official Record of the Durbar noted:

> India has always had its royal progresses and pageants, its coronations and durbars. From the dawn of history, and before, the stories that come down to us are all of kings and princes, their successions and conquests, their bounties and bans. The Mahabharata tells us of a vast amphitheatre shaded by canopies of brilliant colours and resounding with a thousand trumpets, erected on an auspicious and level plain outside what is now the city of Delhi, where the princes and citizens took their seats on platforms to witness a ceremony of high state. (*Historical Record* 1914:3)

The British monarch simply, and inevitably, took the place of the former rulers, amid great color and visual spectacle. Yet although the British assimilated the techniques and iconography of the durbar, this hybrid form also became a site for the production of difference, on grounds of race and gender. A recurring theme is the pointed assertion of difference between the new regime and the colonized peoples who formed its passive audience, a contrast emphasized through the description of male clothing. The appearance of the "Indian princes" is constantly, if implicitly, compared with the restrictive codes of dress for Victorian and Edwardian men in Britain (Harvey 1995).

> It would be impossible [recalled the Hon. John Fortescue] to describe the richness and variety of colour displayed by the dresses of the native princes. The head-dresses alone would require several pages, from the voluminous turban of Kashmir to the small jewelled cap (I know not how else to describe it) of Travancore, and the pagoda-like structures of Burma. (Fortescue 1912:157)

Care was taken to emphasize a contrast between the "hard blue and scarlet of the uniforms of the troops" and the colorful, feminized spectacle of the local aristocracy, those "loyal Indian feudatories" now subordinate clients of the British Raj (Cohn 1983:180). It was as if, while producing a spectacle whose appeal to the senses was vivid, powerful, and expansive, the British authorities wished to disavow the very sensory forces they had unleashed.

Figure 6.2 "The Durbar: The Arena and Spectators' Mound from the Top of the Stand," from The Hon. John Fortescue, *Narrative of the Visit to India of their Majesties King George V and Queen Mary and of the Coronation Durbar held at Delhi 12th December 1911* (London: Macmillan, 1912), opposite p. 139

Music and the Sonic Spectacle of Empire

Central to this production of sensory drama was the intersection of sound and sight, music and art, which had lain, too, at the core of Mughal court culture. Under the Mughals, great public events were celebrated with fanfares on drums, horns and conches (Wade 1998:106). When the Emperor Akhbar (reigned 1556–1605) returned to Fatehpur Sikri on December 1, 1581, "The noise of the drums and the melodies of the magician-like musicians gave forth news of joy. Crowds of men were gathered on the roofs ..." (quoted Wade 1998, 166). Massive processions, with the Emperor mounted on a elephant, and a spectacular orchestration of color and decoration, were a major feature of Mughal ceremonial, often recorded by the increasingly naturalistic Mughal miniature painters. But music and art also held a high position in the private life of the court. For instance, the singer *Tansen* or *Tan Sen* was a highly regarded member of Akhbar's entourage.

Music, too, had a key role to play in the promotion of a modern imperial culture, both in performance and through the medium of mechanical reproduction. While popular songs, circulated as sheet music and as gramophone records, often promoted imperial ideologies, the manipulation of sound to overwhelm the audience's sense of hearing was as central to the imperial durbar as to its Mughal predecessor. Although the fundamentally Western forms of music promoted by the Raj must have been striking to the Indian participants in the Durbar for their radical difference from indigenous forms of music-making, it is important to acknowledge the extent to which the brass band and military band had earlier entered the culture of colonialism through military and civilian routes (Zealley 1926; Boonzajer Flaes 2000). Although the material culture of the musical instruments of the military band differed radically from the multiple traditions of the subcontinent – which include the cacophonous outdoor music of Mughal celebration and the ancient lineage of the Hindu *raga* (Massey and Massey 1993) – the parade-ground lineup of brass, woodwind, and percussion had become widely assimilated into Indian culture by the mid-nineteenth century.

The *Proclamation Music* for the 1903 Durbar, by Captain G. Batthyany Sanford of the Indian Army, made its appeal to the senses through sheer quantity. The score noted that "massed bands, field trumpets, bugles, and drums numbering in all 1850 performers, [were] conducted by the composer" (Sanford, 1903, title page). The music is scored for full military band, in which each part would have been rendered by up to ten players – flute and piccolo, oboe, clarinets in B*b* and E*b*, alto saxophone, first and second bassoon, bugles, four cornet parts, and trumpeters in the band, with a second division of "field trumpets" and a full complement of lower brass and percussion. The side drum, bass drum, and cymbals added the expected martial sonorities, while large items of tuned percussion such as timpani, which could only be manipulated by the cavalry, were also included. The composer was faced with substantial practical difficulties in coordinating these massive forces; furthermore, the harmonic possibilities were limited by the presence of brass instruments such as bugles which could only play the natural harmonic series. Accordingly, the musical effects of Sanford's score rely on a familiar repertoire of antiphonal exchanges, repeated rhythmic patterns and fanfares. Naturally, marches played a leading role, and the steady beat of rhythms in a square four-in-a-bar, pounded out by percussion, must have been audible to all throughout much of the ceremony. Indeed, the sensory affect of regular march rhythms undoubtedly exceeded in the impact of any melodic or harmonic device employed by the composer. As with the insistent tramp of Kipling's famous lines "Foot—foot—foot—foot—sloggin' over Africa/Boots—boots—boots—boots movin' up and down again" (Kipling 1931:541–2), the foursquare plod of parade ground music provided a visceral metaphor for the inexorable progress and discipline of the British Empire. Only in the *Proclamation March Suite*, a longer piece following the construction made famous by Elgar's *Pomp and Circumstance March* No.1 (1901), does a more reflective note enter Sanford's music, with a lyrical trio section framed by longer sections of blazing martial music. In addition to Sanford's workmanlike contribution, a far more distinguished composer with a similar name, Sir Charles Villiers Stanford, contributed a more inventive *Flourish of Trumpets*, scored for 12 trumpets, timpani, side drums, cymbals, and *gran cassa*, which makes greater use of syncopation and adopts a stately pace, *moderato maestoso* (Stanford 1902). Again, however, the steady underlying rhythmic pulse of Stanford's music provides a metaphoric link with the supposed solidity and permanence of empire, and a contrast with the perceived excesses of Asiatic culture. This pulse, slower than that of the human heartbeat, offered a sensory corrective to the collective excitement of the crowd, a subliminal reminder of the disciplinary apparatuses underpinning and constantly struggling to stabilize and prolong the colonial regime.

If the 1903 festivities largely replicated parade-ground practice from Britain, King George and Queen Mary's trip in 1911–12 comprised almost a month of festivities in which epic visual effects were heightened by the widespread use of music with some Indian participation. On "The Children's Day," for example, *The Times of India* observed

> Twenty-six thousand children in their best clothes and all happy!... A military band played to them, and four pipers of the Cameron High-landers delighted them with their magnificence and their music ... [God Save the King] was sung in English and then in Gujerati ... The representatives of the different languages took up the tale in turns, first English, then Gujerati, Marathi and Urdu. The Mohomedan boys who sang last had the best opportunity, if they were not the most tuneful songsters; and their gay clothes, smiling faces, and attitude of prayer added greatly to the effect of their song which already lacked nothing in volume. (Reed 1912:51)

The singing of the British national anthem in translation provided a fairly straightforward demand for conformity to the culture of the imperial center. But there were more subtle forms of imperial power at work here too. The inclusion of the Cameron Highlanders – symbolic of the suppression of the 1745 rebellion and the subordination of the Highlands to English rule – was a sure a sign of an imperialism within the British Isles as well as beyond it, an impression confirmed by the common use in debates about empire (as today on American television) of the terms "England" and "Britain" as interchangeable.

In 1911 the Durbar took place against a wall of sound both magnificent and disciplined. Fanfares were provided by the Royal Heralds, with the State Trumpeters, which was a mixed group, Indian and British, of trumpeters kitted up in embroidered heraldic outfits. In a nice

Figure 6.3 "The Royal Heralds," from Stanley Reed, *The King and Queen in India: A Record of the Visit of their Imperial Majesties to India from December 2nd, 1911 to January 10th 1912* (Bombary: Bennett, Coleman & Co, 1912), p. 67

synecdoche of imperial overreach, however, even this battery of musical artillery could not quite conquer the awesome spaces they aspired to master:

> The massed band, which consisted of over 1,600 performers drawn from seventeen British and twenty-six Indian regiments, played selections of popular and patriotic music from the hour of half-past ten, but the enormous distances in the area robbed the music of much of its impressiveness. It was conducted by Colonel Summerville, commandant of the School of Military Music, and conducted by Major Stretton of the same institution, both of whom had come from England for the purpose. (*Historical Record* 1914:217)

There was no doubting the ideological import of this display of triumphalism, a musical parallel to the assertive rows of red and blue uniforms and weaponry which characterized the parade. Yet in the era before electronic amplification, sight proved ultimately more effective than sound over the huge spaces of the Durbar field.

It was the arrival of the veterans, war-tested heroes of earlier military campaigns (including over a hundred survivors from the Indian "Mutiny" more than fifty years earlier) which marked a sentimental, and musical, climax of the event:

> Shortly after the troops were all steeled in their positions, cheering and the strains of music were heard on the west of the arena as the veterans of the Army marched through. They advanced to the well-known tune of "See, the conquering hero comes", the troops in the arena saluting them successively as they came up, and a sudden silence fell on the assembly as it rose to pay its tribute to this pathetic company. As they filed to their seats on the east wing of the inner theater, the band played "Auld Lang Syne". (*Historical Record* 1914:217)

The affective appeal of these music numbers was directed mainly toward the British and military participants – a chorus from the opera *Judas Maccabaeus* (1747) by Georg Friedrich Handel long since transformed into a classic of the Hanoverian parade ground – and a sentimental Scottish ballad which emphasized the distance from "home" for the British participants in the event. The underlying theme of both, loyalty, echoed the visual statement made by the celebration of loyal war veterans from the "Mutiny," the great moment of crisis for British India.

In the absence of mechanical amplification, and given the multiple languages of the crowd, the spoken word was useless in the context of the Durbar. Music and other sonic effects served to announce the arrival of significant personages, otherwise indistinguishable to the crowd from other distant, uniformed and mounted figures:

> Shortly after this there was a sharp note on the bugle, and the troops throughout the arena sprang smartly to attention. A few seconds later, the waving of pennons at the eastern side of the amphitheatre indicated the entry of a procession. It was that of the Governor-General... (*Historical Record* 1914:217)

About twenty minutes later,

> the first gun of an Imperial salute announced the arrival of the Sovereign's carriage at this point. The feeling in the arena now rose to its highest pitch, and the effect of this, and of the long, glittering line of the troops slowly unwinding itself to the splendid music of Meyerbeer's Coronation March from *Le Prophète,* was a marvel of state pageantry. (ibid.:221)

This recourse to European musical tradition (the German composer Meyerbeer worked mainly in Paris) perhaps reveals the underlying insecurity of *"Das Land ohne Musik."* It was not the only non-British contribution, however. Indigenous cultural forms, hybridized to suit the occasion, were also pressed into service:

> After the National Anthem had been sung in many tongues came the singing and dancing of the Garbi. The Garbi, which is sung on various auspicious occasions, and by Hindus at Devali in particular, is a comparatively modern form of dance ... Whatever the origin and esoteric meaning of the Garbi it is now eminently a dance for *la jeune fille*. It has nothing in common with the nautch or with the *bayaderes* admired by Loti; it has even escaped being influenced by fashionable Russian dances. On the Maidan it was performed by 230 girls of the Gujarati communities, grouped in three concentric circles. (Reed 1912:51)

Finally, Fortescue recalled,

> The King and Queen rose; the pages gathered up the purple trains; the massed bands blared out a march; and the whole assembly sprang to its feet ... The trumpeters ... numbered twenty four, drawn in equal numbers from British and Indian cavalry regiments, with one drummer from the Thirteenth Hussars ... were dressed in the crimson and gold worn by the state trumpeters at home, the British wearing white helmets, the natives white and gold turbans; and all of course were mounted on white horses. (Fortescue, 1912, 158–9)

In this martial context – and in contrast to the dress of the Native Princes – the lavishly embroidered and fanciful clothing of the heralds (pure, rather than colonial, Gothic) signifies as masculine rather than feminized.

The Delhi Durbar was effective precisely because of its superior manipulation of, and appeal to, the senses. Like Mughal Durbars before it, and like totalitarian political rallies after it (at Nuremberg and elsewhere), the Durbar relied on an overwhelming build-up of sound, of color, and of texture, in order to persuade a mass audience of the immutable quality of the regime and to speak directly to a mass audience. In the early days of the Indian National Congress, with a newly confident resistance to imperialism growing in Britain and in India, the British Raj attempted to assert its permanence in Indian and world politics. This impression was, of course, backed up on the parade ground with what appeared to be an overwhelming military force, though when severely tested the imperial forces were actually barely capable of controlling the peninsula, as the experiences of 1857 and 1947 demonstrated.

Edward Elgar and *The Crown of India*

Events in London responded closely to those in Delhi. *The Crown of India: An Imperial Masque* which was produced at the Coliseum Music Hall in London in March 1912, was an allegorical representation, for the London public, of the Indian Coronation and Durbar. Both carried the grandest official imprimatur; both were attended by the King and Queen; both promoted a particular vision of empire. Each event, too, conformed to David Cannadine's recent analysis of the "Ornamentalism" of the British Empire, displaying a marked concern with the promotion of a notional pan-imperial, quasi-feudal social hierarchy (Cannadine 2001). The overriding issue of class status was intended to subordinate questions of race, national identity, and gender.

A key figure under investigation here is Sir Edward Elgar (1857–1934), who composed the score for *The Crown of India* and whose presence

Figure 6.4 *The Crown of India* tableau, from *Daily Sketch* 12 March 1912. Reproduced in Jerrold Northrop Moore, *Elgar: A Life in Pictures* (Oxford: Oxford University Press, 1971), p. 70

in the pit, as musical director, gave the production its unique imprimatur of artistic quality. Elgar's symphonic music has long been taken to epitomize Edwardian imperialism. A rather fierce debate between Elgar's detractors and his partisans has, in recent years, centered on whether to characterize the composer as a brash, social-climbing advocate of imperial triumphalism, or a deeply sensitive individual tortured by a sense of loss and persecuted as a result of his Catholicism and lowly social origins, hiding behind a protective façade (Richards 2001:44–87). The extensive surviving documentation reveals that he was, of course, both of these things, combined in a complex admixture. Elgar's programmatic music offers hints, at least, of the intermingling of imperial and domestic themes. The concert overture *Cockaigne: In London Town* of 1901 is a clear example. On the cover for the score, published by Lesley Boosey rather than Elgar's usual publisher Novello, an illustration by Patten Wilson brilliantly indicated the combination of Gothic-revival medievalism and pictorial depiction of the modern city which underpinned Elgar's glittering exercise in program music. One particularly graphic sequence, in which – according to Elgar's own description – a military band marches past, is illustrated on the cover by troops wearing Indian army kit, including helmets specially adapted to avoid sunstroke, a precaution strictly unnecessary "in London town." In 1933 Elgar's contemporary, Basil Maine, noted the "close inter-relation of the music and the age," adding

> It is not easy for the present generation to realise how firmly Imperialism gripped the imaginations of those who were young men and women at the beginning of the century ... A discussion of the pros and cons of imperialism would be irrelevant. The point is that, right or wrong, salvation or stumbling-block, Imperialism coloured the whole life of the nation during the early years of the century; and to say that Elgar's music during this period was coloured thereby is only another way of saying that it was a reflection of the nation's life. (quoted in Richards 2001:68)

Elgar was perfectly happy to be the official minstrel of British imperialism. In bullish mood, in a much-quoted interview with the *Strand Magazine* in 1904, he asserted:

> I like to look on the composer's vocation as the old troubadours or bards did. In those days it was no disgrace to be turned on to step in front of the army and inspire people with a song. For my part, I know that

there are a lot of people who like to celebrate events with music. To these people I have given tunes. Is that wrong? (quoted in Redwood 1982:123)

Between 1901 and 1930 Elgar would produce a series of orchestral marches under the title *Pomp and Circumstance*, derived from *Othello*:

Farewell the neighing steed, and the shrill trump
The spirit-stirring drum, the ear-piercing fife,
The royal banner, and all quality,
Pride, pomp and circumstance of glorious war!

Elgar later claimed that it was "at the suggestion of King Edward VII" that he transformed the great march tune from *Pomp and Circumstance* March No.1 into the central theme of the *Coronation Ode*, with the addition of words by A.C. Benson, "Land of Hope and Glory" (Young 1973, opp.144). This was to become the most significant musical expression of imperialism to emerge from the British Empire:

Land of hope and glory,
Mother of the free,
How shall we extol thee,
Who are born of thee?
[...]
Truth and Right and Freedom,
Each a holy gem,
Stars of solemn brightness
Weave thy diadem.

Elgar's music, however, which preexisted the words, explores a far wider and more complex emotional compass. The wide intervals, typical of patriotic music (such as "The Star Spangled Banner") are inevitably followed by drooping cadences harmonized to suggest a sense of melancholy and retrospect. After an introduction of blazing splendor, the theme's first appearance in *Pomp and Circumstance* March No.1 is hushed and quiet – *piano, legato e cantabile* – with the melody played low in the register of the first violins, shadowed by clarinet and horns to add tonal richness, and accompanied by two harps. This is hardly the instrumentation of the parade-ground. Perhaps Elgar noted that the quotation from *Othello* began with the valedictory "Farewell." Yet Elgar told *The Strand*

We are a nation with great military proclivities, and I did not see why the ordinary quick march should not be treated on a large scale in the way that the waltz, the old-fashioned slow march, and even the polka have been treated by the great composers; yet all marches on the symphonic scale are so slow that people cannot march to them. I have some of the soldier instinct in me ... (quoted in Moore 1984:339)

The Crown of India, celebrating the Indian coronation of George V, finds Elgar in this demotic vein, as a bard of toe-tapping popular imperialism. While the suite derived from Elgar's score has achieved some prominence through recordings, the visual aspects of this now obscure orientalist concoction have been entirely neglected. *The Crown of India: An Imperial Masque* was written by Henry Hamilton, a minor dramatist whose previous productions include *Ordered to the Front: a Patriotic Address* written during the Boer War (Hamilton 1899). It offers an allegory of Indian history in which the British imperial power inevitably plays a redemptive role. The first tableau – "The Cities of Ind" – opens with scenery which invokes a homogenized essence of India, featuring the building made iconic above all by eighteenth-and nineteenth-century British travelers:

A Temple typifying the legends and traditions of India. At the back is a view of the Taj Mahal at Agra. In front of it and occupying the entire scene is a semi-circular amphitheatre of white marble, its boundary defined by tiers of steps at the summit of which is a semi-circle of sculptured and fretted seats of marble, for the Twelve Great Cities of India – in the Centre being a wide marble throne for India herself. The names of the Cities are inscribed on the plinth beneath the seat of each. (Hamilton 1899:6)

As the lights rise, a "NATIVE CROWD" is revealed, played by British actors in a modified form of "blackface," with "some characteristic FIGURES lying and squatting across the full width of the stage." At one end is "A NATIVE MUSICIAN with a tom-tom, at the other a couple of SNAKE CHARMERS with pipes." Both these, the stage directions continue, "are employed to chime in with the incidental music." Elgar's music bears only a tangential relation to traditional Indian musical forms, despite the availability of these in Edwardian London (Farrell 1997). Rather he employs an orientalist style which nicely conforms to Edward Said's thesis of 1978. He contributed twelve discrete segments of music, with arias, dances including one for "nautch girls," and marches.

Notable orientalist touches include the extensive use of percussion, such as the tambourine and a specially designed gong.

Particularly significant is the way in which, despite the chronology of British imperialism in India, which reaches from the sixteenth to the twentieth century, a key point of reference both for Elgar's music and for the anonymous set designs is medieval Britain, or rather the idealized version of it produced during the Gothic revival of the nineteenth century. Although Elgar once memorably claimed "I am English folk music," he was in fact the court minstrel of Colonial Gothic. His music served the same purpose as Pugin and Barry's designs for the interior of the Palace of Westminster, and in particular the House of Lords Chamber, which opened in 1847, which utilized the latest production techniques to create a vibrant simulacrum of a medieval interior, conveying a sense of irreproachable historical legitimacy on the proceedings within. Social hierarchy is the dominant concept in the design, underpinned by romantic ideas of chivalry and visualized through the colors and designs of heraldry. Elgar's musical imagination was stirred by similar images: his 1890 overture *Froissart* is based on the fifteenth-century chronicler's tales of a perfect Gothic Europe. Elgar prefaced the score with an epigraph from Keats: "...when chivalry/ Lifted her lance on high." Hearing this music for the first time, Ivor Atkins noted "the surge of the strings ... the sudden bursts from the horns, the battle call of the trumpets, the awesome beat of the drums and the thrill of cymbal clashes" (quoted in Moore 1984:153). It was Elgar's first major composition in the ceremonial vein, replete with fanfares and prominent percussion, which would provide the most impressive musical contribution to British occasions from the *Imperial March*, for the Diamond Jubilee of Queen Victoria in 1897, to the *Empire March* for the British Empire Exhibition at Wembley in 1924. These scores are the epitome of colonial Gothic.

The set design for *The Crown of India* recalls an orientalized version of the Gothic flummery of the state opening of Parliament, with Britannia crowned and ensconced in a throne receiving loyal obeisance from female figures allegorically representing the Indian cities. Generally speaking, the appropriation of aspects of Indian artistic traditions – whether the arabesques and repeating patterns of the raga or the brass and percussion of the processions of the Mughal emperor – into Western forms created unstable hybrid structures, emblematic of the power structures and instabilities of the British Empire itself. Elgar, perhaps aware of the dangers of such hybridity, largely steers clear of citing Indian musical forms, preferring instead simply to garnish his already opulent orchestral palette with more percussion than usual.

The climax of the drama is reached when the production concludes with a loyal (if awkwardly rewritten) rendering of the British national anthem. The familiar tune receives new words, expanding the already bellicose nationalism to apply to an entire continental empire:

> God save our Emperor!
> Hear Now as Ne'er before
> *One* India sing.
> Send him victorious
> Happy and glorious
> Long to reign over us
> God save our King. (Hamilton 1912:24)

It was accompanied by the following visual effects:

> The Banners are raised and waved – the INDIAN PRINCES and ALL on the stage again make obeisance to the SOVEREIGNS who rise and again extent their sceptres towards all, as INDIA kneels with arms outstretched towards them. (ibid.)

This historical pageant of loyalty recalled exactly the symbolic structure of the Durbar, acting out in miniature on a London stage the vast field of activity outside Delhi a few months earlier. There was no acknowledgement of India's modernity – of the vital financial importance of Indian textiles to the British economy, or of the extraordinary achievement of the Raj in laying in a railway infrastructure across the subcontinent. Rather, the masque operated in a colonial Gothic sphere of allegory.

The musical climax of *The Crown of India* – interestingly – arrives long before this trite conclusion, during the historical pageant in which the major cities of India are reviewed. A marginal gloss in the text notes "India recalls the distracted state of her Empire previous to its Peoples being welded into one beneath the British Raj and panegyrises the Pax Britannica." For this, Elgar provides a far from "distracted" score; rather, he offers a superb piece of theatrical music, *The March of the Mogul Emperors,* which accompanied the following action: "Enter from the Arch the Mogul Emperors, Akhbar, Jehangir, Shah Jahan and Aurungzebe, each attended by a retinue of courtiers, guards etc." Through a series of contrived encounters with the personified cities of India, each Emperor somehow implies that his major significance was as a harbinger of the imminent arrival of the British. Elgar's music, however, has a swagger and a heady barbarism which clearly differentiates it from the chivalric "nobilmente" of his five *Pomp and Circumstance* Marches. Un-English though it is, there is no sense of weakness or dissolution in the music, no hint of that feminization of Asiatic culture which was such a feature of the Delhi Durbar of 1911; rather, it is bold, muscular and victorious in tone. Most notable is its powerful rhythmic emphasis: the deliberate, heavy tread of the "March of the Mogul Emperors" surely implies the stately gait of the elephant. And here, a direct connection was forged with the modern spectacle of the British Empire. Among Elgar's audience would be many readers of *The Times*, whose Empire Day issue in 1911 had included an article on "Previous Durbars," providing a build-up for the forthcoming event in Delhi in January 1912. Recalling Curzon's great Durbar of 1903, *The Times* noted:

> The incomparable feature of the 1903 Durbar, the feature that can never be reproduced again, was the State entry into Delhi. It was the elephant procession that made it so unique. Lord Curzon elected, like Lord Lytton [in 1877], to enter the Imperial city upon a gigantic elephant, and all the princes of India, similarly mounted, followed in his train... The Viceroy and Lord Curzon [entered Delhi] on an elephant bearing a howdah covered with silver inlaid with gold. The huge saddle-cloth or *jhool* was stiff and heavy with gold embroidery. The elephant was surrounded by spearmen and by *chpbdars* carrying maces and staves. (*India and the Durbar* 1911:42)

Describing the massive procession of "native Princes," *The Times* noted: "It was a barbaric display, if you will, but it epitomised the wealth and magnificence of the immemorial East. On they came, till one almost fancied that the heavy tramp of the elephants shook the ground. The bells hanging from the howdahs clanged like cathedral chimes" (ibid.:43). Elgar, who may well have read these words, was able to fuse in his score for *The Crown of India*, the colonial Gothic elements of Mughal "barbarism" with British imperial triumphalism, the glitter of percussion evoking the brilliant flash of silver in the sun, the menacing brass providing a hint of military splendor, and the heavy percussion evoking the motion of an army of "gigantic" elephants.

The *Crown of India* gained such popularity that it became the climax of a suite arranged for concert use, and was recorded for HMV by Elgar himself, with the London Symphony Orchestra, in 1930 (Moore 1974:113–16). The *March of the Mogul Emperors* was released on a 78rpm record coupled with the *Pomp and Circumstance* March No. 5, one of Elgar's last works, completed in 1930. The twin aspects of colonial Gothic were paradoxically united on the two sides of an electrically recorded shellac disc.

Elgar's own attitude to *The Crown of India* was, however, by no means straightforward: its huge popular and financial success was galling in relation to the paltry rewards on offer for his other music:

> When I write a big serious work e.g. [*The Dream of*] *Gerontius* we have had to starve & go without fires for twelve months as a reward: this small effort allows me to ... buy books ... Then I go to the N. Portrait Gallery & can afford lunch – now I cannot eat it. (Elgar to Frances Colvin, 14 March 1912, quoted in Moore 1984:630)

Critically, too, the *Crown of India* has long been considered a blot on Elgar's record. In a an interesting echo of *The Times*'s description of the Durbar, the Bloomsbury critic Cecil Gray described *The Crown of India* as the work of "a barbarian, and not even amusing one"; this score was, for Gray, "the worst of the lot" (quoted in Richards 2001:73). Yet even in ceremonial mode, Elgar's music tends to melancholy and nostalgia, a celebration, if of anything at all, then of things lost in the mists of time and memory. *The Crown of India* minimizes this vein, but all the major works of the same period enshrine at their heart long sequential passages with drooping cadences hardly likely to provide uplift for the imperial project. There seems to have been an awareness in 1911–12 that despite the presence of George V (mounted, bathetically, on a horse rather than an elephant), the glory of the 1903 Durbar could hardly be rekindled. Curzon's Durbar "marked the end of a great and picturesque era," *The Times* had sorrowfully noted in 1911, "rather than the beginning of a new period" (*India and the Durbar* 1911:40). In language which closely resembles Elgar's own abiding theme of melancholy and nostalgia, the newspaper continued:

> India has changed greatly in the last ten years. The motor car was still an object of some curiosity and there were very few of them at Delhi. The princes brought with them swarms of retainers in medieval garb, and it was no uncommon experience to encounter a troop of warriors in chain armour, with casques and nodding plumes. The great array of elephants dominated the entire spectacle. The elephant was the symbol of the last Durbar: the taxi-cab seems likely to be the keynote of the next. (ibid.:40)

Perhaps the glorious, barbaric "Emperor" conjured up by Elgar's imagination was not Jahangir and Shah Jahan, but the King-Emperor Edward VII, to whose memory his elegiac Second Symphony, premiered to a muted response in 1911, was dedicated. Or perhaps the vision of a handsome leader, bedecked in finery and borne upon an elephant might echo images of Lord Curzon, who appeared from Elgar's Tory perspective as the greatest of all Viceroys, banished from power by the new Liberal administration. This note of retrospect renders Elgar's barbaric march, paradoxically, a kind of "Recessional" (to quote the title of a poem by Kipling which Elgar planned to set to music) for the British Raj. Elgar's formidable musical imagination was consistently inspired by the melancholy spectacle of lost golden ages – whether of Rome (in the overture *In the South*), ancient England (*Caractacus* and *The Banner of St George*), or the medieval era in *Froissart*. His moments of blazing triumphalism were surely haunted by the Gibbonian certainty that Britain's imminent fall was an inevitable part of the historical process. The next major orchestral work Elgar would compose after *The Crown of India* would return to England's golden age, the founding moment of the British Empire: *Falstaff*, a "symphonic study" vividly evoked the most sharply etched of Shakespearean characters. For all his bluster and bravado, Falstaff is revealed as a countryman dreaming nostalgically of the Gloucester meadows of his boyhood. Doubtless Elgar found autobiographical shadows in the ageing knight, not least in the final rejection of the jocose knight by Henry V: despite the baronetcy, Order of Merit, and Companion of Honour, and all the baubles of colonial Gothic bestowed upon him, Elgar never reached the inner circles of the British establishment as Tan Sen had at the court of Akhbar.

Empire Music Hall

Despite its pretensions to high status, culturally and socially, *The Crown of India* took place in the music hall, a contested social milieu which was foundational in the development of modern British popular culture. The earlier halls thrived on double entendre and salaciousness, attracted prostitutes and their clients, and relied on the sale of alcohol for their profits. But the Coliseum, opened in 1904 by the theatrical entrepreneur Oswald Stoll, was intended to transform the music hall into a respectable form of entertainment for professional men and their families (Perkin 1989). Acts at the Coliseum were banned even from using the word "damn," and alcohol was not served. Sarah Bernhardt and Ellen Terry were prominent stars, but the home-grown darling of the Music Halls, Marie Lloyd, was blacklisted because of the double entendre which was her hallmark ("A Little of What You Fancy Does Yer Good"). But one element remained which linked Stoll's sanitized and respectable

Coliseum with the speakeasies and pubs, which were its unwanted forebears: a focus on popular imperialism (Summerville 1986). One of the earliest music halls on Drury Lane, opened in 1847, was known as the "Mogul Saloon" (Mander and Mitchenson 1974:33). Singers would often impersonate the English "Tommy" or common soldier, as can be seen from the following libretto from "A Gaiety Girl", performed at the Prince of Wales Theatre in 1894:

> And whether he's on India's coral strand,
> Or pouring out his blood in the Soudan,
> To keep our flags a flying, he's a doing and a dying,
> Ev'ry inch of him a soldier and a man. (quoted in Summerville, 1986:37)

By the 1890s, imperialism had become the lingua franca of the conservative working classes, a staple population of the London music halls. Profit-making entrepreneurs colluded with the authorities to popularize the idea of empire.

Such theatrical productions as the Indian Durbars called out for treatment on the London stage, and short extracts of films of the Durbars were shown in music halls before the development of purpose-built cinemas (MacKenzie 1984:34; Low 1973:146). In 1912 the Durbar made its way into a hit musical, *The Sunshine Girl*, by Paul A. Rubens, to words by Rubens and Arthur Wimperis, in which the music-hall star Connie Ediss sang "I've been to the Durbar." In this light-hearted waltz, neither melody nor harmonization makes the slightest gesture in the direction of orientalism.

> I've been on a trip
> On board of a ship
> Where do you think I've been?
> You'd never guess my foreign address
> You don't know where I mean.
> What do you say to India, eh?
> Care of the King and Queen.
> CHORUS: I've been to the Durbar
> Didn't I have some fun!
> I was feeling run down with the season in town
> And I wanted "a place in the sun"!
> I saw the King at the Durbar
> And the King saw *me!* (Rubens 1912)

There was little Elgarian grandeur or complexity to *The Sunshine Girl*, but such popular forms of imperialist entertainment won establishment endorsement nonetheless. The advent of the Royal Command Performance, in which leading music hall acts performed for the King and Queen, came at the Palace Theatre on July 1, 1912, just after the *Crown of India* had finished its run. On the bill was G.H. Chegwin's celebrated performance as "The White Eyed Kaffir" (Mander and Mitchenson 1974:211) and the show opened with a full orchestra playing the overture *Britannia* by Sir Alexander MacKenzie. To conclude the evening, the baritone Henry Claff, riding in on a charger, sang verses of the national anthem "dressed in the armour and sword of the White Knight, quite a figure of Chivalry" (*The Era*, 1912, quoted in ibid.:157). Popular entertainment and colonial Gothic were fused into one unmistakably modern form, in an appeal to the senses less formal but no less effective than that of the great Durbars. The modern individual consumer in the marketplace of the mass media would become the key spectator in the twentieth century's narrative of imperial decline.

Recessional

The cultural promotion of the British Empire was prosecuted through a range of practices, from ceremonial to theater and music hall. Techniques of spectacle, visual and aural, were used in order to project a sense of inviolability and invulnerability to the British Raj to carefully selected Indian audiences through the manipulation of the senses on a massive scale. Similar techniques, as has been less readily recognized, involving both sight and sound, were employed in Britain to promote the imperial ideal. Yet the more bombastic the rhetoric, the more obviously it revealed the fractures and incoherences at the heart of the imperial project. Pressures both at home and abroad – constitutional crisis, the suffragette movement, Indian and Irish nationalism in London; mounting popular involvement with the Indian National Congress on the sub-continent – led directly in 1911–12 to the most spectacular avowals of the imperial ideal. The involvement of complex and conflicted individual artists such as Elgar, furthermore, inevitably led to the inscription within the colonial text of counter-ideological elements: doubt, melancholy, nostalgia; even confusion and panic. Yet while the sensory allure of empire's pageants spoke of the immemorial glory of empire, the radical instabilities of cultural and economic modernity eroded the certainties of the Victorian social settlement and the Raj's control over the vast Indian territories. Legible on the glittering surfaces of the audio-visual spectacle of empire was the immanence of empire's dissolution.

References

Barringer, Tim. 2005. *Men at Work: Art and Labour in Victorian Britain*. New Haven and London: Yale University Press.

Boonzajer Flaes, Robert M. 2000. *Brass Unbound: Secret Children of the Colonial Brass Band*. Amsterdam: Royal Tropical Museum.

Brady, Erika. 1999. *A Spiral Way: How the Phonograph Changed Ethnography*. Jackson, MS: University Press of Mississippi.

Cannadine, David. 1983. "The Context, Performance and Meaning of Ritual: The British Monarchy and the 'Invention of Tradition,' c.1820–1977," In *Invention of Tradition*, ed. Eric Hobsbawm and Terence Ranger. Cambridge: Polity.

——. 2001. *Ornamentalism: How the British Saw their Empire*. Oxford: Oxford University Press.

Cohn, Bernard S. 1983. "Representing Authority in Victorian India." In *The Invention of Tradition*, ed. Eric Hobsbawm and Terence Ranger. Cambridge: Polity.

——. 1996. *Colonialism and its Forms of Knowledge*. Princeton, NJ: Princeton University Press.

Collingham, Elizabeth M. 2001. *Imperial Bodies: the Physical Experience of the Raj, c.1800–1947*. Cambridge: Cambridge University Press.

Coronation Durbar. 1912. *Coronation Durbar, 1911: Being a Reprint of Articles and Telegrams previously published in the* Pioneer, Allahabad: Pioneer Press.

Curzon, George [Lord Curzon]. 1906. *Lord Curzon in India, being a Selection from his Speeches as Viceroy and Governor-General of India, 1898–1905*. London: Macmillan.

Davies, Philip. 1985. *Splendours of the Raj: British Architecture in India 1660 to 1947*. London: John Murray.

Dawson, Graham. 1994. *Soldier Heroes: British Adventure, Empire and the Imagining of Masculinities*. London: Routledge.

Farrell, Gerry. 1997. *Indian Music and the West*. Oxford: Clarendon Press.

Feld, Steven. 1991. "Sound as a Symbolic System: The Kaluli Drum." In *The Varieties of Sensory Experience: A Sourcebook in the Anthropology of the Senses*, ed. David Howes. Toronto: University of Toronto Press.

Fortescue, John. 1912. *Narrative of the Visit to India of their Majesties King George V and Queen Mary and of the Coronation Durbar held at Delhi, 12th December 1911*. London.

Haddon, Archibald. 1935. *The Story of the Music Hall: From Cave of Harmony to Cabaret*. London: Fleetway.

Hamilton, Henry. 1899. *Ordered to the Front: A Patriotic Address*. London: Empire Theatre.

——. 1912. *The Crown of India. An Imperial Masque*. London: Enoch & Sons.

Harvey, John. 1995. *Men in Black*. London: Reaktion.

The Historical Record of the Imperial Visit to India, 1911. Compiled from official records under the orders of the Viceroy and Governor-General of India. London: John Murray for the Government of India, 1914.

Hughes, Meirion and Robert Stradling. 2001. *The English Musical Renaissance, 1840–1940: Constructing National Music*. 2nd edn. Manchester: Manchester University Press.

India and the Durbar: A Reprint of Indian Articles in the "Empire Day" Edition of The Times, *May 24th, 1911*. London, 1911.

Indian Princes and the Crown: A Brief Historical Record of the Indian Princes who Attended the Imperial Durbar at Delhi in 1912; Together with a Description of their Territories and Methods of Administration. Bombay, 1912.

Jyoti, Hosagrahar. 1992. "City as Durbar: Theater and Power in Imperial Delhi." In *Forms of Dominance: On the Architecture and Urbanism of the Colonial Enterprise*, ed. Nezar AlSayyad. Aldershot: Ashgate.

Kinnear, Michael S. 1994. *The Gramophone Company's First Indian Recordings, 1899–1908*. Bombay: Popular Prakashan.

Kipling, Rudyard. 1931. "Boots (Infantry Columns)." In *Rudyard Kipling's Verse: Inclusive Edition, 1885–1926*. New York: Doubleday.

Low, Rachael. 1973 {1948]. *The History of British Film 1906–1914, Based upon Research of the History Committee of the British Film Institute*. London: Allen and Unwin reprint.

MacKenzie, John M. 1984. *Propaganda and Empire: The Manipulation of British Public Opinion, 1880–1960*. Manchester: Manchester University Press.

——. (ed.). (1986). *Imperialism and Popular Culture*. Manchester: Manchester University Press.

Mander, Raymond and Joe Mitchenson. 1974. *British Music Hall: A Story in Pictures*. London: Studio Vista.

Massey, Reginald and Jamila Massey. 1993. *The Music of India*. London: Kahn and Averill.

Menpes, Mortimer. 1903. *The Durbar*. London: A. & C. Black.

Metcalf, Thomas R. 1994. *Ideologies of the Raj, The New Cambridge History of India*, Vol. 3, pt. 4. Cambridge: Cambridge University Press.

Millar, Oliver. 1992. *The Victorian Pictures in the Collection of Her Majesty the Queen*. Cambridge: Cambridge University Press.

Moore, Jerrold Northrop. 1972. *Elgar: A Life in Photographs*. Oxford: Oxford University Press.

——. 1974. *Elgar on Record*. Oxford: Oxford University Press.

——. 1984. *Edward Elgar: A Creative Life*. Oxford: Oxford University Press.

Perkin, Harold. 1989. *The Rise of Professional Society*. London: Routledge.

Redwood, Christopher (ed.). 1982. *An Elgar Companion*. Ashbourne: Sequoia.

Reed, Stanley. 1912. *The King and Queen in India: A Record of the Visit of Their Imperial Majesties the King Emperor and Queen Empress to India, from December 2, 1911 to January 10, 1912*. Bombay: Bennett, Coleman & Co.

Richards, Jeffrey. 2001. *Imperialism and Music: Britain 1876–1953*, Manchester: Manchester University Press.

Rubens, Paul A. 1912. *I've been to the Durbar*. Sheet music. London.

Said, Edward. 1978. *Orientalism*. New York: Pantheon.

Sanford, G. Batthany. *c.*1903. *Proclamation Music, consisting of The Summons [of] the Heralds, The March of the Heralds, The Proclamation Fanfares and The Proclamation March Suite*. London.

Stanford, Charles Villiers. 1902. *Flourish of Trumpets for the Imperial Coronation Durbar held at Delhi, January 1st, 1903, by his Excellency Baron Curzon of Keddleston*. Souvenir edn. London.

Summerfield, Penny. 1986. "Patriotism and Empire: Music-Hall Entertainment, 1870–1914." In *Imperialism and Popular Culture*, ed. John Mackenzie. Manchester: Manchester University Press.

Volwahsen, Andreas. 2004. *Splendors of Imperial India: British Architecture in the Eighteenth and Nineteenth Centuries*. Munich and London: Prestel.

Wade, Bonnie C. 1998. *Imaging Sound: An Ethnomusicological Study of Music, Art and Culture in Mughal India*. Chicago: Chicago University Press.

Woodfield, Ian. 2000. *Music of the Raj: A Social and Economic History of Music in Late Eighteenth-century Anglo-Indian Society*. Oxford: Oxford University Press.

Young, Percy M. 1973. *Elgar O.M. A Study of a Musician*. 2nd edn. London: Purnell.

Zealley, Alfred Edward. 1926. *Famous Bands of the British Empire: Brief Historical Records of the Recognized Leading Military Bands and Brass Bands in the Empire*. London: J.P. Hull.

Part 3

Museums

seven

The Museum as Sensescape: Western Sensibilities and Indigenous Artifacts

Constance Classen and *David Howes*

This chapter develops a set of interrelated themes concerning the sensorial dimensions of indigenous artifacts and the sensory typologies of their European collectors. These themes include the importance of touch in seventeenth- and eighteenth-century European collections compared to the dominance of sight in the modern museum; the Western association of the "lower" races with the "lower" senses; the links between museum display and imperialism; and, the complex sensory lives of indigenous artifacts in their cultures of origin. The discussion here builds on the theoretical approach of the anthropology of the senses (Howes 1991, 2003; Classen 1993a, 1997; Seremetakis 1994), extending it to the analysis of the cultural and sensory transfigurations which indigenous artifacts undergo upon accession by Western museums.

The anthropology of the senses emerged as a focus for cultural studies in the early 1990s, partly in reaction to the excesses of "textualism" and "ocularcentrism" in conventional social scientific accounts of meaning, but more fundamentally as a positive attempt to explore some of the basic sensual and existential dimensions of the human condition. The senses are constructed and lived differently in different societies, such that

When we examine the meanings associated with various sensory faculties and sensations in different cultures we find a cornucopia of potent sensory symbolism. Sight may be linked to reason or to witchcraft, taste may be used as a metaphor for aesthetic discrimination or for sexual experience, an odour may signify sanctity or sin, political power or social exclusion. Together, these sensory meanings and values form the sensory model espoused by a society, according to which the members of that society "make sense" of the world, or translate sensory perceptions and concepts into a particular "worldview". There will likely be challenges to this model from within the society, persons and groups who differ on certain sensory values, yet this model will provide the basic perceptual paradigm to be followed or resisted. (Classen 1997:402)

The anthropology of the senses is particularly germane to material culture studies, since every artifact embodies a particular sensory mix. It does so in terms of its production (given the particular sensory skills and values that go into its making), its circulation (given the way its properties appeal to the senses and so constitute it as an object of desire or aversion), and its consumption (which is conditioned by the meanings and uses people perceive in it according to the sensory order of their culture or subculture). In short, artifacts body forth specific "ways of sensing" and they must be approached through the senses, rather than as "texts" to be read or mere visual "signs" to be decoded. Otherwise put, things have sensory as well as social biographies (Howes forthcoming).

In Western museum settings, artifacts are preeminently objects for the eye. Often, in fact, it is only the most visually-striking artifacts which are put on display. Less visually prepossessing objects are hidden in the museum storeroom, no matter how rich their auditory, tactile, or olfactory intricacies. (If they are "nothing to look at," they must be consigned to obscurity.) Susan Stewart has noted that modern museums are "so obviously – so, one might say, naturally, empires of sight that it barely occurs to us to imagine them as being organized around any other sense or senses" (Stewart 1999:28). The same holds true for the artifacts displayed, which become so evidently *visual* signs that it is difficult to attribute any other sensory values to them. Within the museum's empire of sight, objects are colonized by the gaze.

Within their cultures of origin, however, visual appearance usually forms only one part – and often not the most important part – of an artifact's sensory significance. The sensory values of an artifact, further-more, do not reside in the artifact alone but in its social use and environ-mental context. This dynamic web of sensuous and social meaning is broken when an artifact is removed from its cultural setting and inserted within the visual symbol system of the museum. (Of course, much has been written about the "complexities" of visual culture in modernity, and much, no doubt, remains to be written. Yet our academic focus on vision must not be allowed to defer indefinitely the investigation of the social life of nonvisual sensory phenomena.)

To say that an artifact in a museum plays a different role than it did in its culture of production may appear to be stating the obvious – and, indeed, the inevitable. Yet there are many questions and concerns surrounding this process which have, as yet, scarcely been addressed. How is the collection and presentation of indigenous artifacts related to Western notions of the sense lives of indigenous peoples? What are the symbolic attributes and social history of the "sensescape" of the museum? What is missing from, or repressed within, museum representations? What are the implications of the notion of artifacts as multi-sensory embodiments of meaning, as advocated in this chapter, for the redesign of museums? To what extent can one ever apprehend the sensory world of the "other"?

Handling the Collection

In modernity it is usually only owners who have the power to touch collections. It is understood that collections which are not our own are not to be handled. Prior to the mid-nineteenth century this was not the case. Both private and public collections were often touched by visitors, and indeed experienced through a range of sensory channels. The seventeenth-century English diarist John Evelyn, who was an avid visitor to collections across Europe, records feeling objects, shaking them, lifting them to test their weight, and smelling them. In 1702 the English traveler Celia Fiennes recorded a visit she made to the Ashmolean Museum of Oxford:

> there is a Cane which looks like a solid heavy thing but if you take it in your hands it's as light as a feather ... there are several Loadstones and it is pretty to see how the steel clings or follows it, hold it on the top at some distance the needles stand quite upright ... (Fiennes 1949:33)

The Ashmolean's curators at this time were not unconcerned about the deterioration of their collections caused by too much handling. Nonetheless, they were unwilling to forbid such handling, due to the notion that touch provided an essential – and expected – means of acquiring knowledge.

More than eighty years after Celia Fiennes's visit to the Ashmolean, in 1786 the European traveler Sophie de la Roche wrote of her visit to the British Museum:

With what sensations one handles a Carthaginian helmet excavated near Capua, household utensils from Herculaneum ... There are mirrors too, belonging to Roman matrons ... with one of these mirrors in my hand I looked amongst the urns, thinking meanwhile, "Maybe chance has preserved amongst these remains some part of the dust from the fine eyes of a Greek or Roman lady, who so many centuries ago surveyed herself in this mirror ..." Nor could I restrain my desire to touch the ashes of an urn on which a female figure was being mourned. I felt it gently, with great feeling ... I pressed the grain of dust between my fingers tenderly, just as her best friend might once have grasped her hand ... (de la Roche 1933:107–8)

In this remarkable passage Sophie de la Roche indicates how essential her sense of touch was to her experience of the museum collection and how she employed touch as a medium for annihilating time and space and establishing an imaginative intimacy with the former possessors of the articles she surveyed, an intimacy heightened by de la Roche's sensation of coming into direct contact with their bodily remains.

The importance given to touch prior to the mid-nineteenth century and the freedom allowed to its exercise within a museum context is alien to us today. Touch, however, was generally believed to provide a necessary supplement to sight, which sense was understood to be limited to surface appearances. Solely viewing a collection was considered a superficial means of apprehending it. Taking the time to touch artifacts, to turn them over in one's hands, showed a more profound interest. Touch, furthermore, was believed to have access to interior truths of which sight was unaware. Celia Fiennes notes that the cane on display in the Ashmolean looked heavy, but when she picked it up she found that it was light. The deceptions of sight are corrected by touch (see further Harvey 2002).

As the example of Sophie de la Roche strongly illustrates, touch functioned as an important medium of intimacy between the visitor to the collection and the collection itself. Through touch the visitor and the collected are united, physically joined together. Touch provides the satisfaction of a corporeal encounter. By touching a collected object the hand of the visitor also encounters the traces of the hand of the object's creator and former owners. One seems to feel what others have felt and bodies seem to be linked to bodies through the medium of the materiality of the object they have shared.

Exotic Sensations

The objects which particularly elicited a tactile response from early museum visitors were sculptures and artifacts from exotic or ancient lands. With sculptures the lifelike nature of the forms – the drapery which looked so real, the skin which seemed so supple – seemed to invite touching. While appearing real, their inanimacy meant that sculptures – even those of the most august emperor or the fiercest lion – could not resent or resist being touched. Through the three-dimensionality of sculpture one could therefore experience a simulacrum of intimate sensations which one would be unlikely to experience in real life. One could also verify, through touch, that sculptures were, in fact, inanimate, that the lion did not bite back, that the body which looked so soft and supple was indeed cold and hard. Seventeenth- and eighteenth-century visitors to the antiquities of Italy routinely prodded the apparently plump mattress on which lay the statue called "The Hermaphrodite" to feel for themselves its stony hardness, and caressed the spiky bristles of the marble "Wild Boar" until these became shiny with handling (Haskell and Penny 1981:163, 235). Touching statues was not just a question of idle curiosity, however, but of aesthetic appreciation. As the Renaissance sculptor Ghiberti put it: "Touch only can discover [sculpture's] beauties, which escape the sense of sight in any light" (cited in Symonds 1935:649).

Artifacts from exotic lands offered Europeans the possibility of experiencing a safe but nonetheless potent contact with the "other worlds" from which they sprang. It mattered little in many cases what the actual uses and meanings of these artifacts were in their own societies; what mattered was rather the ways in which they could confirm Western representations of non-Western cultures and serve as a springboard for the Western imagination. Thus, for example, what were perceived as distorted, exaggerated features of native masks and statuary were imagined to correspond to a similarly distorted and exaggerated sensuality. A lolling tongue or bulging eyes on a mask or statue invited commentary on the gluttonous or lascivious nature of the society which produced it.

Masks, clubs, "idols," and other characteristic artifacts found in collections fascinated Europeans with their implications of savagery. Touching and holding such "barbarous" objects with their own hands enabled Westerners to vicariously participate in, and confront their fear of, the supposedly brutal lifestyles of "primitive" peoples (see Thomas 1991).

While they often stimulated visceral sensations of horror and disgust, indigenous artifacts might also inspire loftier sentiments. An attractive example of this is the eighteenth-century writer Horace Walpole's reaction to a *quipu*, a recording device employed by the Incas. The *quipu* was a set of knotted cords of different colors hung on a string. The position and size of the knots and the difference of colors served to reference information which the Incas considered worthy of note, from population counts to prayers.

The *quipu* was a very sensual medium, engaging touch and rhythm in the tying of the knots, and involving a wide range of colors and patterns (Classen 1993b:125). The *quipu*, furthermore, was not flat and linear – as is writing. In *Code of the Quipu* Marcia and Robert Ascher write:

> The quipumaker's strings present no surface at all … A group of strings occupy a space that has no definite orientation; as the quipumaker connected strings to each other, the space became defined by the points where the strings were attached … The relative positions of the strings were set by their points of attachment, and it is the relative position, along with the colors and knots, that render the recording meaningful. Essentially then the quipumaker had to have the ability to conceive and execute a recording in three dimensions with color. (Ascher and Ascher 1981:62)

Intrigued by a *quipu* which had been sent to him by a collector of antiquities, Walpole could see in it possibilities for new sensory idioms, such as a language of colors or a tactile language in which one could weave poems and knot rhymes. He wrote to his correspondent that trying to understand the colorful *quipu* was like trying to "hold a dialogue with a rainbow by the help of its grammar a prism, for I have not yet discovered which is the first or last verse of four lines that hang like ropes of onions" (Walpole 1965:261–3).

Walpole goes on to imagine the nature of a language of colors, dwelling on the possibility of making puns through overlapping hues, or of expressing nuances through delicate variations in shade. "A vermilion *A* must denote a weaker passion than one of crimson, and a straw-color *U* be much more tender than one approaching to orange" (ibid.).

The tactile qualities of the *quipu* inspired similar reveries in Walpole. "I perceive it is a very soft language," he wrote, "though at first I tangled the poem and spoiled the rhymes." Indeed, Walpole professed to be "so pleased with the idea of knotting verses, which is vastly preferable to anagrams and acrostics, that if I were to begin life again, I would use a shuttle instead of a pen" (ibid).

Finally the *quipu*, its strings impregnated with ancient odors, led Walpole to reflect on the subject of an olfactory language. He wrote:

> Why should not there be a language for the nose?... A rose, jessamine, a pink, a jonquil and a honeysuckle might signify the vowels; the consonants to be represented by other flowers. The Cape jasmine, which has two smells, was born a diphthong. How charming it would be to smell an ode from a nosegay, and to scent one's handkerchief with a favourite song! (ibid.)

In this flight of fancy Walpole is obviously not accessing any of the indigenous meanings encoded in the *quipu*. Nor does he pretend to. He knows only that the *quipu* was used as a recording device by the Incas. Handling this multisensorial form of "writing" served Walpole as a stimulus to develop ideas about sensory correspondences which were coming into vogue in Europe and which would find further elaboration in the Symbolist movement in the nineteenth century (Classen 1998). However, his physical contact with the *quipu* did potentially bring Walpole closer to the *quipu*'s indigenous significance in at least one sense. Walpole was able to conceive that different sensory aspects of the *quipu* might be used for encoding information, a notion that would later be suppressed by more visualist ethnographic interpretations of the quipu.

Significantly, European collectors and travelers not only brought home specimens of the cultures they'd visited, they frequently had themselves represented as actually embodying those cultures. Thus, in the eighteenth century, Lady Mary Worsely Montagu commissioned a portrait of herself in Turkish costume after her extensive travels in Turkey, while the botanist Joseph Banks was painted wearing a Polynesian bark-cloth cape after his explorations in the South Pacific. In the latter painting Banks holds up a corner of the cape in one hand and points to it with the other, directing us to acknowledge the cloak as tangible proof of his travels and inviting us vicariously to feel the curious weave (Thomas 1991:142–3). Embodying the peoples of other lands through putting on their clothing enabled Europeans to pretend an intimate knowledge of their cultures and played with the European fascination with "going native." Only played with it because the observers of this charade understood that, though the trappings were exotic, the European sensibilities underneath were intact.

The Tactility of the Natives

Europeans perceived themselves to be the rational, civilized, elite among the peoples of the world. As reason and sensuality were traditionally opposed in Western thought, non-Westerners were, by contrast, imagined to be irrational and sensuous. At the same time as they deprecated sensuality, however, Europeans exhibited a vivid interest in, and even longing for, more sensuous ways of life. The sensuous life of the other, to the European mind, was either one of refinement and pleasure or of brutish degradation. The Orient typically served as an imaginary place of exquisite sensory refinements, while Africa was stereotyped as a land of sensory brutality. Both places were, alas, understood to be amoral. However, this only added to their fascination, to their speculative potential as alternatives to Western norms, since none of the social constraints which limited the actions of Europeans need apply.

When Europeans imagined non-Westerners to be more sensuous than themselves, the senses they particularly had in mind were the so-called lower senses of smell, taste, and touch. According to Western sensory symbolism, sight was the highest of the senses and the one most closely associated with reason. As "lower" senses, smell, taste and touch were associated with the body, and with those peoples imagined to live a life of the body, rather than a life of the mind.

Early accounts of indigenous peoples are full of references to their reliance on the proximity senses of smell, taste, and touch. The inhabitants of India are said to have a remarkable tactile acuity, African peoples are described as being ruled by their stomachs, Native Americans are stated to have extraordinary powers of smell, "rivaling that of the lower animals" in the words of one writer (cited in Classen 1997:403).

Many eighteenth- and nineteenth-century philosophers and anthropologists were concerned to depict the "animalistic" importance of smell, taste, and touch in non-Western societies. In his study of aesthetics, for example, Friedrich Schiller stated that "as long as man is still a savage" aesthetic enjoyment occurs by means of touch, taste, and smell, rather than through the "higher" senses of sight and hearing (Schiller 1982:195). In the early nineteenth century the natural historian Lorenz Oken invented a sensory hierarchy of human races, with the European "eye-man" at the top, followed by the Asian "ear-man," the Native American "nose-man," the Australian "tongue-man," and the African "skin-man" (cited in Howes 2003:5).

Their supposed reliance on the "lower" senses, indeed, led indigenous peoples to be likened to the blind by Western theorists. The nineteenth-century physician William B. Carpenter associated the apparent tactile acuity of the blind with the tactile sensitivity of weavers in India. Carpenter added:

> A like improvement is also occasionally noticed in regard to Smell, which may acquire an acuteness rivaling that of the lower animals; and this not only in the blind, but among the races of men whose existence depends upon such discriminative power. Thus we are told by Humboldt that the Peruvian Indians in the darkest night cannot merely perceive through their scent the approach of a stranger whilst yet far distant, but can say whether he is an Indian, European, or Negro. (Carpenter 1874:141)

Similarly to the blind, indigenous peoples were seen as living – both literally and figuratively – in the dark. They were imagined to inhabit dark huts, in dark forests, in dark continents, and to pursue their unenlightened lives in "the gloomy shade" of "absolute barbarism" (cited by Thomas 1991:129).

The Museum of Sight

The more that Europeans emphasized the distinction between the "noble" sense of sight and the "base" proximity senses, the less the latter were deemed suitable for the appreciation and understanding of art and artifacts. In contrast to the multisensory modes of previous centuries, in the 1800s sight was increasingly considered to be only appropriate sense for aesthetic appreciation for "civilized" adults. Thus in 1844 the popular art writer Anna Jameson remarked:

> We can all remember the public days at the Grosvenor Gallery and Bridgewater House, we can all remember the loiterers and loungers ... people who, instead of moving among the wonders and beauties with reverence and gratitude, strutted about as if they had a right to be there; talking, flirting; touching the ornaments – and even the pictures!" (cited by Hermann 1972:126)

Half a century earlier Sophie de la Roche had felt entirely comfortable fingering the exhibits in a museum. By the mid-nineteenth century such behavior had become a sign of vulgarity and insubordination – of a lack of civilized behavior.

The nineteenth century was an era of rising visualism in many ways. Sight was closely allied with scientific practice and ideology, the social importance of which grew immensely during this era. The visual arts were definitively detached from craftwork, which (despite the efforts of the Arts and Crafts movement) was negatively perceived by many as emphasizing the hand over the eye and functional considerations over aesthetic form. The development of industrial capitalism emphasized the visual display of goods, both as a sales incentive and as a sign of material plenty. Visual surveillance, particularly within the context of modern social institutions such as the school and the prison, became a key means of maintaining public order. Furthermore, new visual technologies such as photography made visual representation increasingly central to Western cultural and intellectual life (Classen 2001).

The nineteenth century was also the era of the public museum, and, in its development, the museum reflected many of the visualizing trends of the day. Museums were important sites for testing and presenting visualizing scientific paradigms. They were major sites of display: wealthy capitalist nations needed showcases of cultural capital. Museums were also sites of surveillance and public order. Strict bodily discipline was required from museum visitors who were expected to become as close to pure spectators as possible: not to touch, not to eat, not to speak loudly, or in any way to assert an intrusive multisensorial presence.

Touching the collection was not only deemed to be "uncivilized" in the nineteenth century, it was also considered to be unacceptably damaging. In earlier centuries the distintegration of the less durable parts of collections through handling and haphazard upkeep was common. There was, indeed, relatively little emphasis on conservation. As more and more people gained access to museums during the nineteenth century, however, the potential damage to collections through handling became more dramatically apparent. Since the preservation of collections for posterity was emphasized as a *raison d'être* of the modern museum, it was deemed necessary for collections to be hands-off. Requiring visitors to keep their hands off the exhibits was also believed to have the benefit of fostering an attitude of respect toward collections and their collectors, an attitude that Anna Jameson found so sadly lacking in her early gallery experiences. As in the new era of heightened visualism touch was no longer generally believed to furnish important aesthetic or intellectual insights, the restriction of touch in the museum was not considered to be any great loss. The important thing was to see.

The Colonized Collection

Collecting is a form of conquest and collected artifacts are material signs of victory over their former owners and places of origin. From an early age non-Western artifacts brought home by soldiers, travelers, and antiquity hunters had played the role of spoils. What the modern museum particularly developed, in conjunction with this paradigm of conquest, was a model of colonization, of foreign dominion (Bennet 1995).

Colonel Pitt Rivers, the founder of the Pitt Rivers Museum in Oxford, for example, wished to create a display of artifacts which would show the social evolution of technology from primitive cultures to modern Western civilization. His ideal scheme of display was that of concentric circles, which he believed to be particularly suited to "the exhibition of the expanding varieties of an evolutionary arrangement" (cited in Chapman 1985:38–9). In this system, artifacts from around the world were situated solely on the basis of selected formal criteria (and without regard for their relevant cultural contexts) in an evolutionary scale which culminated in Victorian England as the pinnacle of human achievement. What we see here is clearly more a case of the West (as represented by Pitt Rivers) trying to create a satisfying and self-fulfilling identity for itself through institutional display than a meaningful depiction of the cultures of others (see Figure 7.1).

According to the colonial model of the collection, once artifacts have been acquired or "conquered," they must be integrated into a new social order and made to conform to a new set of values imposed by their governor – the collector or curator. The collection is an unruly mass of displaced natives that has to be disciplined and rendered subservient to its masters. This regulation of artifactual bodies by the regimen of the museum was presented by collectors and curators as being for their own good. Nineteenth-century collectors often justified their removal of native artifacts from their cultures of origin to be placed in Western collections by saying that they were rescuing them from obscurity and neglect. In the words of one collector, the indigenous artifacts he gathered would be "far more valuable amongst the records and treasures of a museum than in the dinginess and filth of their [native homes]" (cited by Thomas 1991:181).

Artifacts were better off in the clean, bright, protected environment of the museum under the aegis of knowledgeable Western scholars. Ironically, the implied conclusion was that indigenous artifacts were misused by their original owners and that it was only when they entered

Figure 7.1 Pitt Rivers, typology

the Western museum that they were used properly. The ethnographic museum was a model of an ideal colonial empire in which perfect law and order was imposed upon the natives. This colonial modeling was made even more explicit in the nineteenth-century world fairs in which fake colonial villages with specimen natives were exhibited (see Mitchell 1988).

The visual emphasis of the museum contributed to the model of colonization in several ways. Artifacts were required to conform to the sensory order of their new home. This meant being reduced to the visual, or – from a Western perspective – being civilized into the visual. As the artifacts in the museum represented cultures, the peoples providing them also symbolically had their senses and sensory presences disciplined. Through their representative artifacts they were rendered touchless, speechless, and smell-less.

The visual order of the museum enabled artifacts to be examined by scholars according to Western scientific standards, something which was deemed to be difficult within the "dinginess and filth" – and cultural strictures – of their indigenous environments. The ethnographic museum usually also functioned as a kind of laboratory in which artifacts might be made to reveal their secrets to the penetrating gaze of the scientist. The visual display of the artifacts in their glass cases further allowed visitors to dominate the collection through their gaze (Bennett 1995). In the colonial empire of the museum it is not only the curators who are the governors but also the visitors, who can assert their superiority to the collection and masterfully survey the kingdom conquered by their own civilization. The visitors can come and go as they please. The collection remains trapped, captive – the canoe hangs still from the ceiling, the drum is silent on the wall, the amulet is powerless in its case.

Outside the Glass Case

One anthropologist of the 1920s, trying to explain to a European readership the indigenous value of certain religious objects from Papua New Guinea, wrote that, while such artifacts might appear to be simply "absurd creations of wicker-work," they were "possessed of another meaning in the dimness and obscurity of their own environment" (cited by Thomas 1991:182). The unintended implication of this position was that, if natives could only see more clearly, they would give up their absurd wicker-work and create Western-style artworks. In the meantime it was the task of the anthropologist to try to shed light on their dim practices.

Even when anthropology left behind crude Victorian typologies of natives, the multisensory dynamics of indigenous cultures remained obscure – and often unimportant – to Westerners. For example, when the creative styles of non-Western cultures began to influence Western art in the twentieth century (such as the influence of African masks on Cubism), their varied sensory dimensions were typically ignored, and only a semblance of their visual façade retained. This was not a negative development in itself, as migrant artifacts must necessarily begin a new cultural and sensory life in their new home, but it contributed to a one-sided representation of indigenous cultures.

Indigenous artistry eluded Western concepts of aesthetics in the complexity of its cultural values and in its engagement of a plurality of senses. The visual, museum model of the artifact is what in most cases entered the Western imagination, not the dynamic multisensory life of the artifact in its culture of origin.

This remains generally true today. In some ways it has been heightened by contemporary anthropology's rejection of the trope of indigenous peoples as tactile beings who place a "bestial" emphasis on the lower senses. It was partly to avoid this stigma that many anthropologists came to treat indigenous peoples and their artifacts as though they were as visually oriented (and therefore civilized) as Westerners (Howes 2003).

Furthermore, Western anthropologists have studied indigenous cultures through the visualist models which dominate in their own society, notably photographs, films, and texts. Visual Anthropology developed as an important subfield of Anthropology. There is no Tactile Anthropology. Therefore it should not surprise us to learn that, for example, a cross-cultural analysis of the aesthetic values of even so apparently tactile an art form as pottery is undertaken by Western scholars entirely on the basis of photographs of pots (see for example Iwao and Child 1966).

The anthropology of the senses, as developed in the last decade or so (Howes 1991, 2003; Classen 1993b, 1997), asserts that every society has its own sensory order – that is, its own unique mode of distinguishing, valuing, and combining the senses. Material culture gives expression to this sensory order; every artifact embodies a culturally salient, sensory combination. This is what makes the study of indigenous artifacts in situations of "cross-cultural consumption," like that of the museum, so potentially problematic and at the same time so revealing of imputed intentions and unintended uses (Howes 1996).

What might happen if we were to conceptually remove indigenous artifacts from their glass cases and try to understand them within their original cultural and sensory contexts? Is there really that much more to learn about a Tukano basket or a Navajo sandpainting, for example, than what we can see of them in a museum?

Sensography of Basketry and Sandpainting

The basketry created by the Tukano people of the Colombian rainforest can serve a variety of purposes. In fact, it includes not just baskets, but also mats, fans, sieves, and even houses, which may have walls of interwoven palm leaves. Aside from its practical functions, basketry plays an important symbolic role in Tukano culture. The process of weaving basketwork is compared by the Tukano to the life process. The act of procreation is likened to pressing grated manioc through a sieve. The fetus is said to float in the "river" of the amniotic fluid wrapped up in a plaited mat. When shamans are undertaking a curing ritual, they often invoke magical woven screens which will admit only healing colors. The cosmos itself is conceptualized as a weaving of threads of light and wind (Reichel-Dolmatoff 1985:6–23).

All the sensory elements of their basketwork have meaning for the Tukano. The different odors, shapes, and textures of the reeds, vines, wood fibers, and palm fronds which are used in basketry refer to elements of Tukano mythology. The red, yellow, and brown colors employed are respectively symbolic of male fertility, female fertility, and maturity. When a basket turns from green to brown in the process of drying, it is said to represent a transformation from immaturity to a state of procreative ripeness. The geometric patterns of the different weavings reflect patterns the Tukano see in their hallucinogenic visions. The shapes of different baskets, trays, and mats refer to such culturally charged concepts as food, wombs, animals, and constellations of stars. The seeping of water, smoke, and other fluids through the baskets and trays stands for the dynamic relationship between the Tukano and their environment (ibid.:24–39).

The aesthetics of Tukano artifacts lies not in the perfection of their form, but in their ability to evoke fundamental cultural ideals through all of their sensory attributes:

> [Tukano art] is never an end in itself; it can never be more than a means through which the highest cultural values and truths can be expressed. For this reason, artistic and technical skill are not of the essence ... What counts is not form but content; not performance but meaning ... In fact, shamans warn people not to be too form-perfect; not to be too impressed by appearances. (ibid.:17)

As it is meaning that is valued rather than form, there is no attempt by the Tukano to conserve their artifacts. Whatever happens to the artifacts, the ideals and meanings they embody will remain untouched.

Tukano basketry is not greatly valued by first-world collectors and tourists because of its unassuming appearance. The subtle combinations of smell, texture, shape, and pattern, and the myriad cultural meanings which these encode, are usually beside the point for collectors, who look primarily for visual display. In this regard the more ornamented and colorful baskets of certain neighboring Amazonian peoples are much more to the taste of foreign buyers (ibid.:40). This emphasis on the visual reflects the role that an Amazonian basket will play when it enters Western culture: it will above all be something to *see*.

Navajo sandpaintings, by contrast, have been greatly admired in the West as an ingenious, primitive form of visual art. Sandpaintings, however, are created by the Navajo for purposes of healing rather than for aesthetic display. The shaman covers the floor of a ceremonial house or *hogan* with dry sand and sprinkles colored pigments on top to create an image of the cosmos. He sings as he works, calling the deities to inhabit their representations in the sand. When the painting is complete and vibrant with divine energy the patient enters and sits in the center. The shaman transfers the positive energy of the painting to the patient by rubbing sand from the different parts of the picture onto the patient's body. After the ritual is finished the sandpainting is swept away (Gill 1982:63).

While the importance of the sandpainting for the Navajo lies in its ability to channel healing power, it has primarily been appreciated by Westerners as an exotic counterpart to a Western painting – a work of "primitive art" preservation. (See Witherspoon 1977 on art as dynamic process rather than timeless object in Navajo aesthetics.) In order to incorporate sandpaintings into Western aesthetics, however, it is essential to make them durable, for a painting made out of sand defies the whole Western system of art collection and preservation. The sandpainting must furthermore be changed from something one sits on (the last thing one would do with a Western painting) to something at which one simply looks.

The simplest way of accomplishing this transformation is to photograph or draw sandpaintings. For the Navajo, the correct view of a sandpainting is that of the patient sitting at the center. From a Western perspective, however, the only satisfying view of a sandpainting is the view from above, which allows the painting to be seen in its entirety. Photographers who wished to capture "complete" images of sandpaintings were therefore obliged to climb on top of the hogan and photograph the sandpainting below from a hole in the roof (Gill 1982:64–6; Parezco 1983:31). Another method of preserving sandpaintings is to glue them to a canvas. Once it is fixed in place, the sandpainting, like a Western painting, can be hung on the wall, bought and sold, and preserved for all time. Several ethnographic museums have tried to achieve greater authenticity by having the sandpainting created within the museum and then covered with a glass case (although in such cases vibrations eventually cause the sands to shift) (Parezco 1983:39).

Traditionally, sandpaintings were destroyed by the Navajo by sundown of the day in which they are made. Blindness, in fact, was held to be the punishment for looking at the sacred symbols for too long (ibid.:38, 48). As with so many other creations of indigenous cultures, however, the influence of Western aesthetic and market values has had the effect of abstracting sandpaintings from their traditional cultural context, divesting them of their multisensory meanings, and transforming them into static visual images, at which one can apparently gaze indefinitely with no fear of reprisal.

The case of the Navajo sandpaintings demonstrates that museum exhibits not only desensualize objects as regards their extension in space, they desensualize them as regards their development through time. Few objects live the artificially atemporal life of museum artifacts. Sandpaintings are eminently ephemeral, created of shifting sands and disassembled the day they are made. Their sensuality unfolds within a sequence of ritual events which are key to their cultural significance. The same point can be made of a Japanese tea bowl, for example. In the tea ceremony the bowl is incorporated into a complex series of rites in which visual and auditory sensations recede and sensations of smell, touch, and taste are brought to the fore (Kondo 2004). When an artifact such as a tea bowl is "frozen" within a museum setting, this sequentiality of sensory experience is disrupted. It seems possible to encompass the nature of the artifact with a glance. In fact, one could say that it is only *when* an artifact is frozen within a museum setting – like a still, stuffed carcass in a nature display – that it *becomes possible* to master it through sight alone. Outside the museum, other sensory dimensions and possibilities intrude. Hence, the museum "holds still" the objects in its collection so that they can be visually appropriated, and then "holds still" the process of sensory revelation at the moment of visual epiphany. The beauty of "letting go" (see Ouzman, this volume chapter 10) is not well understood or appreciated.

Contemporary ethnological museums have sometimes attempted to create more interactive environments for their collections. In some cases these innovations have been the result of pressure put on museums by indigenous groups. For example, under its Sacred Materials Programme, the Canadian Museum of Civilization has "an agreement with the Hodenosaunee to provide corn meal mush and burn tobacco for the false face masks and other sacred objects from the Six Nations Confederacy in the museum, and representatives come to the museum twice a year at the museum's expense to do so" (Laforet 2004). In general, however, what *The* [London] *Times* wrote of the World Exhibition of 1851 still holds true today: "We want to place everything we can lay our hands on under glass cases, and to stare our fill" (cited by Mitchell 1988:20). Despite a number of innovative challenges to the glass-case model, an increasing reliance on visual technologies for documentation and dissemination (as in the case of the "virtual museum") make museums more sight-bound than ever. In her study of the role of photography in museums, Elizabeth Edwards describes the standard accession practices of the modern ethnographic museum. She observes that the museum object is

> defined by a series of documenting photographic practices: accession photographs, conservation photographs, X-ray and infra-red photographs revealing unseen depths of the object – procedures that often address the part, rather than the whole of the object. There is a sense in which the museum object becomes a sum of its photographs. (Edwards 2001:77)

Edwards suggests that there is a "seamless continuum" between photography and museum display.

In this context one can understand how many curators would hardly see the point of allowing visitors access to the non-visual dimensions of artifacts which they have not seen fit to consider themselves. The issue of tactile access to collections is usually only raised as regards the visually impaired (Candlin 2004), the assumption being that those who can see have no need to touch. (Indeed, with even curators donning gloves to handle artifacts, who can now test the veracity of Ghiberti's statement that certain works can only be properly appreciated by touch?) It is, in fact (except occasionally in the case of musical instruments), not a question of exploring the non-visual values of collections, but rather of using ever-expanding visual technologies to gain ever more "insights" into artifacts. It might be argued that the untouchability of the modern museum is due to a purely "practical" concern for conservation, rather than to a shift in sensory values. Yet the increased concern over conservation in modernity is not a "natural" museological development, but is itself the expression of a changing ideological and sensory model according to which preserving artifacts for future view is more important than physically interacting with them in the present (see Classen 2005). It has been claimed, furthermore, that curatorial practice often has more to do with the conservation of expertise than with the conservation of objects (Candlin 2004).

Despite the hypervisualism of contemporary culture, however, most museum-goers are not solely interested in apprehending the formal appearance of the artifacts on display, but in establishing a connection with those artifacts and with the people who created them. (Why else would the average museum visitor balk if told, for example, that every item on display was merely an excellent replica of the original artifacts safeguarded in the museum storeroom?) Museum-goers do not just want to visually process information. Like Sophie de la Roche in the eighteenth century, museum-goers want to feel physically linked – "in touch" – with other peoples and worlds through their material effects. A case in point would be the "Touch Me" exhibition presented at the Victoria and Albert Museum as this book goes to press. The starting point for this exhibition of contemporary designer objects is "the idea that we live in a touch-starved society and that the quality of touch interaction with most products is nothing to what it might be." By showcasing the work of craft makers, and encouraging haptic interaction with the collection, the curators "aim to show that we all have a latent capability for more creative and communicative touch" (see at http://www.hughalderseywilliams.com/projects/touchme.htm).

Alternative Paradigms of Perception

The task facing anyone who wishes to explore the sensory dimensions of artifacts across cultural borders is complex. On the one hand, there is the difficulty of transcending one's own cultural sensory model with all of its potent symbolic associations in order to become open to the alternative paradigms of perception that may be embodied in artifacts from other cultures. On the other hand, there is the difficulty of conveying the multisensory nature of indigenous artifacts by means of the prevalent visual or audio-visual media of communication in use today. Even if a variety of sensory channels are used, to what extent can the intricate symbolism embedded in artifacts by their cultures of origin be rendered comprehensible to members of another culture?

In a nineteenth-century novel, Thomas Edison is presented as musing on the metaphorical blindness of native peoples with respect to the values of Western art: he asks himself

> suppose I place the *Mona Lisa* of Leonardo da Vinci in front of a Pawnee Indian or a Kaffir tribesman. However powerful the glasses or lenses with which I improve the eyesight of these children of nature, can I ever make them really see what they're looking at? (L'Isle-Adam 1982:15)

The same might be said in reverse of Westerners. However much we are encouraged to handle indigenous artifacts, can we ever really understand what we are touching?

The answer must almost certainly be that we who are cultural outsiders cannot. Yet we can recognize what the limits of our understanding have been and we can try to grasp more than we have in the past. It is on this basis that some of the most innovative work in material culture is currently being undertaken. From Marcia Pointon's (1999) examination of the tactile values of Victorian hair jewelry to Nicholas Saunders's (1999) comparison of the sensuous and social values of pearls in Native America and Europe to Sven Ouzman's (2001) analysis of the nonvisual qualities of African rock art, the groundwork is being laid for a full-bodied approach to the study of artifacts which is responsive to the interrelationship between their sensuous materiality and their cultural import (see also Seremetakis 1994; Dant 1999; MacGregor 1999; Stahl 2002). Even the Inca *quipu*, so long silenced, is being revisited as a medium of communication which functioned on several sensory levels. The *quipu* scholar Robert Ascher writes that if Western academics had a less visualist sensory order

> we might understand [*quipu*] writing as simultaneously tactile and visual, and probably more. Being that we are who we are, it is difficult to internalize this notion so that it becomes a part of us, but I think that it is the next step that must be taken in the study of Inka writing. (Ascher 2002:113)

Sensorially-minded curators of ethnographic collections, in turn, must grapple with the fact that, while museums are true to their own cultural background – that is, they are clear products of Western social history – they are untrue to the other cultures they represent. The traditional glass cases of the museum present little impediment to the eye but they are not ideologically transparent. As we have seen, glass cases are ideological framing devices within the larger frame of the museum itself.

The "solution" to this problem (which can never be completely solved given the ultimate incommensurability of cultures) is not necessarily to oppose the visual model of the museum with a "synaesthetic" model of sensory totality (Sullivan 1986). This would be to follow the example of the "open-air" museum or exotic theme park and attempt to create an encompassing cultural and sensory environment, where artifacts are displayed within a mock village, with typical houses, food, music, and "inhabitant"-guides. One difficulty with this model is that the sensuous, simulated reality of the display site might appear to encapsulate, and vie for authenticity with, the actual culture represented. At least when artifacts are presented in vitrines, most visitors realize that they are not seeing the "whole picture." If a whole "living" village is represented, the distinction is less clear.

It is impossible to create a museological model which is free of issues of domination and misrepresentation. The museum is, after all, a tightly controlled site of containment, a cultural zoo, however naturalistic its setting may be made to appear. One intermediate alternative to the "museum of sight," however, would be to allow visitors more possibilities for dynamic interaction with, and a contextual understanding of, the collection, without making a pretense of total sensory immersion. Visitors could be drawn into the physical space of other cultures through full-scale replicas of local buildings, without necessarily creating (or perhaps deliberately inhibiting) an illusion of actual cultural relocation. The issue of conservation might be addressed by having a place within the museum where visitors could handle reproductions of the objects on display. As noted above, however, mere tactile engagement with an artifact will not necessarily deepen one's understanding of its cultural role. Sensory content, therefore, would need to be placed in cultural context. This could be accomplished through such aids as descriptive texts, audiotapes, films, and interactive computer programs – and potentially through other sensory stimuli such as incense – as well as by live presentations and workshops (in which artifacts might occasionally leave their cases). Here the seemingly atemporal character of museum artifacts – and, by extension, of their cultures of origin – could be countered by reference to their social and material mutability and to the realities of cultural change. Of key importance would be to bring out some of the political and social history behind how the artifacts came to be in the museum in the first place (see Gosden and Knowles 2001). A museum exhibit might be most effective when visitors realize that it's not simply a "pretty picture," that it shows the marks of social contacts and conflicts.

This diathetical mode of museum display might be called "stereo-scopic" or "bisensual," for it promotes an interplay of Western and non-Western "worldviews," or "sensory cosmologies." It does not simply strip artifacts of their sensory identities in order to reinscribe them within a hegemonic visual regime – as in the traditional ethnological museum. Nor does it attempt to create an illusion of cultural authenticity by masking the signs of external control and mediation – as in an "open-air"-style cultural recreation. It acknowledges the ideological and sensory trajectory and limitations of the conventional museological model on the one hand, while on the other it opens a breach in that model to allow for a more dynamic, multisensorial, and culturally aware museum experience.

Acknowledgments

The material in this chapter is based on research generously supported by the Social Sciences and Humanities Research Council of Canada, the Fonds pour la Formation des Chercheurs et l'Aide à la Recherche du Québec, Concordia University General Research Fund and a CUPFA Professional Development Grant.

References

Ascher, Marcia and Robert Ascher. 1981. *The Code of the Quipu: A Study in Media, Mathematics and Culture.* Ann Arbor: University of Michigan Press.

Ascher, Robert. 2002. "Inka Writing." In *Narrative Threads: Accounting and Recounting in Andean Khipu*, ed. J. Quilter and G. Urton, 103–15. Austin: University of Texas Press.

Bennet, Tony. 1995. *The Birth of the Museum: History, Theory, Politics.* London: Routledge.

Candlin, Fiona. 2004. "Don't Touch! Hands Off! Art, Blindness and the Conservation of Expertise." *Body and Society* 10(1): 71–90.

Carpenter, W.B. 1874. *Principles of Mental Physiology*, London, Henry S. King & Co.

Chapman, William. 1985. "Arranging Ethnology: A.H.L.F. Pitt Rivers and the Typological Tradition." In *Objects and Others*, ed. G. Stocking. Madison: University of Wisconsin Press.

Classen, Constance. 1993a. *Worlds of Sense: Exploring the Senses in History and Across Cultures.* London: Routledge.

——. 1993b. *Inca Cosmology and the Human Body.* Salt Lake City: University of Utah Press.

——. 1997. "Foundations for an Anthropology of the Senses." *International Social Sciences Journal* 153: 401–12.

——. 1998. *The Color of Angels: Cosmology, Gender, and the Aesthetic Imagination.* London: Routledge.

——. 2001. "The Social History of the Senses." In *Encyclopedia of European Social History*: ed. P. Stearns, 355–63. New York: Charles Scribner's Sons.

—— (ed.). 2005. *The Book of Touch*. Oxford and New York: Berg.

Dant, Tim. 1999. *Material Culture in the Social World*. Buckingham: Open University Press.

de la Roche, Sophie. 1933. *Sophie in London*, trans. C. Williams. London: Jonathan Cape.

Edwards, Elizabeth. 2001. *Raw Histories: Photographs, Anthropology and Museums*. Oxford: Berg.

Fiennes, Celia. 1949. *The Journeys of Celia Fiennes*. London: Cresset Press.

Gill, Sam. 1982. *Native American Religions: An Introduction*. Belmont, CA: Wadsworth.

Gosden, Chris and Chantal Knowles. 2001. *Collecting Colonialism: Material Culture and Colonial Change*. Oxford: Berg.

Harvey, Elizabeth (ed.). 2002. *Sensible Flesh: On Touch in Early Modern Culture*. Philadelphia: University of Pennsylvania Press.

Haskell, Francis and Nicholas Penny. 1981. *Taste and the Antique: The Lure of Classical Sculpture 1500–1900*. New Haven: Yale University Press, 1981.

Hermann, Frank. 1972. *The English as Collectors*. London: Chatto & Windus.

Howes, David (ed.). 1991. *The Varieties of Sensory Experience: A Source Book in the Anthropology of the Senses*. Toronto: University of Toronto Press.

——. 1996. "Introduction: Commodities and Cultural Borders." In *Cross-Cultural Consumption: Global Markets, Local Realities*, ed. D. Howes. London: Routledge.

——. 2003. *Sensual Relations: Engaging the Senses in Culture and Social Theory*. Ann Arbor: University of Michigan Press.

——. forthcoming. "Scent, Sound and Synaesthesia: Intersensoriality and Material Culture Theory." In *The Sage Handbook of Material Culture*, ed. Christopher Tilley et al. London: Sage.

Iwao, S. and I.L. Child. 1966. "Comparison of Esthetic Judgments by American Experts and by Japanese Potters." *Journal of Social Psychology* 68: 27–33.

Kondo, Dorrine. 2004. "The Way of Tea: A Symbolic Analysis." In *Empire of the Senses: The Sensual Culture Reader*. Oxford: Berg.

Laforet, Andrea. 2004. "Relationships between First Nations and the Canadian Museum of Civilization." Paper presented at Haida Repatriation Extravaganza, Masset, B.C., May 22.

L'Isle-Adam, Villiers de. 1982. *Tomorrow's Eve*, trans. R. Martin Adams. Urbana IL: University of Illinois Press.

MacGregor, Gavin. 2001. "Making Sense of the Past in the Present: A Sensory Analysis of Carved Stone Balls." *World Archaeology* 31(2): 258–71.

Mitchell, Timothy. 1988. *Colonising Egypt*. Cambridge: Cambridge University Press.

Ouzman, Sven. 2001. "Seeing is Deceiving: Rock Art and the Nonvisual." *World Archaeology* 33(2): 237–56.

Parezo, Nancy J. 1983. *Navajo Sandpainting: From Religious Act to Commercial Art*. Tucson: University of Arizona Press.

Pointon, Marcia. 1999. "Materializing Mourning: Hair Jewellery and the Body." In *Material Memories*, ed. M. Kwint, C. Breward and J. Aynsley. Oxford: Berg.

Reichel-Dolmatoff, Gerardo. 1985. *Basketry as Metaphor: Arts and Crafts of the Desana Indians of the Northwest Amazon*. Los Angeles: Museum of Cultural History, University of California.

——. 1987. *Shamanism and Art of the Eastern Tukanoan Indians*. Leiden: E.J. Brill.

Saunders, Nicholas J. 1999. "Biographies of Brilliance: Pearls, Transformations of Matter and Being." *World Archaeology* 31(2): 243–57.

Schiller, Fredrick. 1982. *On the Aesthetic Education of Man*, ed. and trans. E.M. Wilkinson and L.A. Willoughby. Oxford: Clarendon.

Seremetakis, C. Nadia (ed.). 1994. *The Senses Still: Perception and Memory as Material Culture in Modernity*. Boulder, CO: Westview.

Stahl, Ann Brower. 2002. "Colonial Entanglements and the Practice of Taste: An Alternative to Logocentric Approaches." *American Anthropologist* 104(3): 827–45.

Stewart, Susan. 1999. "Prologue: From the Museum of Touch." In *Material Memories: Design and Evocation*, ed. Marius Kwint, Christopher Breward and Jeremy Aynsley. Oxford: Berg.

Sullivan, Lawrence. 1986. "Sound and Senses: Toward a Hermeneutics of Performance." *History of Religions* 26(1): 1–13.

Symonds, John Addington. 1935. *Renaissance in Italy*. New York: Modern Library.

Thomas, Nicholas. 1991. *Entangled Objects: Exchange, Material Culture, and Colonialism in the Pacific*. Cambridge, MA: Harvard University Press.

Walpole, Horace. 1965. *Horace Walpole's Correspondence with the Countess of Upper Ossory*. Vol. 33, ed. W.D. Wallace and A.D. Wallace. New Haven: Yale University Press.

Witherspoon, Gary. 1977. *Language and Art in the Navajo Universe*. Ann Arbor: University of Michigan Press.

eight

The Fate of the Senses in Ethnographic Modernity: The Margaret Mead Hall of Pacific Peoples at the American Museum of Natural History

Diane Losche

When with closed eyes, on some warm autumn night,
I breathe your bosom's sultry fragrances,
Enchanted shores unfold their promontories
Dazed by a sun monotonously bright ...
Led by your scent to magic littorals,
I see a harbour filled with masts and sails
Still tired from the sea surge, the ocean near ...

Baudelaire, *Selected Poems*

As buildings lose their plasticity and their connection with the language and wisdom of the body, they become isolated in the cool and distant realm of vision. With the loss of tactility and the scale and details crafted for the human body and hand, our structures become repulsively flat, sharp-edged, immaterial, and unreal. The detachment of construction from the realities of matter and craft turns architecture into stage sets for the eye, devoid of the authenticity of material and tectonic logic.

Pallasmaa, "Architecture of the Seven Senses"

Introduction

This chapter suggests that modernity has two opposed and sometimes contradictory discourses regarding the sensory Imaginary in the museological tradition.[1] In one of these, following Foucault, the gaze becomes a new kind of power through an apparatus, such as a panopticon, which distances the observer from the observed and reduces sensory input other than the visual to a minimum. In this way the viewer can scan the object of the gaze and gains knowledge through a distancing effect or apparatus. The idea of the museum as a panopticonic apparatus has been developed in an influential book by Tony Bennett (1995) that examines the nineteenth-century museum. However there is another discourse in modernity, and this is that of poets in particular, a discourse in which the viewer is immersed, once again through an apparatus, for example words or sounds, in a sensescape, a particular imaginary sensorium. In this discourse a sense of immersion rather than a viewpoint of distance is sought. Baudelaire is only one of the most outstanding examples of this utopian quest. There have been postcolonial critiques of both modes of representation (Bennett 1995; Said 1994) which have pointed out that both discourses involve forms of colonization of an "other." In the poetic form of representation the "other," be it the body of woman, or the territory itself, is invaded and traversed. (In fact Baudelaire weds the two. In his poem, quoted above, the reader is carried via the body of woman to a distant scape.) This discourse is intertwined with naturalism in poetic modernity, as the true, real, and authentic is evidenced through the visceral and the experience of the senses.

These countervailing tendencies, distance versus immersion, torque about one another, and are often constructed as opposed poles of comprehension. Immersion is seen as an attempt to recuperate authentic experience, lost through the distancing lens of science, rationality, and detachment. Different senses occupy very different spaces in relation to the real, the imaginary and the virtual, and the visual is more readily associated with fact, truth, and science than with the other senses. It is the implications of these divisions, and the struggle with these different discourses in ethnographic exhibition development, that will be the topic of this chapter.

These multiple discourses about the senses are often segmented into different disciplines, institutions, and spaces. Poetry and the other arts, film, the novel, and dance, explore the immersive path, while institutions, such as museums and art galleries, are seen as dedicated to the panopticonic survey and "rational" and classificatory understandings. The two passages that began this chapter represent the apparent opposition between these sites. In these particular statements the contrast is between a poetry whose luxuriant language is the vehicle for the reader to enter via a woman's body, a foreign scape and an architecture critiqued for its "flat, sharp-edged" structures divorced from the human body. Or so the story goes. But, as anyone who has been to a contemporary art space knows, the story is not so simple – in fact contemporary artists (at this moment Damien Hirst is only the most obvious) constantly try to unravel the distancing structures of gallery and museum, and often use viscerality and immersion in senses other than the visual to do this. Whether they succeed is an interesting question but not one for this discussion. The point here is not only that the various discourses of modernity are always hybrid and contaminated by each other but that in any particular case these multiple discourses are, to use the words of Bruno Latour, an "imbroglio."[2] This term was originally used by Latour to describe the way that everyday knowledge, for example that found in a reading of the daily paper, involves us in tangled networks of information which, if followed, show how the worlds of politics, science, medicine, the arts, etc. are necessarily connected with each other in significant ways. The important point of Latour's concept is that this hybridity and interconnectivity is also, simultaneously, ignored. Rather than tracing networks and interconnections there is a constant resort to rigid and outmoded categories of knowledge. Latour's sketch of an imbroglio is worth quoting for his elaboration of the concept. He uses the daily newspaper as an example of a situation that presents the reader with the need to trace significant connections between apparently different domains, pointing out

> those hybrid articles that sketch out imbroglios of science, politics, economy, law, religion, technology, fiction. If reading the daily paper is modern man's form of prayer, then it is a very strange man indeed who is doing the praying today while reading about these mixed-up affairs. All of culture and all of nature get churned up again every day ... yet no one seems to find this troubling. Headings like Economy ... Science ... Local Events remain in place as if there were nothing odd going on. (Latour 1993:2)

He gives a specific example of such an imbroglio in a description of the accounts of the AIDS virus:

On page six I learn that the Paris AIDS virus contaminated the culture medium in Professor Gallo's laboratory; that Mr. Chirac and Mr. Reagan had, however, solemnly sworn not to go back over the history of that discovery; that the chemical industry is not moving fast enough to market medications which militant patient organizations are vocally demanding; that the epidemic is spreading in sub-Saharan Africa. Once again heads of state, chemists, biologists, desperate patients and in- dustrialists find themselves caught up in a single uncertain story mixing biology and society. (1993:1–2)

Latour suggests that the networks of what he calls translation between these separated domains need to be investigated in order to understand how the real world works, in spite of the barriers of official compartments of knowledge classification. Knowledge needs to be recast and remade, according to Latour, for these hybridized interactions and networks are – and this is a significant facet of his analysis – not commensurable with each other:

The same article mixes together chemical reactions and political re- actions. A single thread links the most esoteric sciences and the most sordid politics, the most distant sky and some factory in the Lyon suburbs, dangers on a global scale and the impending local elections or the next board meeting. The horizons, the stakes, the time frames, the actors – none of these is commensurable, yet there they are, caught up in the same story. (1993:1)

This chapter makes use of Latour's notion of the imbroglio, particularly the issue of commensurability and translation, to describe the creation of an exhibition about Pacific peoples at the American Museum of Natural History in New York. This analysis will also extend Latour's concepts to suggest that it also provides a way to understand particular outcomes of projects that involve incommensurate forms of knowledge as well as the roles of particular agents and their relationships with each other.

Anthropology, one of the hybrid sciences born of modernity, has constantly struggled, not always self-consciously, with compartment- alized forms of knowledge. The hybrid nature of the discipline was something of which most practitioners were well aware; however, the incommensurable nature of the activities being hybridized was simultaneously recognized and ignored. Many of ethnography's most interesting products are those that reveal the contradictions and rifts between these incommensurables. Such contradictions can be seen in one of ethnography's major twentieth-century products in particular, the ethnographic exhibit.

In the present discussion, it will be suggested that what characterizes the twentieth-century liberal and progressive museum tradition is a dual goal: to present a panorama to observers, but also to immerse them in a foreign place via the construction of an imaginary sensory environment that transports the viewer. From this perspective the senses are a kind of surface material by which curators construct an imaginary environment while simultaneously conveying a panoramic and rationalized view of culture. This attempt to combine immersion with a rationalized visual system is not always successful but, following Latour, the failure to combine the two in an exhibition reveals interesting imbroglios of modern ethnographic knowledge. When it comes to notions of the senses, what needs investigation is how the conditions of the imbroglio are set in place and enacted via institutions and individual agents.

One major and largely unexamined condition of the museum tradition in anthropology is the control of space via architecture and design[3] and it is the interaction of ethnography with architecture that needs investigation in studies of exhibitions in museums. The power of architecture, and the control of space is, since Foucault, a cliché, but one that is seldom apparent to most professional anthropologists except for those involved in creating exhibits. The fact that architecture can constrain and dominate in ethnological exhibitions is most often ignored by museum anthropologists although they encounter architecture head-on in planning exhibitions. Despite this there is little theorization or consciousness about the implications of the entwinement of these practices in exhibitions. Thus, how architecture translates anthropology in exhibitions needs investigation. The case I will examine here is a collaboration between the ethnographic and the architectural in the attempt to create a modern exhibit in which scientific and rational knowledge were combined with a sensory environment in order to produce knowledge in a form which was both sensual and scientific. That this collaboration was widely thought to be a failure as an exhibitionary spectacle makes this an interesting case to study because it illuminates the difficulties faced when the attempt is made to orchestrate, in one space, the contradictory impulses of modernity. This chapter identifies the dilemma in which the curator and designer found themselves as they created the Margaret Mead Hall of Pacific Peoples at the American Museum of Natural History as an imbroglio in Bruno Latour's sense.

Margaret Mead, Anthropology, Art and Science

The main narrative of this chapter tells the story of the creation of that exhibition. It will be useful, however, to outline briefly Margaret Mead's biography, because it demonstrates how the attempts to wed art and science, the academic, and the popular that characterized the Peoples of the Pacific Hall also formed strands of her entire career. One of Mead's overarching aims was to wed these discourses, a utopian quest inspired by a number of motives (Lutkehaus 1995), among them the quest of anthropology, as a modern discipline, to find an identity of its own during the first half of the century. Mead often used lyrical written descriptions of foreign sensescapes to convince the reader of a point that she believed also had a scientific validity, particularly in those writings that were designed for a wider, nonacademic readership. Texts such as *Coming of Age in Samoa* (Mead 1923), for example, contain many such passages. From the reader's viewpoint this immersion provided evidence of a real, true, and authentic experience and served as a gateway to understand a foreign place. Mead's writing styles are a well-known facet of her role as a public intellectual. Lutkehaus analyzes these styles and the frequent criticisms of them by (often male) social anthropologists. As Lutkehaus points out, Mead's desire to communicate to different audiences was intrinsically bound up with her mode of writing, and she quite consciously varied her style to suit her audience. Mead's notion of herself as a public intellectual and her rhetorical modes were, in turn, related to her utopian vision of anthropology as capable of changing society and culture. This desire for a scientifically credible anthropology needs to be emphasized, especially since, with her death and Derek Freeman's subsequent critique (1983), she seems to have become identified as only a princess of the popular. But, as Lutkehaus suggests, "more than many anthropologists, Mead consciously valued the practice of writing as integral to the practice of science..." (1995:188). Mead was most able to change and adapt her writing styles for different audiences and there is a significant strand of Mead's writing in which the scientific was foregrounded with little attention to immersing the reader in place, for example "Kinship in the Admiralty Islands" (1934) and "The Mountain Arapesh I" (1938). All of these different texts illustrate her self-conscious awareness of and ability to change from one discourse to another depending on the audience she hoped to address.

What is significant here is the extent to which both Mead's writings, in all their various modes, and the equally well-known critiques obscure the shifting and unstable nature of anthropology as a united and coherent discipline with clearly understood modes of knowledge production and communication during the first part of the twentieth century. Mead, for example, was well aware that anthropology is a "conglomerate of disciplines – variously named and constituted in different countries as cultural anthropology, social anthropology, ethnology, ethnography, archaeology, linguistics, physical anthropology, folklore, social history, and human geography" (Mead 1975:3), but at the same time she constantly reiterated that anthropology was a science. Peter Worsley, whose critique of Mead's style is analyzed in depth by Lutkehaus, is also of the clear opinion that anthropology should be a science, as signaled by the title of his critique "Margaret Mead: Science or Science Fiction?" (Worsley 1957). He asks whether Margaret Mead's writing is scientific or fictional precisely because of its lyrical, poetic and, as he suggests, subjective mode. Again, what both Mead and Worsley elide is the very insecure and unstable status and identity of anthropology as a science – a classic Latour imbroglio in which the incommensurable nature of many different kinds of knowledge and institution is evident but simultaneously ignored. This modernist suppression of the degree to which anthropology could be a science also carried over into Margaret Mead's work at the American Museum of Natural History, where she was Curator of Pacific Ethnology from 1926, the year she joined the Museum, until her retirement in 1969, after which she remained at the Museum as Curator Emeritus until her death in 1978. Mead's Hall of Pacific Peoples, opened in 1971, will be the focus of the rest of this discussion.

If anthropology as a whole was embroiled in modernist imbroglios of art and science and the popular and the academic, the museum was one institution where these dilemmas became most visible because of the multiple tasks required of curators. Curators were usually required not only to conduct research but also to superintend collections and to acquire artifacts. They also had important educational and public roles, the most significant of which was to curate major Halls of Ethnology, more or less permanent displays about the culture area they were responsible for. These multiple roles plunged a curator into the intersection of a number of potentially contradictory modes of knowledge and representation: the popular and the scientific, art versus science, as well as one other that will be of particular concern in this chapter, the mode of visual versus written representation. Once again Mead, if anyone, was able to adapt to this role and develop it because she was so aware of both the limitations and the possibilities of writing.

She was a pioneer in the use of different forms of visual recordings available for recording data. Her innovative use of film and photography is well documented (Mead and Bateson 1942; Jacknis 1988) and she also constantly championed visual anthropology and castigated the discipline for neglecting the documentation of the visual and auditory aspects of cultures (Mead 1975). Although a devotion to visual as well as writerly modes of representation does not necessarily signal a sensitivity to multiple sensory modes, Mead's recognition of multiple modes of communication and her desire to immerse readers/viewers in a culture boded well for the new gallery. Creating an exhibition, especially one on the scale of a permanent gallery at a large institution such as the AMNH, draws the curator into association with a team of people through whom his or her ideas are translated. Most importantly for this chapter, the curator's intentions are carried out via the medium of architecture and design.

Museums, Anthropology, and Architecture

In the twentieth century large museums, such as the American Museum of Natural History, had important design and exhibition departments specially devoted to the production of exhibitions. The exhibition and display divisions of museums grew enormously in size and influence in the postwar period (Brawne 1965). By Mead's time the days were long gone when the curator herself placed objects in cabinets (Griffiths 2002). The AMNH was a pioneer in the use of the diorama, two-dimensional, curved, painted landscapes in front of which objects were placed. The curvature of the diorama and the artifact installation were specifically created to convey a sense of immersion to viewers, and even though they were, in fact, usually looking through glass, the illusion of being in the landscape became a part of the exhibit itself (Griffiths 2002:17).

The exhibitions and permanent halls of the AMNH have been marked not only by the innovative development of the exhibition diorama, but also by major stylistic changes in architecture and design. If one wanders the halls of the museum, which has maintained some galleries for decades, one sees an archaeology of architecture since the turn of the twentieth century. The period in which an exhibit was designed is marked by the most influential and, often, the most cutting-edge architectural design of the era, and designers necessarily experimented in the exhibition space (Harraway 1989:26–59; Staniszewski 1998:98–9; Griffiths 2002:3–45).

By the 1960s there was a highly developed theory and practice of exhibition design and architecture associated with the concept of the "New Museum" (Brawne 1965). New York, the city of the Guggenheim and the Museum of Modern Art was, not surprisingly, one of the most significant sites for the development of these ideas about the modern and the new. Examples abounded of the major innovative style of the period, which, although known by many terms, is often referred to as modernist formalism. This style emphasized contemporary materials, minimalist decorative features, and, most significantly, a foregrounding of the function of a space. One architectural text of the period gives a sense of how these rules carried over to display in the "New Museum:"

> Each ... visual and tactile [experience] is intended to sharpen the encounter between object and observer, to make possible a communication between artifact and individual... Successful communications depends on the clear reception of signals and this clearly is dependant on the absence of interference-of "background noise," that is to say of any intruding element. (Brawne 1965:7)

Lighting, air control and other design elements such as color and texture all flowed from the purist premise, expressed here by Browne, that, under proper conditions, the viewer could have a pure and unhindered communication with the object displayed. This mode of installation has been a major influence on the display of contemporary art to this day. However, these ideas about the ideal conditions in which to view objects also had a significant influence on museums of natural history (Brawne 1965:7; Staniszewski 1998:98–9) through the influence of individual architects who struggled to implement new design features in ornately decorated nineteenth-century buildings. For this chapter, the significant point about architectural modernism is the impact this style would have on the ambience of the Peoples of the Pacific Hall at the AMNH.

The Margaret Mead Hall of Pacific Peoples: Modernity and the Sensory Surround

An in-depth look at the plans for Margaret Mead's exhibition about the Pacific at the AMNH is possible because she together with her large team of assistants ensured that many of the documents associated with the development of the Hall were archived in the Anthropology Department of the Museum. This remarkable archive represents one of the fullest records of the creation of a large, permanent anthropology hall held by a major museum.

The Margaret Mead Hall of Pacific Peoples opened at the American Museum of Natural History in New York in 1971, the product of many years of planning. Mead stated in a filmed interview that she had been, "promised a new Hall of the Pacific People in 1926, when she first arrived at the museum" (Abinader 1994). It had thus taken almost fifty years to complete the exhibition. The first documents in the substantial archive date from 1945, and it is possible to glean from these an idea of the initial plans for the Hall. They illustrate that Mead as curator had, from the very beginning of her planning, very specific ideas about the ambience of the gallery, particularly about space, light, and sound and how these elements would place the visitor in a particular kind of "other" space. The archives indicate that Mead's intent was always to convey the entire ambience though the creation of a mimetic environment that was generically, perhaps even stereotypically "Pacific," but at the same time modern.

This is articulated with particular clarity in a document written in 1960, one of several different moments when she thought that the actual construction work on the gallery would soon begin. Entitled "Outline Plan of Ideas To Be Emphasised and Cultures to be Included" it begins with a section entitled " Basic Assumptions," which states:

> 5. The Hall will be designed to give an impression of islands and sea, with a feeling of lightness and distance, and the occasional density of the deep bush.
>
> 6. Sound effects of the sea in all its moods, the pounding of the reef, lapping of waves on the beach, the occasional roar of the tempest will be used. (This is especially important because this is a terminal hall, and the sound will lead people on). (PPHA 1960)

Mead's outline of the "ambience" she hoped to create in the Hall is an extension of a briefer document which she had sent to Dr. Harry Shapiro, then Head of Anthropology, in 1955. There the same points are made, with the same wording, but more briefly:

> 5. The Hall would need to give an impression of islands, sea and deep bush, changing lights.
>
> 6. If sounds were used, different kinds of breaking waves, from heavy reefs to lapping waves, could be used effectively. (PPHA 1955)

The designer of the Hall, Preston McClanahan, joined the team in 1960. How he attempted to translate Mead's ideas into the structure of the Hall will be discussed later.

A long delay in completing the Pacific Peoples Hall was caused by the financial difficulties of the City of New York, on whose support the AMNH partially depended. Nevertheless by the late 1960s Mead had assembled a large team of young anthropologists, some in graduate school in New York City, to assist in the curatorial development of the gallery. The assistants were usually vetted by Mead before being hired, and each was assigned a particular research task. The importance Mead attached to sound in the gallery is evidenced throughout the archives. By the later stages of planning the generalized sound ambience tape had became a complex research project which involved not only musical instruments as forms of material culture, but also the transferring to audio tape of music from the culture areas represented in the gallery. At any given time at least one research assistant, and often more, were involved in work on the sound tapes and on research on the musical instruments for the display cases. This research appears to have been one of the more difficult and time consuming tasks of Mead's research staff because, although sound instruments were traditionally archived in museum collections, the sounds they made were not. In addition, the use of ambient sound in a hall of such size (over 9,000 square feet) was experimental. Since music samples were not widely available in the New York of the 1960s, the researcher's job involved hunting down places and/or individuals who held such recordings and deciding which were of a good enough quality to be used in a large space and which would require significant amplification. The final tape had ambient sounds of waves as well as music from various parts of the Asia-Pacific. In comparison with other museums and art galleries in New York during this period, the scale on which the AMNH used sound ambience and music was innovative and unusual.

There is no doubt that Mead also put great emphasis on the way in which the Hall should immerse the visitor in the environmental ambience that she associated with the Pacific and, at the same time, give a panorama of the entire region. In an article about the Hall for *Redbook Magazine* she begins with a very concrete description that beckons the reader into the space of the hall to a large map of the Pacific:

> In May, at the American Museum of Natural History in New York, a new Hall of the Peoples of the Pacific will open its doors to the public. Just inside the entrance to the hall, where you begin to hear the sea sounds

of waves and wind, there is a great map showing the vast expanse of the Pacific. (PPHA 1971a:1)

The Pacific Hall designer, Preston McClanahan, was an architect for whom Mead had great praise. In the same *Redbook* article she speaks of McClanahan:

As so often in my life, I was lucky. Preston McClanahan, my designer, was a young man, eager and responsive to new things. He read books, he looked at film, he came to lectures. In fact once I was formally rebuked for allowing him to become so interested; designers are supposed not to read, but to design. But he saw what I had in mind.

I had decided that the hall in every detail of its construction must reflect the islands – the blue of the sea, the bright sky, the far vistas and sunlit shores, only relieved in some areas by the jungle darkness of the interior of the larger islands and the pale desert colors of Australia. (ibid.:4)

In an interview with the well-known TV commentator Edwin Newman, Mead emphasizes how specific aspects of the ambience are possible in the modern museum because of technological developments associated with modernity. Newman asks: "If this Hall had been completed 45 years, or thirty years ago, would it have been very different from what it will be?" Mead replies with a long statement in which she emphasizes the political changes that the Hall documents, such as the emergence of independent nation-states, but she also focuses on the modernity of invention, which allows the conveyance of ambience:

We wouldn't have had the materials we're using in the Hall now. We wouldn't have been able to put things on the kind of plastic supports so they look as if they were floating. We would have had to have iron clamps or wooden things or something. We wouldn't have had this Hall or this special – this ceiling with this special kind of ceiling for sky, you know – for the sky over the islands. We wouldn't have been able to give this sort of impression. We couldn't have had the sound in the Hall that would have worked. We could have had a phonograph record, but we'd have had our troubles. Now we're going to have sound put on a tape and on it will be music that's been collected since then – since 45 years ago by people who have gone all over the world with tape recorders that they could get the sound with. (PPHA 1971c:2)

Mead doesn't underestimate the difficulties carrying out the ambience, including sound design. In an unpublished document, she writes:

> Sound was another problem. The music of these diverse islands runs the gamut from the simplest kinds of music known to the complex polyphony of Indonesian gamelan. Originally there was a plan to put the music of each area – which meant the music to go with each areal alcove – on the audiophone, and have in the Hall itself only the sounds of the sea, from the gentle lapping of the waves to the pounding on the reef and the occasional roar of a hurricane. But audiophones are unstable, sometimes working and sometimes not, so the plan was changed so that sea sounds intervene between the bursts of area music that comes from each alcove, in turn, but not close together enough to clash in listeners' ears. (PPHA 1970:2)

She sees the musical punctuation as a metaphor for the relations between islands:

> The sea sounds intervene between one musical style and another, just as the surrounding sea made it possible for each island to develop its own art style. (ibid.)

Great attention was also paid to the issue of scale in the gallery. The press release about the new hall issued by the AMNH features scale as a dominant attraction:

> The problem of scale was considered; there are three scales – life size, for the actual artifacts; ⅜ inch to the foot for the miniature diorama and the exaggerated sizes used in much of the Pacific area art – i.e., the huge Easter Island head replica. (LC 1971a:1–2)

Mead herself had a love of the miniature, which she put to use in the Museum as early as the early 1930s:

> On my return from Manus I worked with the department of preparation on a miniature model of a whole Manus village, one of our first less than life size models, just 4 by 4½ feet. Then it was something of a curiosity. But now, when a whole generation has grown up looking at the world on the television screen, the scale has become familiar. In the new hall I have had the models – a Manus village, a Balinese trance dance, a Samoan tattooing ceremony and an Australian totemic rite – made with

removable domes and set on castors, so that they can be wheeled out and filmed in color from all sides. In this way they can be shared not only by the millions who actually visit the museum, but also by television viewers in the most far away places. (PPHA 1971b:4)

McClanahan was, from Mead's perspective, well equipped with the knowledge necessary for successful translation of the ambient environment, an idea he was committed to, into the structure of the Hall. The press release states:

Mr McClanahan's basic idea was that an exhibition Hall such as this is both an environment and an extension of the diorama principle pioneered at the Museum around the turn of the century. He felt that a hall such as this should reflect the natural surroundings of the artifacts to be shown. Therefore the hall gives the feeling of the open horizons of the Pacific region. (LC 1971b:4)

By all indicators the Pacific Peoples Hall should have been a "successful" endeavor, especially in terms of reaching its stated goals of being a space that immersed the viewer through the senses in the environment from which the artifacts came. However, precisely because McClanahan was a cutting-edge architect, he was dedicated to the view of modernity current in his own field. His translations of Mead's sense of ambience were carried out using a minimalist architectural formalism that used new, experimental techniques and hard-edged building materials so popular in the New York of the 1960s and 1970s. The most prominent components of the gallery were the floor, the roof materials, the lighting, and the cases. Each of these was designed, somewhat experimentally, on the scale of the Pacific Hall, to convey the sense of a great ocean space and, in particular, the quality of light in the region. The Hall also conformed to the aims of the "New Museum" as described by Brawne (1965) – to heighten and purify the encounter between object and observer through the reduction in the number of design elements that interfered with this communication. This was particularly evident in the minimalist design of the glass cases, which were intended to detract as little as possible from the objects themselves. As Mead described in her interview with Edwin Newman the objects would appear to float in space because of the use of clear plastic mounts. The press release gives a good summary of these features, of their importance, and of the work that went into designing them: Despite its self-serving language, the intent and mechanics of conveying the ambience come through:

> The Hall is spectacular in both its design and content. With more than 9200 square feet of floor room it is extraordinarily large, even by the standards of the AMNH. Its ambience is that of limitless space, idyllic climate, exotic styles, and art works that are both beautiful and mysterious... The spaciousness of the Pacific Ocean is suggested in an overhead lighting system softened by a diffusion structure called "Leaf-Lite" which gives the illusion of bright tropical sunlight softened by the blue of the ocean. More than a thousand overhead fluorescent tubes run the full 154 foot length of the room above the leaf lite. Dozens of spotlights are also used, to highlight the specimens.
>
> The hall is washed by the sounds of the Pacific Ocean. Interspersed with the sounds is the music of the various culture areas... The Columbia University recording project directed by Alan Lomax assisted with the sound track... (LC 1971a:2)

The intention behind the design of the floor, a beautiful turquoise blue terrazzo, was to summon a sense of the ocean beneath the viewer's feet, while the ceiling, with its complex reflective leaves, would evoke the sky overhead, and the glass modular showcases, experimental at this scale, would not only highlight the artifacts, but also increase the sense of light and space in the Hall. The ambience, its modernity and its intent to immerse the viewer using very modern materials, whose innovative qualities fostered this sense of submersion, was featured as a central facet of the new Hall. The idea seems thus to have been to maintain a minimalist formalism while at the same time evoking a certain, stereotypically "Pacific," light and space. The mimetic effect, however, could only be partial because the materials differed radically from those of the original environment.

The Hall: Its Reception and Revision

The history of the Pacific Peoples Hall is a chequered one after its opening in 1971. Anyone who has worked in a museum and curated a gallery knows with what great difficulty any objective judgment of the "success" or "failure" of a gallery can be reached. Does one interview dazed museum visitors? How does anyone factor in the multiple influences – administrative neglect, faulty light bulbs that aren't changed, unfortunate placement of the space within the Museum? Nevertheless the aura of success and failure is part of the life cycle of a hall and this one has its own story. Certainly many of the professional visitors I spoke to, some of whom were at the 1971 opening, expressed disappointment at its ambience, especially the "cold, flat" lighting. Margaret Mead's daughter, Mary Catherine Bateson, sums up some of the problems with the Hall and its rather sad role in her mother's life:

> For years there was talk of finally doing "her hall," a new hall of the peoples of the South Pacific, but it was not actually opened until 1971, after she had formally retired – and by the time of her death it had been closed up and packed away to allow for a change in floor plan. The image she tried to build into her Hall was that of a multiplicity of islands, each elaborating different cultural themes, divided by wide stretches of blue, the reaches of sea and air and sky, crisscrossed in perilous voyage. The displays were meant to be suspended in light in their transparent cases, while others suggested shadowed jungle. The rationale is elegant but the hall itself was disappointing, with sections of exotic material not quite integrated into a whole. (Bateson 1984:69)

In informal conversation, museum workers and others who remember the 1971 Hall highlight the failure of the lighting: it was too cold and there was too much reflection from and between the glass cases. These criticisms suggest specific design misjudgments in the carry-out between design intention and solution. However, I would suggest that the Pacific Hall, if looked at from the viewpoint of Latour's idea of an imbroglio, cannot be dismissed as a simple failure of vision or technique. A gallery is created by translations at many levels, between anthropology and architecture and techniques, between word and image, between the quality of sunlight and that of artificial light. Both of the collaborators discussed here, Margaret Mead and Preston McClanahan, were skilled practitioners. Both were committed to modernity and both seem to have failed to notice the chasms that separated an actual Pacific environment from words, verbal descriptions, and the overriding mini-malist architectural rules of the New York of the 1960s and 1970s. It is precisely because both participants were committed to a particular brand of modernism that the PPH is better characterized as a scandal of modernity rather than a failure. By shifting from the notion of failure to that of scandal and imbroglio, one can see more clearly that the failures of the Peoples of the Pacific Hall are systemic failures of the ethnographic exhibition project. This perspective highlights the fact that both collaborators were already dealing with a stereotypical view of the sensory imaginary of the Pacific. Both were, I suggest, already invested in an imaginary Pacific sensescape, one that they believed could be translated and packaged into paint, glass, terrazzo, and steel.

Perhaps it is because they held this fixed and stereotypical idea of the area that they had the courage – or, depending on one's perspective, the audacity – to attempt a Hall in the first place. Each of the principal participants seems to have "failed" to notice the incommensurability between realms, between writing and architecture, between the Pacific and a museum gallery in New York, between the ocean and terrazzo, or the sky and neon and metal. If this is "failure" it is one repeated throughout institutions of modernity, and it is so systematic a failure that, as Latour suggests, it appears to be a major feature of communication in modernity and a part of its very fabric and structure.

Farewell Baudelaire: The Redesign of the Peoples of the Pacific Hall

1978 is a very poignant, sad year in the Margaret Mead archives. It is the year of her death and, reading through the material with retrospect, one knows how ill she was at the time of her struggles over planned renovations to the Hall, which had been closed in 1977. A memo, dated January 23, 1978, contains notes that Mead made about a meeting with Museum staff. A few quotes give some sense of her frustrations:

> I outlined the plan for the hoteal [sic], the way the ceiling and floor were not as planned, and how other things interlocked. The designer has only seen the hall now, bad, flat light, everything in a mess...
> Nickilsen [Director of the AMNH] thinks the hall is flat doesn't stand out, everything two [sic] uniform ... I stressed as much as I could how much any change would upset the mesh, but they all want to get their fingers in, don't like modules, don't like the fact that you can see through ... essentially I think don't like the Hall ... Only real hope of saving things will be to convince them its too expensive to change things ... (LC 1978)

Margaret Mead died in November of that year, not having succeeded in convincing the Museum administrators. Documents indicate that the designer of the new renovations, Eugene Burgmann, was presenting Mead with plans as late as July of 1978. Although it is possible that she saw mock-ups of the new plan, there is no archival record of her response. Burgmann's plans highlight perceived flaws in the 1971 Hall. Some changes are clearly there to redress specific design flaws but his designs attempt to maintain the ambience originally imagined by Mead while increasing intelligibility.

The renovated Hall opened in 1984 in an entirely different location in the Museum, one floor directly beneath the original Hall. The terrazzo floor was replaced by color-coded carpeting. The problematic ceiling in which Mead and McClanahan had invested such hope and which turned out to be so problematic, was lowered and the neon lighting and "Leaf-Lite" grid disappeared to be replaced by hidden lowlights in the ceiling and spots in wooden painted display cases. Burgmann's plans are of interest in that they show his attempt to deal with the Hall's problems while maintaining ambience, once again primarily with glass and lighting. One section of his redesign, titled "General Ambience," indicates:

1. Bright Hall but not the intense glaring light of existing hall.
2. Blue "sky", "blue" Ocean, colored carpeting.
3. Artifacts in cases bathed in a warmer light, with a more dramatic highlight and shadow effect than now exists. (PPHA, Burgmann 1978)

Most of Burgmann's redesigns are attempts to retain this blue sky/ocean effect but create a "warmer" and more intimate ambience. His designs also attempt to make the Pacific Hall's organization more intelligible by color-coding the Culture Area Sub-Divisions (e.g. Australia, Melanesia, Polynesia, etc). Today the Hall stands pretty much as Burgmann redesigned it, although it was subsequently closed for several more years. The ceiling is low and blue, and there are several colors in the carpet and wooden painted display cases. Australia is, for example, an ochre-like orange. The ambient lighting is kept low, with bright spots highlighting particular objects in cases, which are no longer all glass but, rather, enclosed in wooden painted cases which are also color-coded, turquoise or orange, to designate area.

There are many suppositions one could make about the "failure" of the ambience of the 1971 version of the gallery. One could suggest that warmer lighting would have solved all problems – but I doubt this. Rather, what I would suggest here is that the 1971 Gallery actually suffered from a contradiction in desires, contradictory desires which are built into modernist ethnology. Indeed Mary Catherine Bateson in her remarks about the gallery suggests one problem with the gallery that others commented on. She suggests that the gallery, despite having many fascinating individual sections, fails to knit into a whole for the viewer. Stated in other terms, what Bateson is suggesting is that the gallery failed to provide a panopticonic view of the Pacific for the viewer, and that thus one has only a feeling of bits and pieces. The point is, however, that this modern desire to see over – and thereby gain a sense of control over – an area requires a viewer to be placed in a particular and distanced vantage point from that which is able to be seen. It is only in this way that the whole can be seen. As stated in the beginning of this chapter, there is an opposed desire in modernity to immerse the viewer in the sensory surround of the place. The AMNH has had a long tradition of using up-to-date techniques to convey a sense of the environment to viewers and, in fact, is still an institution strongly associated with the diorama. In its traditional form the diorama is visually parallel with the panorama and the panopticon in that it provides a long-distance view of a landscape. By mid-century, however, the diorama – à la McClanahan's intentions – came to surround the viewer with the diorama, a very different proposition from the original since the exterior position of the viewer, outside of the diorama, vanishes.

Once McClanahan made the exhibition itself the diorama, with the observer walking through it, the diorama loses its perspectival dimension, the horizon disappears and the gallery becomes an environment. The problem for the Peoples of the Pacific Hall was that the very immersion in the environment fragmented knowledge, and viewers were frustrated in attempts to gain a panopticonic view over the Pacific. From this perspective the PPH was not the failure of individuals so much as a conjuncture of contradictory impulses of modernity, the desire to see over an area as opposed to the desire to be immersed in a far-away space.

Notes

1. Here I follow the notion of discourse used by Martin Jay in *Downcast Eyes* (1993:15–20), where he states that "By choosing to call the complex ... a discourse, I am fully aware that I am invoking one of the most loosely used terms of our time ... Despite these contrary and shifting usages, discourse remains the best term to denote the level on which the object of this inquiry is located, that being a corpus of more or less loosely interwoven arguments, metaphors, assertions, and prejudices that cohere more associatively than logically in any strict sense of the term (ibid.:15–16). I agree with Jay and find this notion of discourse useful in this context, not only because it expresses the order of the phenomenon I want to examine here but also allows for the notion of contradiction and contestation between discourses to emerge.

2. I want here to thank all of my colleagues from the Wenner-Gren Conference, Sintra, Portugal 1994. I have never enjoyed so much such stimulating company in such beautiful surroundings. Thanks to everyone, especially Wenner-Gren for its generosity and marvellous organization. I believe that it was Chris Gosden who suggested to me that the situation I describe in this chapter could be illuminated by Latour's notion of the imbroglio. I am much indebted to that idea, as will be seen – and much indebted to Chris and all my colleagues for their great ideas. The research on which this chapter is based was carried out at the American Museum of Natural History, New York, where I received the most generous support and assistance from the wonderful staff of the Anthropology Department and Library.

3. Peter Vergo in the New Museology (1989) pointed out "...the creating and the consuming of exhibitions remain, to my mind at least, curiously unreflective activities." (Vergo, P. 1989:43) Although the situation has changed somewhat since his perceptive comments, there are still relatively few in-depth studies of exhibition production. There is almost no ethnographic theory given over to the production of exhibitions.

References

Archive Sources

Peoples of the Pacific Hall Archives (PPHA), American Museum of Natural History (AMNH), New York

1955. Document. Conceptual Memos File. Anthropology Department.
1960. Document. Conceptual Memos File. Anthropology Department.
1970. "PPH first draft, mm November 28, 1970." Anthropology Department.
1971a. *Redbook*. "A New Hall – Behind the Scenes." Draft. May 1971.
1971b. Document. February 2, 1971. Anthropology Department.
1971c. M. Mead and E. Newman. WABC TV Program. Transcript of Interview dated April 17, 1971. Anthropology Department.
1978. E. Burgmann. Document. Anthropology Department.

Library of Congress (LC), Mss Div, Margaret Mead Papers (MMP), Washington, DC

1971a. Press Release, May 11, 1971. Department of Public Relations. AMNH MMP Mss Div, LC.
1971b. Press Release May 19, 1971. Department of Public Relations. AMNH MMP Mss Div, LC.
1978. Document dated January 23, 1978. Box K9. MMP Mss Div, LC.

Books and Articles

Abinader, Geralyn. (Film Director) 1994. *Margaret Mead at the American Museum of Natural History*. New York: Film Dept. American Museum of Natural History (AMNH).

Bateson, Mary Catherine. 1984. *With A Daughter's Eye*. New York: William Morrow.

Baudelaire, Charles. 1975. *Selected Poems*. Harmondsworth: Penguin.

Bennett, T. 1995. *The Birth of the Museum: History, Theory, Politics*. London: Routledge.

Brawne, M. 1965. *The New Museum: Architecture and Display*. London: Architectural Press.

Freeman, D. 1983. *Margaret Mead and Samoa: The Making and Unmaking of an Anthropological Myth*. Canberra: Australian National University Press.

Griffiths, A. 2002. *Wondrous Difference: Cinema, Anthropology & Turn-of-the-Century Visual Culture*. New York: Columbia University Press.

Haraway, D. 1989. *Primate Visions: Gender, Race and Nature in the World of Modern Science*. New York and London: Routledge.

Jacknis, I. 1988. "Margaret Mead and Gregory Bateson in Bali: Their Use of Photography and Film." *Cultural Anthopology* 3(2): 160–77.

Jay, M.1993. *Downcast Eyes: The Denigration of Vision in Twentieth-century French Thought*. Berkeley: University of California Press.

Latour, Bruno. 1993. *We Have Never Been Modern*. trans. Catherine Porter. Cambridge, MA: Harvard University Press.

Lutkehaus, N. 1995. "Margaret Mead and the 'Rustling-of-the-Wind-in-the-Palm-Trees' School of Ethnographic Writing." In *Women Writing Culture*. ed. Ruth Behar and Deborah Gordon. Berkeley and London: University of California Press.

Mead, M. 1928. *Coming of Age in Samoa*. New York: William Morrow.

——. 1934. "Kinship in the Admiralty Islands." *Anthropological Papers of the American Museum of Natural History* 34(2): 183–358.

——. 1938. "The Mountain Arapesh I. An Importing Culture." *Anthropological Papers of the American Museum of Natural History* 36(3): 139–349. Reprinted 1970 in *The Mountain Arapesh II: Arts and Supernaturalism*. Garden City, NY: Natural History Press.

——. 1975. "Visual Anthropology in a Discipline of Words." *Principles of Visual Anthropology*. ed. Paul Hockings. The Hague and Paris: Mouton.

—— and Bateson, G. 1942. *Balinese Character: A Photographic Analysis*. New York: New York Academy of Sciences.

Palaasma, J. 1994. "An Architecture of the Seven Senses." In *Architecture and Urbanism: Questions of Perception: Phenomenology and Architecture*, ed. S. Holl, J. Palaasma, and A. Perez-Gomez. Special issue, July: 28–37.

Said, E. 1994. *Culture and Imperialism*. London and New York: Vintage.

Staniszewski, M. 1998. *The Power of Display: A History of Exhibition Installations at the Museum of Modern Art*. Cambridge, MA and London: MIT Press.

Vergo, P. (ed.). 1989. *The New Museology*. London: Reaktion.

Worsley, P. 1957. "Margaret Mead: Science or Science Fiction." *Science and Society* 21: 122–34.

nine

Contact Points: Museums and the Lost Body Problem

Jeffrey David Feldman

This chapter addresses the problem of the body in current museum theory and practice. It considers what is lost by a museum paradigm that emphasizes visual display over other embodied experiences. Where do the senses enter into museum discourse? How do museum objects give rise to particular sensory regimes? Subsequently, how are the senses excised or excluded from both the agency and critique of display? This discussion also questions the historical and political distortions that result from these oversights. Can a critical focus on material culture and the senses in museums lead to more expansive theoretical discussion of colonialism? To examine these questions, there is a focus here on a particular type of museum object emergent from the history of anthropology and the Holocaust, as well as theoretical discussions from the phenomenology of perception, postcolonial theory, museum studies, and literary critique. At its broadest, this is an attempt to connect the study of museums to the question of the body.

The discussion begins with two types of object created in the first half of the twentieth century and displayed in contemporary museums; its central claim is that these two examples constitute one genre of museum object. The opening vignettes, thus, serve as heuristics for the central issue in the discussion: the process whereby the body enters into but is then eliminated from museum discourse. I call the result of this process a museum "contact point." Intended to evoke but not be limited by the experience of colonialism, "contact point" describes as a general category of object that results from physical contact with the body, and then the subsequent removal or destruction of the body. In some cases, a contact point is produced entirely within a museum discourse, while in other cases they result from other discourses, only to arrive in the museum at a later date. Paradoxically, while contact points are visually compelling, the act of looking at them often proves insufficient as an analytical strategy for understanding them. This is because the complexity of contact points unfolds at the intersection of what is present and what is absent in them – between the haptic contexts of their production and the circumstances of their display.

A theoretical focus on contact points offers a critical counterargument to the visual hegemony that dominates museum discourse. Contact points open onto not only the sensory experience of creating specific museum objects, but also the theoretical discussion of how museums constitute generalized discourses of colonialism and genocide. Contact points pose key critical questions about representation, embodiment, and value, and suggest new avenues for understanding museums as "zones" of social interaction.

In current postcolonial theory, the term "contact" has been used to signify a particular critical emphasis on "copresence" as constituted through social interaction and a certain conceptions of shared cultural practices (Pratt 1991:6–7). While helpful in understanding certain broad elements of colonial experience, all too often this social conception of "contact" in critical theory results in the unfortunate displacement of the sensory experience of contact, the actual feel, smell, and sound of colonialism. Theories of museums that pick up this use of contact as a heuristic for social interaction, thus, risk dampening the deeply embedded experience of the body in colonialism. Rather than stripping "contact" of its power as a social metaphor, I consider the distinction between contact "zones" and contact "points" as a strategy for relocating the sensory within anthropological theories of colonialism.

Theorizing the relationship between contact zones and contact points is a key aspect of the much larger project of defining colonialism in relation to the senses. In social theory, studies of colonialism rarely focus on the senses, but are more often grounded in history and exchange. Thus, definitions of colonialism begin with notions of historicized social process, the unequal encounter in the past between Western colonizers and the non-Western colonized. For critical museum studies, however, the urgency of understanding colonialism begins with the inherited legacy of material objects and materializing practices forged out of those social encounters.

Building from Pratt's perspective, I define colonialism as the experience of contact. Accordingly, the field of colonial analysis is the contact zone as delineated by ongoing systems of domination, not by geography.

Contact points, thus, are the sensual products of unequal encounter that materialize in the contact zone, ranging in durability from the most fleeting sensation of sound or touch to the most durable products of colonial labor set in stone or steel.

For various reasons stemming from the conditions of their production, contact points carry forward various sensory experiences that might otherwise be associated with the memories. The idea of the contact points in this respect builds on the broader discussion of collective memory (Halbwachs 1980). Here, the problem is the historical and experiential distance between the individuals who experienced the sensory aspect of the contact point and those who simply view it as a museum object years later. Contact points from this perspective are embodied memories whose conventional presentation in museums often limits the ability or dulls the will of museum visitors to perform the "memory work" necessary for comprehending them (Young 1993:5). Thus, the visual emphasis of museums can often limit or confuse the visitor's ability to remember the colonial past. This point is a crucial one. Museums do not eliminate contact points so much as they leave their sensory complexity unarticulated. In this respect, museum displays risk reinscribing the silences and eliminations that gave rise to the contact point in the first place. When left unexplored, contact points in museums risk becoming sites where memory is subverted, similar to the way in which memorials in other aspects of the public sphere risk becoming passive "sites of memory" (Nora 1989).

This is not to suggest that museums are somehow capable of banishing sensory experience completely. In the most sensory or sterile of gallery environments alike, the contact point engages the visitor's senses on multiple levels. There is not, in other words, a simple solution to presenting contact points in museums such that visitors can adequately engage with them. Instead, the goal should be to theorize these objects so that visitors can be more open to the sensory agendas of the museum space themselves.

Thus, the discussion of contact points also casts light on the need for a deeper analysis of the relationship between objects and subjects posited by much of museum theory. Just as the intersection of museum discourse and post-enlightenment individualism has been critiqued by postcolonial anthropology, more critical attention should be paid to the interplay between museums and Cartesian dualism. Accordingly, this discussion takes clues from Merleau-Ponty's problem of the body (1958:77), Bergson's question of what the body does (1991:17), and Bourdieu's conception of the body as geometer (1977:114). At its broadest level, therefore, this reframes the conversation object and cultural embodiment (Csordas 1990), and tests the limitations of understanding objects through current theories of history, politics, and culture.

The Lost Body Problem

During a recent visit to the Anthropology Museum at Rome's La Sapienza University, I came across a display of human faces eerily similar to death masks. The faces were painted plaster casts known as "racial types" or "face models," and were created by Italian anthropologists conducting fieldwork in colonial territories during the 1920s and 1930s. Before each mask could be created, a negative mold had to be created by applying wet plaster to the surface of a subject's face. Multiple plaster masks could then be pulled from the mold. Each plaster face was remarkably naturalistic, albeit only capturing the front half of the head from the hairline to the neck. The masks were screw-mounted onto several large boards. In this way, the installation demonstrated a variety of face types from Africa, Asia, and Europe. The text accompanying the display explained how all anthropology museums in Italy once contained this type of mask collection, but that, today, these racist displays are used solely to illustrate anthropology's history of racism.

The display was troubling. While the text provided some historical context, it did not explain why some faces were expressionless, while others appear to grimace with pain. All the faces had closed eyes, but some had visibly furled brows and smiled as though their faces were in the process of being burned by the hardening plaster. The faces were not only different in color, but were different in personality. Even worse: the darker-toned more "African" looking faces appeared to be almost dead, while lighter-toned "Asian" and "European" faces appeared to be alive. The process of making a mask was not the same for every subject. The casts captured not only a wide variation in surface morphology, but also a noticeable variation in embodied reaction to the process of having one's face covered in plaster. Despite the centrality of these faces in the gallery, the embodied experience they so vividly captured had been overlooked in the exhibition. With that oversight, a key aspect of the relationship between Italian colonialism and material culture had been lost.

The director of the museum explained that the displays had been completely renovated in 1993 (Cresta 1993). Walking to the back of the gallery, he pushed open an ordinary looking door off to one side of a display about early hominid ancestors. It felt as if we had stepped a century back in time to the first days of the museum. The dark back room, roughly twice the size of the main museum gallery, was packed with dozens of tall display-storage cases, filled with human skulls and bones. A typical physical anthropology museum design, its founder Giuseppe Sergi (1841–1936) intended it to be a site where skulls on display were retrieved from shelves and examined on central tables (Manzi 1987). In one of the display cases, I noticed a few racial type masks of the same genre as the display I had just observed. They were stacked haphazardly, leaning against some skulls. The masks leaned against the skulls in such a manner that it seemed as if they were the separated sections of the same bodies. The image of disembodied faces was both suggestive and unsettling, as it demonstrated how the body of the cast subject had been lost on multiple levels – cast out of the final museum product, leaving behind the negative space of the mask, and cast out of museum practice. The living bodies of colonized natives so central to the creation of museum objects were at once so noticeably missing from the current museum.

Having seen the back room, I looked at the public display of masks in a new light. I had been mistaken. There were, at minimum, two levels of embodiment that were missing from the display of the masks – indeed from the very convention of displaying the masks as objects: the embodied experience of the masks being produced in the colonies and the experience of the masks being used in the museum. Both were intertwined, and both were separated off from the display.

My response to the display in Rome reminded me of a similar unease I once felt upon seeing a display of 4,000 shoes piled in a steel cage in the United States Holocaust Memorial Museum. The shoes had been brought to Washington, DC, from Majdanek, a former extermination camp set up in the Polish colonies that the Nazis referred to as "The German East." Upon arrival by train, prisoners were forced to drop their belongings and disrobe. In some instances, prisoners' heads were shaved and they were issued camp uniforms, while in other cases they were killed immediately. Once imprisoned or killed, the personal effects left behind were sorted into piles by orderlies, with the goal of organizing them to be shipped back to the German population as wartime supplies. The purpose of the display was to visualize the evidence of lives lost in the Nazi camps.

If the lost feel of hot plaster on skin in the masks had made me uneasy, the palpable effluvium of mildew mixed with rotting leather in the shoes had nauseated me. While visually overpowering, what caught me by the throat was not the quantity of shoes, but their smell. The odor could have come from the moldy leather, the decomposing rubber, or even embedded human sweat. I turned to the accompanying text for more information, but there was none. As a result, the smell rendered the visual message of the memorial disconcerting and ambiguous. The shoes all looked the same from a distance, but I suspected that the particular experiences that led to their being in this pile were varied. While the size of the pile made a powerful statement, the experience of the people being forced to remove their shoes had been disregarded, and as such the crucial link between German colonialism and the relics of the Holocaust was missing.

Subsequently, I learned that the shoes on display in Washington were collected not just from a pile of shoes in Majdanek, but from a similar memorial display in Majdanek museum. As was the case in other concentration camps, the piles of shoes left by Holocaust victims were turned into museum memorial displays long before the opening of the memorial museum in Washington, DC. As the status of Poland switched from German- to Soviet-occupied territory, the concentration camps became museums warning of the dangers of fascism. The shoes, together with piles of hair, suitcases, and eyeglasses, became powerful installations viewed by millions of people in the Soviet memorials that predated the term "Holocaust" or any global historical recognition that Nazism came close to complete genocide of European Jewry. In many ways the pile of shoes is about traces of the body.

Multiple levels of embodied experience had been lost in the shoe display. Not only was any attempt to include or recapture the physical distress soaked into the shoes missing from the display, but also missing were the decades of sensory encounter with the very same display of shoes. Gone was the history of the smell of genocide, and gone was its embodied record of Jewish and Polish experiences under successive waves of violent European expansion. Here the lost body tension was different from what I had experienced in Rome. While the living African body was so palpably absent from the anthropology museum in Rome, the living Jewish body was well represented at the Holocaust museum. Jews were present as both visitors and museum workers. But the lost body of the children who had worn the shoes was still present and disconcerting.

Museum Visuality

The masks and shoes were contact points. Though the body was instrumental in creating the masks, the masks became body surrogates in museum discourse. What fascinated me about the installations I encountered was the gulf between the visual emphasis of the displays and the rich sensory information accumulated in the objects. Contact points are not, in other words, fully compatible with the visual logic of museums. To explore the full significance of contact points, it will first be necessary to critique the centrality of looking and seeing in museums. How does visuality constitute a set of routines that define museum practice? What is the relationship between the objects in a museum and a museum's visual logic? Can museum objects open onto questions of the body beyond the visual?

Michael Fehr's avant-garde museum exhibition "Silence" (1988) offered one set of answers. In his first exhibition as curator of the Karl Ernst Osthaus-Museum in Hagen, Germany, Fehr chose to remove all objects from the museum rather than install a new arrangement. The elimination of all visual cues from the museum was inspired by John Cage's avant-garde music compositions. Accepting Cage's idea that the absence of sound could be arranged into a musical composition, Fehr looked for similar ways to treat the absence of sight as the basis for a museum exhibition. Following this logic of silences, as his core curatorial principle, Fehr demonstrated that the visual was not an ephemeral feature of museum practice that dissipated when museum objects were removed. In recounting his most striking experience in the three-day exhibition, Fehr drew attention to how the visual was not limited to the display of things, but was embodied through the actions of the museum visitor:

> The public not only behaved as usual and walked through the empty spaces just as if something were on display, but also began to recollect the previous placement of the collection and to discuss the works of art I had taken away. Moreover, the architecture of the building, stripped bare, came into view and became the main topic of conversation. In the end everyone focused on one architectural feature, an elaborate art nouveau-style wooden railing that I had not been able to demount or cover. And this is how I learned from some of the older visitors that this railing, which I had believed to be a relic of the old museum, was in fact a replica manufactured in the early 1970s when the building had been extended and renovated. (Fehr 2000:43)

Note the persistence of a routine interaction with museum display even when the visual cues of that display had been taken away, which suggested that museum display in Hagen was a generative principle in museum practice. It unfolded in the interplay between museum structure, exhibition history, and the agency of the public. The curator's emphasis on sound did not displace the tendency of the public to approach the exhibition primarily through sight. Despite this persistence, the emphasis on silence and absence brought to light knowledge that had been otherwise concealed by the unchallenged logic of seeing the museum collection.

Curiously, some visitors to the Hagen exhibition interpreted Fehr's silent and empty galleries as a replaying of episodes in the 1930s when the Nazis confiscated large segments of the museum's collection. The empty galleries elicited these memories. By disrupting the visual hegemony of his museum, visitors reconnected with important knowledge about the objects in the collection, about the history of the museum's display of those objects, and ultimately about the local experience of Fascist cultural entrenchment. The museum exhibition, thus, became an instrument of engagement with multiple levels of local knowledge that had been concealed by visual surfaces and routines of display.

Just as pitting the visible against the visual led to serendipitous results in Hagen, the absence of such creative confrontation has lead to contestations of a much more damaging sort. One such example was *Mirroring Evil*, Norman Kleeblatt's much-maligned exhibition at the Jewish Museum of New York (2002). According to Kleeblatt, the exhibition was intended to show how artists had begun to use Nazi and Holocaust imagery in their work over the past ten years. Concluding that pieces like Zbigniew Libera's *LEGO Concentration Camp Set* seemed "disturbing, yet significant" Kleeblatt set out to exhibit similar work (Kleeblatt 2001:ix). While the exhibition was a success in terms of attendance, it elicited a disconcerting response by Holocaust survivors who felt that the exhibition belittled their experiences in the camps. In the most memorable moment of protest, camp survivors stood on the steps of the museum and pulled back their sleeves to reveal numbers which had been tattooed onto them upon arrival in Auschwitz. The gesture of pulling up one's sleeve to reveal the tattoo was a powerful reminder not only that the body had been lost from museum representations of the Holocaust, but that the tattoo marked the experience of the Holocaust on the body through the pain and penetration of human skin.

Street protests are not the only instances in which the visuality of the museum has been challenged. The boundaries of the display paradigm have been transgressed not only in the trenches of exhibition controversy, but also among the literati of museum design. Through diverse strategies, the museum in recent years has become a space that guides visitors to confront their own expectations about encountering legibility, leading them to wrestle with various penumbrae of representation. The problems of representing Jewish history in Berlin, the slave trade in Ghana, and the destruction of the World Trade Center in New York have each constituted a broad emptying of the display paradigm as a result of critical encounters with such diverse terms as "diaspora," "genocide," and "loss" (Young 2000; Finley 2001). New forms of museum design are the products of an increased critical awareness of the social elements of museum representation in current theory, as well as of the increased value placed on museums in the global culture industry.

My discussion of the visuality of museums suggests an important tension between the body qua the person in the space of the museum, and the body qua the lost agent in the social and cultural production museum discourse. It is easy to "see" the visitor in the museum, but "seeing" as an analytical strategy is less useful in reaching the multiple aspects of agency that resulted in, for example, a plaster mask. These types of perception resonate in an uncanny encounter with a particular installation, in dramatic gestures of a museum protest, and in the subversive designs of new museums. They also begin with new starting points for theory. The contact point as an analytical focus has the potential to include a wider range of sensory experience through which museum objects – and culture discourse – come into being. Accordingly, contact points can serve as the basis for museum theory that engages the visual through a more flexible model of sensory embodiment.

Zone Work

One of the most important critiques of museum practice in recent years has been James Clifford's thesis that museums are not simply places where people look at, or talk to each other about, objects, but are social and political "contact zones" (Clifford 1997:192). When Clifford first used the contact metaphor, his goal was to draw attention to the museum as a space of ongoing encounter between colonizers and colonized, a site where historically diverse and separated people "come into contact with each other" (ibid.:192). Despite the importance of this reading, however, the contact zone has become shorthand for the more cumbersome leitmotif of postcolonial museum studies, that museums are not static containers of objects, but arenas of social encounter. Indeed this has been an important insight. But as was the case with Benedict Anderson's phrase "imagined community," much of the initial intent behind the idea that a museum is a contact zone has been replaced by a more general conception that museums are places about people not things. The specificity of Clifford's argument has been diluted by more general ideas about museums as sites of social encounter.

By suggesting that museums are contact zones, however, Clifford did not fully leave the realm of the visual, nor did he fully examine the problem of the body in museum objects. "Contact" in Clifford's estimation was in many senses a stand-in for "conflict" – a signifier that he kept close at hand when explaining why particular exhibitions became controversial: "The museum became an inescapable contact (conflict) zone" (Clifford 1997:207). "Contact" was not in Clifford's use a synonym for touch, but was a metaphor that interrogated the idea of equal exchange. Disturbed by the inequalities between a group of Tlingit elders and a group of museum workers during one such consultation in the Portland Museum of Art, Clifford concluded that the museum:

> became something more than a place of consultation or research; it became a *contact zone* ... "the space of colonial encounters, the space in which peoples geographically and historically separated come into contact with each other and establish ongoing relations, usually involving conditions of coercion, radical inequality, and intractable conflict." (Clifford 1997:192)

Clifford was careful to overtly specify Pratt's idea of "spatial and temporal copresence of subjects previously separated by geographic and historical disjunctures" (ibid.:192). The type of contact he discusses, therefore, is social not physical contact, primarily Native Americans engaged in the act of cultural consultation with museum workers in collection rooms.

What strikes me about Clifford's discussion, and in particular his ethnographic vignettes, is the extent to which he never addresses bodily "contact" as the basic act of creating museum objects, and the extent to which this absence of the body has been absorbed into the critical discourse around museums in general, far beyond Clifford's particular paradigm. Contact does not involve the body at all, and is not a sensory mode, but is more akin to a structural principle emergent from interaction between social and material forces. Clifford sees contact happening when natives, anthropologists, and museum staff are negotiating in the presence of objects, and speaking to each other through historical memories and counter-histories. Contact, thus, reframes the museum space as a site where words – in addition to things – are presented, exchanged, and, unfortunately, manipulated for cultural profit. Contact is reduced in critical discourse to the strategies that museums demonstrate for appropriating cultural capital and for maintaining legitimacy through the storm of multiculturalism.

While the contact zone includes many options for resistance, it delimits the body to the boundaries and actions of the political person, overlooking the possibility of the body as a material discourse. It redefines the museum-container as the museum-space, and displaces material collection with narrative recollection as the central act of museum practice. Arguably, however, these concerns lie well outside of Clifford's discussion which is aimed at the discovery of inequalities that are reaffirmed within a discourse of equality, or cultural chauvinism within multiculturalism. Theorizing museum objects themselves is not a concern.

While indispensable as a frame for the politics of museum encounters, it is helpful to augment Clifford's contact zone with the idea of contact points. Expanding the idea of contact to reclaim the senses is possible if the museum is conceived as a social world shaped by the experience of the body. This reclamation occurs when the frame of museum contact is recalibrated from museum space to museum object. It begins by tracking "what the body means and does" for museum objects (Bergson 1991:17), or by imagining "one's own body" and museum objects (Merleau-Ponty 1958:112), or by seeing the "socially informed body" (Bourdieu 1977:124) in museum objects. We begin by considering museum objects before the model separates them into bodies and things, and focus on the processes whereby the thing as object replaces the body as subject – by considering the museum at the moment the body is lost.

When museum objects are treated as contact points, the senses become historical links between histories and representation, thereby opening onto unexpected discourses of domination, agency, and material value that might otherwise be silenced or excluded by critiques of museums as markets. Here it is critical to specify that not all contact points are the result of imitating the body through such representational intimacies as plaster casting. There are many types of contact points, but within the general category, it is helpful to posit a broad range of possibilities from the mimetic to the metonymic.

Specifically, we are facing two forms of indexical trace, the first being the plaster cast itself and second being the impression of living feet in the shoes. Racial casts, with their simulated representations of the body in the plaster, epitomize the mimetic contact point, distinguished by the persistent impression of the body in the object itself. Here, the visual cues of the body open onto a much broader experience of the body. In some cases the mimetic contact point results from one action, while in other cases it is the product of a more drawn-out series of actions – such as measuring or photographing the body, then producing a reproduction of one or more parts. The metonymic contact point, by contrast, retains nothing of the body, but is an object associated with one part of the body that stands symbolically for the whole. As for the mimetic contact point, the metonymic contact point begins with a visual association that opens onto a more expansive discourse of embodiment. Holocaust shoes typify the metonymic contact point in museums. In some cases, the metonymic contact point comes into being directly as museum objects, while in other cases it falls into disuse or abandonment for an intervening period prior entering into museum discourse.

Mimetic Casts

In 1932, Italian anthropologist Lidio Cipriani (1894–1962) published *In Africa from the Cape to Cairo* which included 286 photographs produced in Africa during multiple fieldwork trips (1927–32) (Chiozzi 1994:92). The book also included several images related to the production of racial typology masks of the sort subsequently displayed at the La Sapienza Museum of Anthropology.

Like photographs, masks were produced in the field and were central to the project of data collection at the core of European anthropological practice. A mask was made in several stages. First, a subject was positioned so that he or she was lying face up on the ground and several pieces of hollow straw placed in the mouth or nostrils. A batch of plaster was then mixed in a shallow bowl. Cipriani would straddle the subject's chest with one knee on the chest, while his assistant kneeled just above the subject's head so that he could hold it steady on both sides. Cipriani would then slap plaster onto the subject's entire face, from the bottom of the chin to just above the hairline, building up the plaster as much as possible before it began to set. After about five minutes of holding everything still, the mold was removed from the face and set aside to dry further. Once the subject was freed from the plaster, Cipriani's assistant would describe the subject's skin and eye color using standardized racial typology charts. This casting technique captured an exact impression of the face in a negative mold that could then be used to produce multiple "masks" of the subject's face (Cipriani 1932:33).

The visceral experience of being cast gave shape to both positive and negative ideas about Europeans. During one attempted casting, Cipriani noticed not only that all the members of his subject's band had vanished, but also that she was trembling too intensely for the plaster to set without being ruined. Despite all efforts, he could not secure her head firmly to the ground. After slapping the plaster on her face and wiping the excess on his shirt as best he could, Cipriani tried gripping her hair with one hand, fashioning a pull out of a lock of hair a few inches above her forehead while pressing down on her neck with the other hand. With plaster dripping down her ears and clavicle, Cipriani then place his knees on her shoulders, which only caused her to squirm more as his weight opened a painful gap between bone and muscle. Here, contact was more struggle than science. Sand, sweat, and hair had mixed together with the plaster making more of a mess than a mask. Eventually, Cipriani abandoned the attempt, peeling the plaster from her skin in rough, uneven chunks as the woman pushed him off and ran away with white pieces still stuck to her neck and scalp. Despondent that he would no longer be able to carry out his work, Cipriani was surprised when, soon after the incident, an elderly male leader of the group returned with a dozen more men. While not interested in being cast himself, the man offered the other men to be cast in exchange for trade goods (Cipriani 1932:167).

While always disconcerting physically, being cast by an Italian anthropologist posed a personal threat and an entrepreneurial opportunity for the Bushman. The experience was sought out and feared. Despite what the experience meant to the Bushman, however, for the anthropologist casting always constituted a process of contacting and then discarding the body. The body entered into the museum discourse as it was extended onto the ground, but it began to vanish by the time the plaster hardened:

> The method for obtaining [the masks] was easy, but as in many other cases, the difficult part was convincing the Bushman not to grimace until the plaster on their face had hardened. With patience and gifts it was possible and there is now an effort to deposit the eleven models in the National Museum of Anthropology and Ethnology at the University of Florence. (Cipriani 1932:21)

Placing his knees on the subject's shoulders, holding the head in place, and providing the right amount of gifts to avert a grimace – these were the basic prerequisites for insuring that a sufficient likeness of the face would be absorbed into the plaster, thereby allowing the model to mimic the body in museum discourses.

The creation of Bushman casts was a contact point of colonial activity. The gifting of trade goods was a prerequisite for achieving the physical submission necessary for the casting to succeed: "Gifts of tobacco and sweets were always sufficient means to win over the Bushmen, who were always good people with me" (ibid.:167). Contact, therefore, was scientific and social, physical and economic. The gift initiated a process that the plaster completed. Similar to other mimetic processes, the plaster effectuated the "swallowing-up of contact ... by its copy" (Taussig 1993:22), giving the mask its value and obscuring the body from the discourse of the face. Thus, valueless plaster took on the value of the body. Plaster casts traveled well, could be easily reproduced, and could be fine-tuned with a paintbrush to match previously codified racial data. The plaster mold, unlike the Bushman's body, could be used again and again.

The economics of Cipriani's Bushman casts is not meant as evidence against the more typical conclusions about the violence of anthropology's encounter with the Bushmen. Casting constituted one part of a violent encompassment of the Bushman by the state. Casting was one aspect of much broader museum exploitation of the Khoisan, according to Pippa Skotnes, curator of *Miscast* (South African National Gallery, Cape Town, 1996), the controversial exhibition about the image of the Bushman in South African history. The Bushmen were not just cast in plaster, Skotnes argued, but were "cast out of time, out of politics and out of history" (Skotnes 1996:16). For the Khoisan who came to the exhibition and who voiced protests against it, however, *Miscast* misfired. They recognized in the cast an entire set of "other embodiments" (Taussig 1993:14–16) germane to their experience of politics, history, and economy.

As Shelly Ruth Butler argued, the Khoisan from contemporary Kagga Kamma used the museum images of their own relatives to reconstitute community, to fortify the value of their tourist performances and, broadly speaking, to seek greater control of their own cultural capital (Butler 1999:87). At best, therefore, Skotnes' conception of the Khoisan image was incomplete. At worst, it reinscribed a common analytical mistake inherent in the idea of "misrepresentation," the idea that Western representations mask "true" aboriginality. The idea that the meaning of the casts was the sole product of a visual encounter was unquestioned by Skotnes even as it was reiterated by the Khoisan from Kagga Kamma.

The discussion of casting and miscasting raises the vexing problem as to why objectification techniques that resulted in the loss of the body should add such value to the objects – value for the people who control them and value for the people whose bodies they represent. Here, Cipriani's anecdotes and museum larceny must be read in concert with the reactions of the Bushmen to *Miscast*. The value contained in the casts is not merely commodity value as manipulated by the museum market of scientific artifacts, but a much broader social value with origins in the point of contact between the Bushman and various colonial forces. The casts are not just representations, but records of the process of encounter, a type of social script of how the experiential was injected into the casts.

Different from anthropological casting, metonymic contact points are often created through acts of violence wholly disconnected from museums, only to enter into museum discourse after an intervening period of time. Metonymic contact points, therefore, are often given meaning within discourses of memory and relics, as opposed to discourses of science and types. What distinguishes the metonymic contact point from an ordinary object, however, is the physical, sensory experience of the body that it symbolizes. A shoe may stand as an example for one or many categories of shoes. As a metonymic contact point, however, it stands for the relations between persons and objects in the contact point.

Reliquary Metonyms

First thrust into public view during the Eichmann trial in Jerusalem (1960), the shoes of Nazi concentration camp victims have become the most powerful material relics exhibited in museums. In a now famous moment of that trial, a witness stood on the stand and testified to having seen the Treblinka concentration camp after liberation covered in bones, skulls, and shoes, whereupon Israeli Attorney General Gideon Hausner unwrapped one pair of children's shoes to corroborate the story (Cole 2000:61). As one audience member at the trial later recalled:

> For seemingly endless seconds, we were gripped by the spell cast by this symbol of all that was left of a million children. Time stood still, while each in his own way tried to fit the flesh to the shoes, multiply by a million and spin the reel back from death, terror and tears to the music and gay laughter and the animated joy of youngsters in European city and village before the Nazis marched in. (Pearlman 1963:304)

What fascinates me in this quote is Pearlman's struggle to push past the archival isolation of the single pair of shoes and to reconnect with the tactile sensation of a child's skin pressing against leather. This initial desire to reclaim the contact between skin and shoe is a key aspect of what would transform Holocaust shoes into such powerful metonymic contact points. The results of violent genocidal acts, the shoes bear impressions of the people who wore them, contain links to the earth, and symbolize – both individually and in large quantities – the entire process of the concentration camps. Here it is important to specify that the shoes do not simply stand for death, but for a particular, industrial process of death. It is that process, with its recyclable byproducts, that transformed the shoes into relics and gave them resonance as museum objects.

The shoes in the museum, therefore, open onto a broad range of sensory experience that constituted the Jewish, German, and Polish encounter in the Holocaust. Thus, the question emerges as to whether or not the Holocaust is best understood solely as a process of destroying Jews through violence, or as an industrialized colonial encounter between multiple social actors, which produced a broad range of contact points. Indeed, the difficulty that theory has in coming to grips with the Holocaust is not the sole result of the violence or inhumanity of it. The difficulty of documenting and theorizing an industrial genocide is similar to the problem of documenting and theorizing colonialism. The experience of contact is, at one and the same time, destructive and productive, wasteful and efficient, automatic and creative. The main difference between colonialism and genocide, therefore, can be found most noticeably in the manner in which each is framed by the state, the former depicted as geographic appropriation for national profit and the latter cast as demographic purification for national survival. Indeed, the difference between casting and killing is one of context more than one of degree.

After the Eichmann trial, a pair of children's shoes found in the ruins of a Nazi concentration camp became a symbol for all children killed in the Holocaust when it was displayed at the Historical Museum at Israel's Yad Vashem (Cole 2000:62). The metonymic quality of the shoe was clearly relative to the mimetic of the Bushman masks. The shoe contains the trace of "the flesh," but not the actual impression. The presence of the body must be "fit" back to the object through memory. Moreover, while the physical encounter of Cipriani and his assistant pressing the Bushmen's head against the dirt was menacing, it was not murderous. For the shoes, the contact point gives rise to a violent encounter – the trampling of the body, or worse: the thunderous march of Nazis' boots multiplied "by a million."

Since Yad Vashem first displayed them, children's shoes have become metonymic contact points within a standardized set of global museum routines. In former concentration camps and in Holocaust museums throughout the world, large piles of shoes and other Holocaust relics have become both standard memorial installations expected by both museum visitors and planners alike. Museum emphasis on Holocaust relics has resulted in stinging critiques of the museums as sites of memorial hyperreality engaged in the obviation of Western and capitalist views of history. Tim Cole, for example, has argued provocatively that display cases "filled with piles of suitcases, shoes, glasses, and women's hair" have transformed Auschwitz into a Holocaust version of Elvis' Graceland (ibid.:98). Once a site of mass murder, Auschwitz has become a tourist destination that sells representations of mass murder to heritage pilgrims. The signifiers of loss are no longer connected to the event, but have been recreated as fetishes in a global memory market. Cole supports his thesis that Holocaust museums worldwide are infected by this fetishization of concentration camp relics by bringing to light the "loan" of shoes, rubble – even entire concentration camp barracks – for the creation of the permanent exhibition at the United States Holocaust Memorial Museum (ibid.:160).

While Cole's is an important critique of the political agendas behind memorials, his emphasis on the banalities of museum representation misses an important aspect of the mimetic contact point. As James Young has argued, the encounter with these large piles of relics itself becomes the key memory for most visitors to sites of Holocaust memory:

> What most visitors remember from trips to the Auschwitz museum are their few moments before the huge glass-encased bins of artifacts: floor to ceiling piles of prosthetic limbs, eyeglasses, toothbrushes, suitcases, and the short hair of women... What precisely does the sight of concentration-camp artifacts awaken in the viewers? Historical knowledge? A sense of evidence? Revulsion, grief, pity, fear? (Young 1993:132)

Young argues that the power of the camp artifacts lies in their quality as "dismembered fragments," not commodities (ibid.:133). The shoes, in other words, contain traces not of the physical bodies that once wore them, but of the social bodies that gave them meaning. Their power, therefore, lies in their ability to conjure images of the social body and in their inability to reanimate the social body. The emphasis on "dismembered fragments," warned Young, would become a problem for

Holocaust commemoration because it displaced the necessarily active performance of memory work with the passive visual encounter. Powerful in establishing the magnitude of the Nazi atrocities, the risk in relying on relics was that they would perpetuate the reduction of concentration camp victims to statistics – albeit visceral statistics (ibid.:133). Ten years after Young's warning, the reproduction of concentration camp "bins of artifacts" either through loan, sale, or photographic reproduction testifies to the prescience of Young's reading.

By bringing to light the importance of the social body, Young engages a critical aspect of contemporary memory work that is lost by the emphasis on mass quantities of relics. Nonetheless, "dismemberment" as a both descriptive and critical heuristic is deeply rooted in visual assumptions about the encounter with museum objects. Considering Holocaust artifacts as disarticulated contact points gives rise to multiple levels of experience not afforded by the idea of social dismemberment. Museum pieces created out of genocidal encounters often exude a discernible record of the body's experience of murder and the object's decades-long abandonment – they smell. Yet, this sensory record is excluded through the visual emphasis of Holocaust museum display. Indeed, the interregnum between death and memorial rediscovery is a critical period often discarded in reliquary discourses focused on the visuality of museum displays.

Approaching relics as metonymic contact points allows for the multiple histories and contexts signified by the shoes to come to light, thereby using a sensory approach to the Holocaust as a strategy for reversing the reduction of victims to disembodied statistics. While the quantity of Holocaust relics clearly signifies the number of people murdered in concentration camps, it also references the overlooked history of Poland as a colonial territory occupied by Nazi Germany. The reason that Holocaust relics survived in such quantities was not simply because of genocide, but that these byproducts of genocide had economic value. Paradoxically, Nazi concentration camps were sites of murder and productivity. Hair was shaved from prisoners for hygienic purposes, and then saved for potential use as insulation. Clothes, suitcases, prostheses, and shoes were removed prior to gas chambers, and then shipped en masse to metropolitan centers. The large piles of shoes seen by the Allied liberators of Nazi occupied Poland were indeed evidence of the violent destruction of Jewish bodies, but they were also the unprocessed reserves of colonial enterprise.

The problem of interpreting Holocaust relics resides precisely in their capacity as contact points to signify multiple activities and experiences through a broad range of sensory information. The core of these experiences involved the violent processing of the body in industrialized extermination camps. Thus, relics such as shoes, hair, and eyeglasses are impregnated with the bodily by-products that resulted from the radical experience of violence, such as the odor of gangrene in shoe leather, the stain of human fluid in cloth, and the rim of a prison cap worn shiny by constant pressing against the forehead. But relics also contain those traces of the whole bodies that were removed, incarcerated, and incinerated – traces of scissors against the scalp that left only a cut of hair, the sudden rip of glasses from a face that left only the thin gold wire frames, and the piercing of skin by the tattoo pen that, despite millions of repetitions, left few living bodies to recount the experience.

Thus, when read as ethnographic observations, not simply as critiques, Cole and Young speak to the complexity of relics as material records of genocide, empire, and European reconstruction. The significance of the relics cannot be reduced to their roles as visual signposts to the past or tourist destination in the present. They are vestiges of the violent act of biological racism layered onto history, and a material journey from personal belonging to museum piece. The shoes, eyeglasses, or hair that one observes in Holocaust museums never appeared "in real life" as they appear in Holocaust exhibits. They are not mere images of the past, but are the sensory products of the brutal genocidal encounter. They are, in other words, the discarded body-objects of a once celebrated, now abhorred, colonial industry – the waste that remained after the body had been harvested, sorted, and destroyed.

Conclusion: A Sense for Contact

As an analytical model, the contact point suggests that bodies and objects are not as separated as the visual logic of museums indicates. It remains difficult to "see" the body in museum objects, however, for three main reasons. First, the cultural routine of looking at museum displays separates the body from the object both pragmatically and conceptually. Second, recent critiques of museum representation have reaffirmed the visual logic of museum objects, albeit through the complex models of political and social exchange, colonial context, and heritage consumption. Third, contact points vary widely in form, location, scale, and – most importantly – meaning. Accordingly, while I have suggested that certain types of objects epitomize the museum contact point, it is less an object category than a theoretical approach.

Rather than creating interpretive problems, any ambiguity in the contact point is analytically productive. The contact point reframes the physical and social conceptions of the museum in sensory terms. As such, the processes by which people and objects associate or dissociate must themselves be reevaluated historically and ethnographically. Through the act of linking agencies and inequalities to sensory cues embodied by museum objects, the visual scripts that dominate museum practice are destabilized, and the museum opens onto more extensive and suggestive interpretive possibilities.

In thinking of a general type of museum object, therefore, it is important to keep in mind that contact points can be the end products of collaboration between anthropologists and subjects, or the remains of less collaborative, more violent interventions. Museum contact points can be the products of science or art, research or murder. A single contact point can express competing political or social valences, and multiple contact points can link objects both in and out of the museum. They can look like all or some part of the body, or they can be devoid of any resemblance of the body. Moreover, the body – even though it has been discarded – can often be more visible than the contact point itself. Qisuk's bones at the American Museum of Natural History exemplify this last case. Brought to New York by arctic explorer Robert Perry, and then housed at the museum by Franz Boas, Qisuk, a Polar Inuit from Smith Sound, Greenland, died of Tuberculosis after a year (1898) living as an anthropological specimen. To avoid arousing the suspicions of his son, workmen replaced Qisuk's corpse with a man-sized log just before his coffin was buried, then dissected and accessioned his body as part of the museum's anthropological collection. The log that took the place of Qisuk's body – carved, buried, and eulogized by museum workers – was a contact point despite being fully hidden from view, and despite the fact that Qisuk's body ended up in a museum collection drawer (Thomas 2000:77–9).

As a result of the violence and inequality often described by the museum contact point, the sudden recognition of museum history and politics can transform them into flash points of cultural struggle. There is no natural relationship, however, between the visible form of a contact point and its potential to explode into controversy. The key factor that delimits the contact point as a category of museum object is not how it appears to the eye, nor where it resides relative to the space of the museum. Rather, the crucial issue is its material reference to the process of the body being eliminated, and its discursive link to museum practice. Contact points signify social processes not just images, interactions not just individuals. Because of the central role of the body, more often than not the contact point frames moments of moral ambiguity and political inequality in the history and practice of the museum.

The contact point poses a critical challenge, in other words, to the commonsense logic that frames conventional ideas of museum categories. It challenges museum theory to recognize the museum encounter as socially and materially enacted, and to consider that the various, separate discourses of global expansion represented in distinct museum displays might in fact be more interconnected than either theory or practice has allowed.

The genocide of European Jewry, for example, was not the only historical event to have left behind objects that did not enter into museums for a considerable time after "contact." The so-called West African "slave castle," such as Gorée Island in Senegal or Elimina in Ghana, is itself a museum contact point whose meaning is deeply rooted in the centuries-long elimination of the body through trade. In the slave castles, as in Holocaust relics, the contact point frames both a history of physical destruction and a history of abandonment, forgetting, rediscovery, and display. The power of the castles does not reside in what can be seen there, but in the way the darkness and dankness of its dungeons open onto the history of human bodies being transformed into property, and then dispatched (Bruner 1996:290).

While former Dutch slave castles are not the same as former Nazi concentration camps, nor plaster casts equivalent to children's shoes, as museum contact points they suggest multiple links and overlaps between otherwise disparate events, people, sites, and things. Indeed, the Holocaust was a colonial process whose moral and material legacy still plagues Diaspora Jewry and post-Socialist Poland. And many anthropological techniques for visualizing the Bushman are eerily similar to the forms of domination and violence associated with genocide. What is to be gained or lost by distinguishing these discourses rather than finding new ways to create dialogues between them?

To some extent, traditional anthropological conclusions about museums provide an answer. Where museums once gave shape to vast scientific paradigms and national culture, they are increasingly understood as records of local history and references for individual identity. While a critical stance toward the identity or representation as "imagined" can be a powerful first step in the ethnography of museums, it can also result in the dismissal or oversight of social experiences with real consequence and value in people's lived worlds. Focusing more closely on the agency and social encounters that give shape to museum objects can help reconnect theory to the grounded products of everyday life.

Contact, therefore, as description and theory begins by reworking the object as the social and cultural nexus linking museums and the modern world. Whereas the act of looking was the starting point for a modern theory of museum visuality, a sense for contact must be the starting point for a new theory of museums. While museums give shape to discourses, they also give rise to meanings and routines that resist, precede, and give shape to concepts.

As such, having a sense for contact can take the shape of noticing a colonized subject grimacing in pain – or reacting to the smell of Holocaust relics that have been rotting after three decades of abandonment. Contact points in the museum can take many shapes, but they involve and are engaged not just through an analytical gaze, but through the full range of bodily senses. In the contemporary world where museums play an every increasing role in global politics, having a sense for contact, therefore, will increasingly constitute the basic act of ethnography and history.

References

Bergson, Henri. 1991. *Matter and Memory*. New York: Zone Books.

Bourdieu, Pierre. 1977. *Outline of a Theory of Practice*. Cambridge: Cambridge University Press.

Bruner, Edward M. 1996. "Tourism in Ghana: The Representation of Slavery and the Return of the Black Diaspora." *American Anthropologist* 98(2): 290–304.

Butler, Shelly Ruth. 1999. "The Politics of Exhibiting Culture: Legacies and Possibilities." *Museum Anthropology* 23(3): 74–92.

Chiozzi, Paolo. 1994. "Autoritratto del Razzismo: Le Fotografie Antropologiche di Lidio Cipriani." In *La Menzogna Della Razza: Documenti e Immagini del Razzismo e Dell'Antisemitismo Fascista*, ed. Centro Furio Jes. Bologna: Grafis Edizioni.

Cipriani, Lidio. 1932. In *Africa dal Capo Al Cairo*. Florence: R. Bemporad & Sons.

Clifford, James. 1997. *Routes: Travel and Translation in the Late Twentieth Century*. Cambridge, MA: Harvard University Press.

Cole, Tim. 2000. *Selling the Holocaust: From Auschwitz to Schindler, How History is Bought, Packaged, and Sold*. New York: Routledge.

Cresta, Massimo, Giovanni Destro-Bisol, and Giorgio Manzi. 1993. "Cent'anni di Antropologia a Roma. Celebrazioni per il centenario dell'Istituto Italiano di Antropologia." *Rivista di Antropologia* 71: 1–29.

Csordas, Thomas J. 1990. "Embodiment as a Paradigm for Anthropology." *Ethos* 18(1): 5–47.

Fehr, Michael. 2000. "A Museum and Its Memory: The Art of Recovering History." In *Museums and Memory*, ed. S.A. Crane. Stanford: Stanford University Press.

Finley, Cheryl. 2001. "The Door of (No) Return." *Common-Place* 1(4). Electronic document: http://www.historycooperative.org/journals/cp/vol-01/no-04. Accessed October 15, 2002.

Halbwachs, Maurice. 1980. *The Collective Memory*. New York: Harper and Row.

Kleeblatt, Norman. 2001. "Acknowledgements." In *Mirroring Evil: Nazi Imagery/Recent Art*, ed. N.L. Kleeblatt. New Brunswick, NJ: Rutgers University Press.

Manzi, Giorgio. 1987. "Il Museo di Antropologia dell'Università 'La Sapienza' di Roma: una testimonianza del percorso intellettuale di Giuseppe Sergi nella seconda metà del XIX secolo." In *Giuseppe Sergi Nella Storia Della Psicologia E Dell'Antropologia In Italia*, ed. G. Mucciarelli. Bologna: Pitagora Editrice.

Merleau-Ponty, Maurice. 1958. *Phenomenology of Perception*. New York: Routledge.

Nora, Pierre. 1989. "Between Memory and History: Les Lieux de mémoire." *Representations* 26: 13–25.

Pearlman, Moshe. 1963. *The Capture and Trial of Adolf Eichmann*. New York: Simon & Schuster.

Pratt, Mary Louise. 1991. *Imperial Eyes: Travel Writing and Transculturation*. New York: Routledge.

Skotnes, Pippa. 1996. "Introduction." In *Miscast: Negotiating the Presence of the Bushmen*, ed. P. Skotnes. Cape Town: University of Capetown Press.

Taussig, Michael. 1993. *Mimesis and Alterity*. New York: Routledge.

Thomas, David Hurst. 2000. *Skull Wars: Kennewick Man, Archaeology, and the Battle for Native American Identity*. New York: Basic Books.

Young, James E. 1993. *The Texture of Memory: Holocaust Memorials and Meaning*. New Haven: Yale University Press.

——. 2000. *At Memory's Edge: After-Images of the Holocaust in Contemporary Art and Architecture*. New Haven: Yale University Press.

ten

The Beauty of Letting Go: Fragmentary Museums and Archaeologies of Archive

Sven Ouzman

There seems to be a constant decay of all our ideas; even of those which are struck deepest, and in minds the most retentive, so that if they be not sometimes renewed by repeated exercises of the senses, or reflections on those kinds of objects which at first occasioned them, the print wears out, and at last there remains nothing to be seen.

John Locke, *Human Understanding*

Archaeology and museology constantly balance their emancipatory potential against their legacies as colonial controlling processes. Do archaeology and museums occupy a key space in contemporary identity formation? Are they part of the modern state's inventory of attributes rather than public "contact zones?" Museums' attempt to reinvent themselves as socially engaged places of memory are hindered by an embedded desire to catalogue, conserve, and display objects. Many of the peoples whose objects are collected and displayed believe in an encultured world in which the decay and death of people, objects, places, and time was and remains expected.

We need to consider how objects work and what their rights might be. Objects, places, and people have typically "messy" biographies that offer points of attachment for a wide range of sensory engagement. Archaeology's two strengths, materiality and context, can productively expose significant ruptures in master narratives through archaeologies of archive that ask how objects come to be collected and displayed (or not) and at what cost. This wider understanding of the archive as multitemporal and multisensorial can show how decay and history intersect with personhood, place, and politics, demonstrating the Beauty of letting go.

Imagine a beautifully designed museum where light, airy galleries enter into contrapuntal conversation with darker, more atmospheric niches. Imagine further that these spaces frame and give texture to thousands of objects[1] collected from near and far, from long ago and yesterday. Now imagine that, intermingling with beautiful and intact, text-accompanied objects, there are hidden display cases, empty or half-filled with tragic and disintegrating objects, some smelly. The visible manifestation of declining funding? The aftermath of "looting" such as recently occurred at the Iraqi National Museum in Baghdad? No. The future of museums and archaeology? Hopefully.

Any talk of the future requires revisiting first principles. One such basic principle concerns how we treat material culture and is encapsulated by asking the simple but salient question "why conserve?" Foregrounding artifacts as always being in states of transformation, some of which may be called "decay," should not be positioned as a shock tactic to spur greater conservative efforts (Page and Mason 2003), but as a comment on culturally specific understandings of the nature of artifacts, time and being. The relevance of museums[2] and archaeology in postcolonial contexts is constantly debated both to score easy political points and to address serious mismatches between museums and the societies in which they operate (for example Davison 1998; Hooper-Greenhill 1992; Karp and Lavine 1991; Pearce 1992; Stocking 1985). The institutional "audit cultures" (cf. Strathern 2000) that determine what is and isn't collected and displayed (Belk 2001), who gets jobs and funding, and what research, collection, and education outputs should be, is a pressure ill-suited to museums and archives functioning for the diverse publics they should be serving. Similarly, in studying the material culture of "other" cultures we oscillate between studying artifacts in embedded physical contexts and by disembedding artifacts for study elsewhere. This latter move typically entails legal ownership justified by neoliberal notions of stewardship and conservation, leading to friction between "an object-centred discourse on ownership, while archaeologists and ethnographers are but part of a larger (perhaps western) academic discourse which values knowledge over property" (Brodie 2003:13). But what saves museums, archaeology, and their attendant archives is their skill at using artifacts as metonyms that have the valence to evoke imaginaries of "other" people, objects, and places (Kusimba 1996;

Simpson 2001). Yet despite this power, few practitioners pay sustained attention to the histories and biographies of their archives (but see Bennett 1995; Fehr 2000; Gosden 1999; Murray 2001; Trigger 1989) or consider how objects work.

At the heart of these techniques of acquisition, research, and display is a particular brand of post-Enlightenment science that stresses the importance of static ocular-centric observation and meta-narratives that James Elkins calls "our beautiful, dry and distant texts" (Elkins 1997). This bias has made largely unproblematic the acceptance of quasi-military techniques like aerial photographs, infiltrative particip-ant observation, and culture-historical mappings to surveille and en-clave the people or "cultures" of specific geo-cultural landscapes (Harley 2001; Werbart 1996). Though social scientists are mostly aware of the problematic construction of sight as the sense of reason (for example Elkins 2000; Jay 1994) dependence on vision remains our single most pervasive epistemological and ontological bias. The scientific gaze is positioned as a neutral but potent vehicle that can access spatially, culturally, and temporally distant knowledge systems. Archaeology and museology trace a genealogy to Robert Merton's contention that the science of studying artifacts and people was portable, replicable, and that the forces generating social phenomena were largely uniformitarian (Merton 1973). Few practitioners today support Merton's assertions, but paradigm lag, familiar institutionalized practices, and lack of pol-itical will are hard obstacles to overcome. But we can try. One way to perceive our faults and institute remedial action is to step outside our normal boundaries – a move Johannes Fabian likens to an "out of body experience" (Fabian 2001). Sometimes we can only "see" ourselves clearly, especially warts and all, when we adopt another's perspective – in this case the "cultures" we display and the real and imagined audiences of those displays. Previously subject and objectified people increasingly are taking control of their identity, biopower, and representations (for example Said 1989; Tuhiwa-Smith 1999).

Allowing such outsiders in can generate innovative display techniques. Fred Wilson – an African-American former museum attendant turned installation artist – culls objects from a museum's collection, which he juxtaposes in provocative and thoughtful ways. In one powerful statement, ragged British and French imperial flags blindfold and gag wooden Zambian masks with the musty naphthalene-ness of the flags warring with the oilier nose of the masks (Wilson 2002–3). This "reverse gaze" (see Clifford 1988:120–1) has the benefit of presencing a counternarrative, but the disadvantage of being easily ignored because it typically is reactive. Rather than a binary "us" : "them" opposition, we can insert the objects we collect, study, and display as agents. Georg Simmel writes powerfully on the politics of numbers: "3," for example, suggests the possibility of an interlocutor and exponentially more connective and disjunctive possibilities than does a binary (Simmel 1950 [1908]:43). This approach grants greater human–object intersubjectivity and coproduction (Latour 1993; Haraway 1991; Polyani 1962) and shows perspective's partiality:

> There is a premium on establishing the capacity to see from the peripheries and the depths. But here lies a serious danger of romanticizing and/or appropriating the vision of the less powerful while claiming to see from their positions ... The standpoints of the subjugated are not "innocent" positions. On the contrary, they are preferred because in principle they are least likely to allow denial of the critical and interpretive core of knowledge. They are savvy to modes of denial through repression, forgetting and disappearing acts – ways of being nowhere while claiming to see comprehensively ... But *how* to see from below is a problem requiring at least as much skill with bodies and language, with the mediations of vision, as the "highest" techno-scientific visualizations (Haraway 1981:191; italics original)

Partial perspectives confer authorship, responsibility, and self-awareness. They ameliorate a top-down scopic stance with a more embodied vision. I attempt the "how" to perceive "from below" by considering how objects work. I then suggest three fundamental rights for objects that, in turn, encourage an archaeology of archive. I conclude by moving beyond the building to consider how "heritage sites" and storytelling offer socially engaged and multisensorial means of identity formation and coming to terms with difficult past and presents. I situate this discussion in post-Apartheid southern Africa, sampling artifacts, museums, and monuments.

Object Logic

What does food want from us?

Aldona Jonaitis, Sintra Conference 2003

When we study or display artifacts we frame our work on concepts of the object's authenticity. Within this frame objects are usually presented as being in either a pristine or a conserved state. Restoration and conservation interventions may even be unvoiced lest they detract from foregrounding the objects' authenticity. Alternatively, interventions may be highlighted to demonstrate conservation science's virtuosity (Crew and Sims 1991). The expertise and power invested in these conservation programs can gloss the fact that the provenance and ownership of artifacts in the archive is contested and suggest that the objects are clearly safer in say, Los Angeles, than wherever they originated, legalities and ethics aside. But conservation interventions are strategic and are not applied to most artifacts as it is expensive and time-consuming. High-profile interventions create the impression of comprehensive curatorial care and deflect attention from artifacts accumulating in and rotting in collections (Beck and Daley 1993). Whichever façade is presented, the object is abject, subservient to a greater project concerned with uncovering original meanings and presenting a pleasing outer surface. What then is the logic of objects? How do they work; how may we know their needs and approach them? One way to understand object logics is through their changing material states and our attendant and unstable perceptions of materiality.

Though now unfashionable in mainstream anthropology, the "fetish" helps connect materiality to human subjectivity. We can trace the fetish to the 1436 CE Portuguese-African encounter in which the medieval amulets called *feitição* (Latin *facticius* – "manufactured") were transferred to seemingly lawless African life that was seen to revolve around "idols" (Pietz 1987). For the Portuguese, "fetish" came to mean a beautiful façade masking something false. But it soon came to mean an object that embodied the spirit of a civilization and that was ultimately incommensurable but integral to cross-cultural colonial encounters. Later, Marx's classic analysis stressed the attribution of surplus value to objects, mis-recognizing human-material coproduction. Otherwise put, material relations between people and objects become expressed as social relations between objects (Marx 1967 [1867]:72–3; also Appadurai 1992). Consequently, social scientists try to decipher residues that accrete and erode on and from objects, giving primacy to meaning rather than to materiality.

Another twist on human-object relations among "Westerners" from Classical times to the near-present concerns the power of objects over people and vice versa. Elaine Scarry traces a shift from when beautiful objects had the capacity to hold in their power people who gazed upon them, to when the beholder's gaze has power over the object (Scarry 1999:120–4). This shift is bundled with a Euro-centric discourse on "beauty" – a quality objects are said to radiate when they bear out the intentions of their makers. When different cultures came into contact through European colonialism, people realized that displaying exotic objects and bodies in museums involved considerable violence to the object and the truth it was meant to convey but could not. Museums violate one of the key tenets of archaeology – the importance of context. Metropolitan museums almost always are disembedded, displaying objects, places, and people from elsewhere in spaces that encourage vision and a relatively fast flow of movement. The spatial and cultural difference between the museum and its objects is often so great that audiences consider it a betrayal. Even grouping objects in dioramic simulacra do not ultimately succeed. People do not have "faith in fakes" (Eco 1986), which utilize mechanical reproductive processes that water down the essential "aura" of a work (Benjamin 1968:221). Unless, of course, the "fake" seeks not to copy but to create and even recreate itself – Las Vegas with its temples, pyramids, and pirate ships being the most outrageous example. Alternatively, copies need not be considered watered-down penumbral phenomena, they actively draw from an original's aura. An example here is Lascaux II – the photogrammetrically reproduced replica of the Upper Palaeolithic rock art site in what is today France. So successful is the copy that it is limited to 2,500 visitors per day, thus both drawing from an aura and becoming an artifact in its own right. Authenticity is a key concept in curators' and publics' perceptions of what is worth keeping, displaying, discarding. But "authenticity" is a malleable concept and can accommodate fakes if they are old, sufficiently spectacular, or endorsed by sufficiently authoritative connoisseurs. Authenticity is also directional. Some people are more concerned with the object as material manifestation while others are more interested in the knowledge and emotions tethered to objects.

Integrating these directionalities is important because glossing detached objects with text compounds confusion. The limitations of language are marked in postcolonial contexts where many people cannot or will not read. Textual alienation stems in large measure from the core epistemology of museums as a visible and repeated disciplining of objects and people into a desired wor(l)d order. Objects are seldom displayed or curated without a caption, label, or description. Branches of archaeology have even considered material culture as "text" in which objects constitute a "record", "syntax," or "code" that can be cracked and meaning read off (for example Tilley 1991). This privileging of language over object stresses an outsider-looking-in stance that does not adequately reference the object's originator community, temporality, or

The Beauty of Letting Go... 275

geography. Words may be thought of as a voice speaking for an object, but a harsh one that is not always well-disposed to that object. For example, the "Yosemite" of North America were so-named by their enemies, the southern Sierra Miwok. Lafayette H. Bunnell of the Mariposa Battalion chanced upon the latter in 1851 CE and believed "Yosemite" to be an emic ethonym. However, "Yosemite" means "there are killers among them" and the "Yosemite" called themselves the "Ahwahneechee" or "people of the gap-mouthed valley" (Gudde 1998). Because of this historical conjuncture their artifacts must now (and forever?) bear an exonym. Ethnonomy – the emic and etic ascription of identities – is a critically important study able powerfully to expose the masking and naturalizing of European colonialism. There are several ways to deal with the tyranny of text. One way, more common to art galleries than to museums, is to display objects unencumbered by text stressing the incommensurability of writing about objects. Feelings of wonder and a greater appreciation of the object as material manifestation are the fruits of such a tactic. If that object can be displayed without impediment, people can experience other attributes such as smell – usually of mustiness, chemicals, or sometimes woodsmoke – and occasionally touch – such as in "blind alphabets" (Coombes 2001:250–1) and discovery rooms. Text can even be used against itself by, for example, hanging opaque text-imprinted plastic in front of objects, actively hindering people's view and understanding of what is on display (see Figure 10.1) (Ouzman 1995:3).

Object Rights

Without accepting the fact that everything changes, we cannot find perfect composure. Because we cannot accept the truth of transience, we suffer.

Shunryu Suzuki, *Branching Streams*

These non- and antitextual interventions help center the object, but they are still subject to human agency instead of a more networked human-object coproduction. Though logically only partially possible, it might be interesting to think about objects as having certain rights, as people do. These rights are not synonymous with "stewardship," "curation," "conservation," and similar interventions that are more accurately characterized as human obligations to objects. The general goal of these activities is to preserve some form of patrimony for the

Figure 10.1 Text on plastic obscuring artifacts. "The Wind Blows Dust ... material culture of the San of southern Africa's central interior" exhibition, South Africa, 1995

benefit of future human generations. Rather than relying on a deferred temporality – a kind of "excavating the future" – object rights stem from environmental politics of the brand that acknowledges the mutuality of "nature" and "culture" (for example Cronon 1995; Pollan 2001; also Ingold 2000). As a result of environmental lobbying, legal rights were granted to singular objects (such as trees) and coagulations of objects (such as a watershed; see Stone 1973) within most Western jurisprudences. These object rights strengthened people's ability to claim aesthetic, posterity, and economic rights bound up in (natural) objects. This approach was initially promising in asking what the needs of natural objects were, but became hijacked by the gentry. Perhaps the approach can be redeemed by using explicitly cultural objects. The most obvious and powerful such cultural object is human remains. The polemic on archiving human remains shows the power of words. What would happen if, instead of using "human remains" we used "humans." This one instance of a common curatorial embracing of the fragmentary, decaying, and incomplete nature of a specific artifact strategically uses a diminished physical state to suggest similarly diminished responsibility to wider society. More complete human "remains" such as mummified or otherwise preserved people tend to evoke stronger reactions from people, and museums almost never "restore" people, though they can simulate them and try to arrest their decay. For example, Oetzi, the c.5300-year-old Tyrolean "ice man" loses about 5 grams of his 14 kg body weight a day, now slowed to 6 grams a month with the construction of a special refrigerated storage facility (SAPA 2003). But apart from being artifacts, archived humans can reasonably be ascribed certain "rights" such as are contained in the World Archaeological Congress's "Vermillion Accord" and various national legislations that regulate the treatment of humans dead and alive. A note of caution is here required. Rights-speak is very common these days and, as Michael Brown warns (2003:229–40), is predisposed to conflictual, antagonistic interchanges rather than committed to finding workable ground. Nor should objects' rights take precedence over human rights. The recent outcry over the destruction of Iraqi archaeological and other heritages was much more muted when it came to speaking out against the loss of human life in the same war (Hamilakis 2003; Ouzman 2003). Further, the "audit culture" that pervades archaeology and heritage provides sufficient noise and business to drown out the concerns of claimants on specific heritages. Perhaps object rights should be meant spelled with a small "r." But some sort of strong object-centric corrective is needed – a robust set of expectations which objects can reasonably expect to have. This is not to argue that we reverse the trajectory from human back to the all-powerful affective object (cf. Scarry 1999:120), but to acknowledge that humans and objects produce and project each other and should have contextually equivalent standing (Latour 1993:142–5; Stocking 1985). What then would objects' "rights" be and how may we accommodate them?

Drawing from recent renewed archaeological interest in "object worlds" – especially those experienced multisensorially (Stahl 2002) – I suggest three basic object rights: the right to a life history, agency, and home. These rights may also be stated in the plural, since most artifacts have long, complicated, and multiple biographies (Hoskins 1998).

First, acknowledging an object as a living entity or having life potential accords with many indigenous conceptions of material culture embodying sentience (cf. Brown 2003, chapter 5). Here the originator or custodial community who have insider knowledge on the conditions of the object's genesis and/or care are key. Some objects are said to have a life cycle, and in these instances "conservation" disrupts the balance between life and death and stigmatizes the archive as a macabre space. It is like life support for a gracious but terminally ailing relative. Conservation and display stress stasis, and though often aesthetically pleasing, this appearance belies considerable violence to the object and to the object's creators. Life and its residues are necessarily multi-sensorial – and archives are not exempt, especially when they can, if pushed, accommodate different sensory registers. For example, in southern Africa, the Bantu-speaking Venda have special drums used to summon rain (see Figure 10.2) (Blacking 1965:22–30). These drums

Figure 10.2 Venda drums safe and "fed" in National Museum, South Africa

are spoken of as being a herd of five cattle that regularly need to have pungent animal fat and red ochre lovingly rubbed into them to make them "well." Pleasingly, this indigenous intervention can fit within existing curatorial practice as fat prevents the wood and animal skin from cracking. That the fat and ochre are modern and not "original" is offset by realizing that these substances add to the drums' archaeology and satisfy their makers' wishes. Further, when these drums are made, the largest "bull" may have the bones of the chief or the stones from a crocodile's stomach with whom the chief is zoomorphized, placed inside it – a perfect embodiment of the inextricable human–material relations. The chief is an active ancestor residing in the similarly active drum, which needs to be kept in a safe place, usually a cave. Though unanimity is a fiction, a number of Venda have expressed their satisfaction that a museum qualifies as such a safe place to keep the drum ancestor.

That the belief in an object's life cycle is not just an "indigenous" concern was forcefully highlighted in 2004, the 500th anniversary of Michelangelo's "David" sculpture, commemorated by a controversial restoration process. In the debate that lost itself in the minutiae of how best to clean the sculpture, art historian James Beck adopted a larger and more sensory perspective by opposing any intervention whatsoever:

> A work of art is pretty much like a human being. We all get battered, we all break bones, they mend, we go and get some disease, we get cured, and then we die. There's an organic life to a work of art, too. It accumulates experience as humans do, and those experiences shape it. Once you've understood that, the idea of going back to the original seems pointless, even if it were possible. (Spinney 2004)

The stains and marks objects acquire and lose over time are part of the process that give artifacts their allure (also Dekkers 2000). Archaeologically, the patina on "David" is a site formation process in miniature, the stratigraphy of years of environmental and social information. Further, basic research suggests that this "grime" is protecting what is really an inferior piece of marble – Michelangelo then being short of money – from more rapid decay. Apart from their politics and financial implications, these restorations draw on a Classical ocular-centric "perfection," which prefers clean surfaces to underlying layers and textures. Such curatorial assumption of single authorship and a relatively brief genesis lead to "pristine" restorations, which project a narrow range of knowable original meanings. This focus on original states explicable by meta-narratives is in need of remedial roughness.

Here conservation mirrors archaeology – peeling back layers to an imagined original state and meaning that is considered more important than the overlying layers and subsequent lives of the artifact these layers represent. Artifacts made for one purpose and then reused at later times for another purpose are usually considered derivative and even decadent.

But these multiple lives highlight the second right of objects – agency. Rather than here tread the well-worn path of active agency, I support a more chaotic and fragmentary agentiveness that would fall within de Certeau's "*docta ignorantia*" (1984), replete with unintended consequences rather that over-determined, all-knowing social manipulation. For example, the social sciences use material culture of people present and especially past as metonyms – "artifacts were seen as standing for an entire human culture" (Dicks 2003). Having imputed into you the capacity to speak for whole cultures and epochs is an enormous responsibility. As a fragment with specific life histories, an object necessarily embodies temporality, but often fragmented with imperfect knowledge of its context. But to assume that our and the object's temporality are commensurate is to assume rather than question that time past connects with time present. Many objects are mysteries – we do not know who made them, why, or for what purpose. But a grid of classification, causality, and consequence can mask this deficiency. Better to foreground the object's right to exist as an interesting but sometimes unknowable and unknowing entity, reining in the portability and replicability of Merton's scientific method. Through the object we may have a more modest but honest view of material and human agency. An interesting convergence of these agencies is provided by bacterium such as *Pseudomonas stutzeri* that are used to clean medieval European frescoes (Arie 2003). Janet Hoskins puts this relationship in a more active but chaotic dialectic: "Not every biographical object is chosen by its subject. An object can at times be imposed or attributed, linked to someone who did not consciously choose it as a vehicle for her own identity" (Hoskins 1998:161). A good example of the sometimes knowing, sometimes recondite object is the "bored stone" – a ubiquitous sub-Saharan African artifact. Usually a hard rock culturally modified into a more or less spherical artifact through which a hole is bored (see Figure 10.3), bored stones are found in many cultural contexts dating as far back as 27,000 years ago to now (Ouzman 1997). A survey of published, ethnographic, and archaeological sources yields no fewer than 43 observed or imputed uses of "bored stones" that range from digging stick weights to spindle whorls to phallic objects. The power

Figure 10.3 Bored stone and less agentive associated artifacts, southern Africa

of language to mask via the generic label "bored stone" compresses disparate millennia, cultures, and geographies into two words. Debate on bored stones' "original" meanings is common. Even when clearly having multiple uses – like when a digging stick weight was used as an upper grindstone – the subsequent uses are seen as derivate and secondary. Technology is an important aspect of this artifact's agency. Many European-descended Africans have difficulty reconciling the huge labor and aesthetic effort of bored stones with their imaginations of, for instance, the San as noble or even ignoble "savages." When people today are allowed to pick up these objects they heft them, feel their weight, peer through their aperture, sniff and tap them, and they wonder, wonder, wonder ... But left at that point, the attraction to bored stones and similar artifacts with laminated histories is indulgent and makes archaeology and museums even easier to marginalize by people for whom ruins have no romance. Here the post-colony's histories add an essential political engagement between archive and audience. Thus, bored stones also presence violence. In central South Africa, Boer farmers would routinely break these artifacts because they associated them with the San who fought tooth and nail against the Europeans over the land. A broken stone is thus no less worthy an artifact because of the manner of its death. Bored stones and similar "special" artifacts have an agency that selects us to collect and display them. We therefore need to temper strong object agencies with "small things forgotten" which have less direct but perhaps no less interesting biographies.

Third, objects have a right to a home. I do not necessarily mean an "original" home but the object's right to integrate with or reject its current surroundings. This requires understanding an artifact's life cycle and biography as always in production. Most archives are concerned with provenance – the succession of homes an artifact has had and owners it has tolerated – which is vital in, for example, countering the illicit antiquities trade (Renfrew 2001). But provenance can be presented piecemeal, glossing dubious, derivative, or violent episodes or stressing an original location. Objects are important per se, but as and even more important are the various knowledges associated with objects that underpin the material's authenticity. Absent objects like the Elgin Marbles help to sustain particular brands of nationalism that would not be as strongly attached had the object not been absent. The most promising way to satisfy an object's right to a home is via an archaeology of archive that traces how objects came to be collected and curated, and their archival life cycle. The archaeology of archive is multiple and even contradictory but has the necessary messiness that people living in previously colonized countries or lands with violent pasts may find more believable than the sterile simulacra approach used in large parts of the heritage industry.

Archaeologies of Archive

Why, if ancient knowledge has been preserved and if, speaking in general, there exists a knowledge distinct from our science and philosophy or even surpassing it, it is so carefully concealed, why is it not made common property? Why are the men who possess this knowledge unwilling to let it pass into the general circulation of life for the sake of a better and more successful struggle against deceit, evil and ignorance?

Peter Ouspensky, *In Search of the Miraculous*

Instead, then, of situating objects as metonymic of far-off places and process, we can use them to speak of their most recent history – in the archive. Archives are created in a bewildering variety of ways – planned, serendipitous, and chaotic. Despite the rapid rate at which we accumulate, we seldom curate as efficiently: most archaeologists, museologists, and similar have no formal training in "collections management," typically a euphemism for "crisis management" (Pearce 1999). Here the schizophrenic ability of archaeology to step outside normal epistemological and ontological bounds by borrowing techniques, methodologies, and theories from other disciplines is useful in generating ideas that can then be developed in ways useful to archaeology by dispersing its objects (Shanks 2001). In this spirit, archive archaeology borrows directly from "taphonomy" – the palaeontological principle that explains the "life" history of fossils from the death of an organism to its moment of human discovery (Behrensmeyer and Hill 1980). This taphonomy incorporates a slew of agencies from how sediments accrete and erode: the effects of acids on soil and bone, climate, earthworm bioturbation, and so forth. Similarly, artifact archives grow and shrink, appear and disappear; but unlike in the case of palaeontology, artifacts can be discovered many times and have ongoing lives beyond the moments of discovery. They have different layers to cater to different audiences with image, text, and sometimes sound, touch, and, rarely, smell. Great effort is put into making these layers seamless. But just as Walter Benjamin, who influenced the Situationists (see for example Debord 1994), remarked that anyone can follow directions but only the truly gifted can use a map to get lost (Benjamin 2002), perhaps greater effort should be put into making sure the overlaid layers are not in perfect registration, but show ruptures – "the process of construction, the backing and forthing of logic, of different logics belonging to the past and the present, piecing together and laying out the contradictions rather than smoothing them over" (Coombes 2001:237–8). Here greater use of the senses can be immensely productive. Smell, perhaps our most evocative and difficult-to-discipline sense, best embodies organic decay, the life of an object ebbing away or transforming into another energy. Similarly, archives, be they books, ethnographic artifacts, and so on, have unique smells and atmospheres that influence how persons move, what they pick up, which drawer or dark corner they are attracted to. Though there are alternatives such as collecting and excavating less and repatriating more, curatorial decisions are tied to enshrined principles of stewardship and conservation and to dominant economic, moral, social, and political climates. These pressures and the haphazard nature of most collecting lead to many occlusions and missing information. But even occlusions leave residues. Just as we can determine the shape of a stone tool from associated lithic debitage even if the tool itself is absent, that a hut was made of reeds because these left impressions in clay walling, or know that as-yet-unseen sub-atomic quarks exist because of their imputed effect on slightly larger and seeable atomic particles, so archived artifacts' lacunae leave traces.

Guess What's Missing?

A series of such gaps and traces is provided through a taphonomic triangulation between an archaeological site, a museum display, and sociopolitical concerns that center on South Africa's new coat of arms (see Figure 10.4a). Unveiled on April 27, 2000 (Smith et al. 2000; Barnard 2003), this most potent of state symbols has at its center a mirror-imaged human figure inspired by a San rock painting from the "Linton Panel." The Linton Panel is a painted rock fragment ("panel" suggests an over-determination to frame and suggest wholeness) displayed at the South African Museum in Cape Town since 1918 (Figure 10.4b). The fragment is ensconced in the type of softly-lit display hall advocated by architect Juahani Palasmaa in his "eyes of the skin" manifesto that seeks to temper the subtext of light as analogous to "reason" with darker locales that allow other more haptic senses and especially the contemplative imagination to play a greater role (Palasmaa 1996). The historic building, soft lighting, and beautiful religious imagery (Lewis-Williams 1988) combine to evoke a reverential aura. To the sacred is now added respect attendant on political power through knowing that one of Linton's human figures (Figure 10.4b inset) is incarnated in South Africa's highest symbol of state. This political knowledge is, however, for a restricted audience as there is no contextual information pointing to the human figure or its journey from religious to political symbol. Indeed, this painting's smallness and low position requires the viewer to contort his or her body – suggesting that "seeing" can morph into a more embodied practice of "looking" (see Okley 2001). Though Linton is a fragment in the intensive care of the display case, museum visitors do not know that this fragment is radically displaced from its home at Linton rock shelter (we do not know its San name) in the remote and high Drakensberg mountains over 1,000 km east of coastal Cape Town. The laconic accession annotation that this fragment was "collected" belies the physical impact on the fragment's home. In removing two[3] approximately 1.85 m × 0.85 m painted rock fragments two approximately 5 m² gaps were left in a painted rock wall (see Figure 10.4c). This physical and aesthetic violence – after 90 years the Linton removal scars still seem fresh with rough and chalky fragments that

Figure 10.4 Life history of the Linton fragment
   a. Embodiment in South Africa's Coat of Arms 2000.
   b. Museum display 1918–present. Inset, rock painting that occurs in coat of arms.
   c. Linton fragment's original home, 2000. Damage done 1916–18.

adhere to one's finger as you touch the scar – is at stark odds with the managed museum space. A further slippage is the huge and unequal labor that went into procuring this artifact. Between 1916 and 1918 three men labored mightily to chisel out the fragments to satisfy the then SA Museum Director Louis Péringuey's desire to display San rock art (SA Museum correspondence, accessed December 4, 2000).[4] But these three men's labor was not equal. Superficially, it cost £122.00 – a considerable sum, worth a year's salary to a skilled worker – for the whole operation (not £30.00 as stated on the SA Museum web site and by

Lewis-Williams 1988). Of this, about £60.00 was paid to Mr. Stephanus Naude, a white stonemason, while his co-workers – "Jonas" and another, unnamed black worker – received around £8.00 each, the rest being spent on materials and transport. This "cost" is a telling indication of the valuation of race-identified labor (Shepherd 2003).

More recently, the Linton fragment has exposed a gap between "value" and "price/lessness." In 1995 Linton and seven other painted rock fragments from southern Africa toured Berlin, London, and New York (no African venue) as part of *"Africa: the art of a continent"* exhibition. Linton was, for insurance purposes, valued at R1-million – a huge sum, the cost of a high-end apartment overlooking the South African Museum today. Insuring collections is common practice, but this sum made its way into the press. Linton's millionaire price tag came to stand as an authoritative valuation of an allegedly priceless heritage. Then working as an archaeologist at National Museum,[5] I received numerous requests from landowners and municipalities to appraise their archaeological "inventories." Though they did grasp the concept of alienable and inalienable heritage (Weiner 1985), the landowner response to the insured sum confirms Igor Kopytoff's observation that restricted-circulation "priceless" objects can only maintain this status by periodically entering a market economy (Kopytoff 1992). "Priceless" thus just means "extremely expensive."

These "missing" episodes in Linton's life history and the slippages it exposes took a new twist two weeks after the coat of arms' unveiling. In an article entitled "Guess what's missing?" journalist Glenda Daniels found it "striking and disturbing that the two human figures in the middle [of the coat of arms] are in attitude and 'giss' (general identification, shape, and size) unmistakably male – two male bonding figures" (Daniels 2000). Comparing the coat of arms figure (Figure 10.4a) to the original rock painting (Figure 10.4b inset) shows that the transformation from museum to state object involved some separation anxiety with the neutering of the state symbol version. Daniels interpreted the figures either as representing "subliminal patriarchy" or, more playfully, as "androgynous" figures. This latter option she dismisses, bringing up the valid point that coats of "arms" tend to be masculinist and seldom incorporate femininity. But her "androgynous" throw-away comment is probably spot-on. The dominant tenor of the rock art produced by diverse southern African gatherer-hunter communities is that their religious import is dominantly shamanistic (Lewis-Williams 1988). Shamanic altered states of consciousness are understandable to us through neuropsychological studies. In these states, gender identity and allegiance is radically and even violently altered. Third and further genders are entirely plausible in the Spirit World (see Butler 1993). Thus, the "androgynous" or "stick" figures[6] in San rock art are probably not "androgynous" or "asexual" but their absence of primary sexual characteristics accurately presences the impossibility of maintaining a simple gender binary. The value of archaeology in approaching Linton's rock art on something approaching its appropriate cultural context points us to its most deafening silence – that of its makers and their descendants. Prior to its removal, Linton lived in an area which nineteenth-century British colonial administrators labeled "Nomansland" to nullify Xhosa and San claims to it. The San of the area fell victim to colonial genocide and assimilation and their absence from displays like Linton is telling (see Mayer 1998). Most displays and dioramas are seemingly politically disengaged yet actively gloss destructive epochs even when the material displayed speaks explicitly to such destruction (Lewis-Williams and Dowson 1993). The lack of respect for this violence is especially acute at the South African Museum. On March 20, 2001 the (in)famous "Bushman diorama," located in the next hall from the Linton Fragment and inter-visible, was closed for fear of offending the public and San descendants despite many of these expressing approval for the diorama and its accompanying contextual and remedial information. The diorama was one of the museum's longest-running (c.1911) and most popular exhibits (Davison 2001; also Skotnes 1996):

> Within the changing social context of South Africa, museums have a re-sponsibility to reconsider their roles as sites of memory, inspiration, and education. The South African Museum, together with the other museums that form Iziko Museums of Cape Town, is currently rethinking directions and priorities. In this context a decision has been taken to "archive" the famous hunter-gatherer diorama while its future is reviewed. It will not be dismantled but will be closed to the public from the end of March 2001. This move shows commitment to change and encourages debate within the Museum, with the public and especially with people of Khoisan descent. South African Museum statement. http://www.museums.org.za/sam/resources/arch/bushdebate.htm, accessed June 8, 2002

The violent process that led to the Linton fragment being in the museum could easily be accommodated into most display techniques, especially since most South African museum visitors are conversant with violence and its effects, given their country's turbulent imperial, colonial, and Apartheid past (Coombes 2002). The museum as a "safe" space is just too much at odds with this history (Herzfeld 1996). Juxtaposing the taphonomic layerings and occlusions of the Linton Fragment's life renders it more believable and even parallels the painful histories and present circumstances of at least local audiences. In a region in which domestic violence, HIV/AIDS infection rates, and abuse of children and elders is marked, southern African archaeology and museology can usefully employ their mastery of larger perspectives of time and human behavior to destabilize demeaning but naturalized modern practices. We can show other possibilities of personhood, thereby demonstrating that hegemonies are not inevitable, and that the present can be remade. Using a life history, taphonomic approach we can show what's missing – and why. This is the muscular, fractious museum as "contact zone" that James Clifford perhaps envisaged (Clifford 1997; also Feldman in chapter 9 of this volume).

Beyond the Building

> If we had a keen vision and feeling of all ordinary human life, it would be like hearing the grass grow and the squirrel's heart beat, and we should die of that roar which lies on the other side of silence.
>
> George Eliot, *Middlemarch*

Elision and violence are familiar parts of archaeology and museum's lexicon (Mayer 1998). Washington, DC's Holocaust Museum and Johannesburg's Apartheid Museum bludgeon the visitor with multiple violences and absences. Few museums have demonstrated the imagination to deal with absence other than as sledgehammer. In Italy, some art museums harness absence by leaving blank spaces on walls from which artworks have been stolen. The slight discoloration of the once-covered wall speaks elegantly of the flow of objects through channels legitimate and non (Mariane Ferme, personal communication, May 2004). The disjuncture between objects, history, and social justice can promote willful amnesia. Some communities choose not to preserve "sites of hurtful memory" such as Chile's National Stadium where Pinochet had "dissidents" dealt with or the Nazi headquarters in Berlin (Dolf-Bonekämper 2002; Forty and Küchler 2001). This approach is perfectly valid and means that history is not supported by an object inventory but by memory and oral histories (Samuel 1994). In a revealing reversal of memorial temporality, Rosemary Joyce in her presidential address to the 2003 Society for American Archaeology conference told how the United States government turned to archaeology for advice on how permanently to mark nuclear waste storage facilities to warn future generations of the site's toxicity. In a supreme irony, the model for permanent marking was held to be the stone and clay-impressed writing systems of the classic civilizations of the Near and Middle East – sites the US invasion of Iraq threatens with destruction.

Staging Stories

The desire to tell and listen to stories is one of the few cultural universals (see for example Dundes 1984; Lakoff and Johnson 1999). By "story" I do not mean a make-believe, politically lame "fairy tale" but a robust narrative born out of a certain soil and people, though it can also have wider relevance. Recently, archaeologists have examined storytelling as a productive trope for conveying the multivocality and ambiguity standard archaeological techniques have so much trouble dealing with (Joyce 2002; Pluciennik 1999). Storytelling is capable of a double centering. First, the storyteller with his or her fund of knowledge, lived experience, and rhetorical skills is able to perform even if he or she is not text-literate, does not have a wide, worldly knowledge, or does not enjoy material wealth. Secondly, the story's stage – the locus at which the story is told or relates to – is brought strongly to the fore. Stories can both accord with and challenge "official" channels of information such as newspapers, television, and other top-down, minimally consultative processes. Stories are much more difficult to discipline because they allow people to interpolate their own voice and interpretations. Storytelling is a credible and democratic alternative to centralized knowledge production, though it runs the risk of becoming locally powerful but weak at transnational or transcultural scales. The /Xam San – a people who suffered physical and cultural genocide – spoke of "Stories that float from afar" to tell how knowledge of the world seemingly travels on the air from far-off places (Lewis-Williams 2000). This seemingly overly romantic rendering of sound and knowledge does have materiality. Indeed, sound is technically a product of vibration and thus arguably part of the sense of "touch." Archaeologically, San sound has a material residue that acted as a powerful vector for identities ordinary and extraordinary (see also Tuzin 1984).

Among the thousands of San rock-engraving sites in southern Africa, there are at least 280 instances where people selected for naturally resonant ironstone boulders (Ouzman 2001:240–2; see Figure 10.5).

Figure 10.5 Gong rock at southern African rock-art site

Either stacked or broken by lightning, heat expansion, or freeze contraction to create a resonator, these "gong rocks" produce the brand of
repetitive, percussive sound and sensation that induces changes in
states of consciousness. These gong rock sites, unconstrained by walls,
nonetheless act like the vaulted cathedrals of Europe that were designed
to frame and direct music on its journey to heaven. Gong rock sites are
located in seemingly endless landscapes where sound travels from its
source unconstrained. Such sites potentially offer a powerfully multisensorial site museum.[7] Producing the sound requires intense bodily
engagement – touch, hearing, perhaps singing, sweating, the release
of natural peptides and endorphins that blur sensory boundaries, even
confusing them so that sounds are touched, colors tasted. Synaesthesia
is a potent gambit in empowering the past and establishing seemingly
familiar knowledge. Even if the gong rocks are left unstruck – perhaps
as a requiem to their absent makers – the landscape can be so quiet as
to induce a constant ringing sound in one's ears – "the roar that lies
on the other side of silence."

Contrast these affirmatory, connective types of sound with Apartheid-
era curfew sirens that were also repetitive and percussive but which
limited rather than liberated. Implications for the heritage industry are

that soundscapes and maintaining an acoustic integrity are important aspects of managing sites and displays. Similarly, silence is perhaps one of the most important constituents of any story – the length, frequency, and quality of pauses can build suspense, deliver a dénouement, or show a necessary fallibility in the teller, the inevitable fragmentation of a narrative thread over time.

Situating silence and narrative thread is crucial. Spatially framing a story in museum originary and imaginary locations requires more than a formulaic object-centric design language. A good example is the Deer Valley Rock Art Center in Arizona, USA. Here, archaeologists let go and allowed architect Will Bruder to highlight essences of both the rock art and its immediate surroundings in ways unusual but interesting for the visitor. Bruder mimicked the profusion of engraved rocks with almost industrial emplacements of concrete clad in a copper-like skin that oxidized in a process analogous to that of the engraved rocks. He installed simple tubular pipes that directed the visitor's gaze to certain engravings and landscape features (Bruder 1997). Taking the notion of a peopled place still further, Estelle Smit applied animation and motion studies at three southern African rock engraving sites that both echo engraved patterns and human movement (Smit 2002). Human movement is a powerful indicator of identity (see Solnit 2000), differentiated on the basis of gender, age, race, urban or rural, outsiders or residents, New Agers and Christians, and so forth. For example, scant attention is paid to the anarchic movement of children – known as NCU's (non-conforming units) in the building trade – yet their passage is often very intuitive and sensuous, not to mention their being numerically the most dominant visitors to museums. Smit's gateways structures include perishable materials that decay and become "messy" over a period of years as, for example, the iron-rich rocks are destroyed by lightning strikes every so often.

Discussion

This creation of emplaced, embedded site museums creates common ground for empathy or even argument. But the enthusiasm for site museums must be tempered by at least two factors. First, transport to non-metropole centers is often prohibitively difficult for many people and only privileged, well-wheeled people get to what become exclusive enclaves (Kirshenblatt-Gimblett 1998). Secondly, "site museums" may perpetuate a provincial relation between "city" and "countryside" rather than permitting each to do different work (Buck 1998; Omland 1997).

Human movement, this time at a larger scale, is again an important consideration. For all the talk of global interconnectedness, tracing flows, destinations, establishing movement patterns, and even identifying travelers is an imprecise science. Jonathan Friedman brings some sanity by pointing out that less than 2 percent of the world's population is on the move and that diasporas have become elliptical rather than linear. People tend now to return and revisit places rather than just "emigrate" or "flee" (Friedman 2002). We are not dealing with "locals" and "outsiders" but with people who move in and out of these states. Movement is far from neutral. Just as rock-painted fragments like Linton were moved against their will, so Apartheid and colonial administrations displaced people and their place-based identities and cultural property (Bender and Winer 2001). Bhabha's contention that hybridity is a "natural" human condition interrupted by the uniformitarian grid of imperial and colonial projects, seems spot on (Bhabha 1994). It is then not surprising that the postcolony offers the most emotionally and socially engaged methods of presenting objects, places, and people in critically defensible ways (Davison 1998). By emphasizing nontextual, more performative ways of conveying knowledge, by representing the past and present, and by using vision as just one of a range of senses and bodily practices helps retain the elements of wonder and awe that are often strangled out by cookie-cutter design languages.

This is both a forward-looking exercise and an opportunity for retrospect. Though reprehensible violences were perpetrated by colonial archaeologies and museologies, some of the techniques we use may be reclaimed and many are empowering. A prime candidate is the curiosity cabinet. Previously a somewhat chaotic attempt to collect and systematize that became part of the apparatus used to exoticize and denigrate, curiosity cabinets have recently been creatively reintroduced into the public domain. The conceptual artist Mark Dion's "cabinets of curiosity" installations for museums and public spaces attract unprecedented crowds (Vail 2001; Weisman Art Museum 2001). If curators were to be brave, then they could place large parts of their archive within the public display space. Of course not all objects are suitable for public display (see Burström 2003 for "the value of junk"), but the common lament of not being able to display would be largely solved by storing collections within display spaces. People could discover the collection in less ascriptive ways while being aware of great absences in their knowledge represented by unopened and perhaps unreachable drawers. This approach is gaining currency, though it has problems of being higher-maintenance and curators fear damage to objects. Creatively used drawers could hold surprises like empty boxes, triggering music when opened, acrid and soothing smells, elegantly faded colors, making the "discovery room" and exhibit halls integrate.

This is not to ally with those destructively self-reflexive brands of social science that fail to recognize that they are authoritative sources of knowledge, but as a shifting set of practices whereby people and objects try to get along in the world and, indeed, help produce and represent each other (McCracken 1991). Archaeology as a set of repetitive and usually laborious techniques forces contemplation of the objects being studied, and helps to a degree in placing the massive violence of colonialism at the kind of distance needed to make intelligible yet emotionally engaged comment. This repetition and labor are analogous to "habit" and "skill" – mechanisms that permit innovation and act as pathways to virtuosity (see for example Hobsbawn and Ranger 1992). To this end, the practitioner has also to place him- or herself under the lens, as one of the most telling absences in most museums is the curator. It is, however, a fine line to tread between a courageous "archaeology of us" (Buchli and Lucas 2001) and an indulgent one, especially if the curator does not also involve multiple perspectives in which are embedded a range of sensory practices (Howes 2003). The challenge to archaeologies and museologies that seek contemporary relevance is how to permit people still to marvel at objects but to do so in ways that make the apprehender aware of the object's place in a continuum of humanistic and material practice. There is a beauty in letting go, but it takes resolve, will and, to reiterate the sentiment that began this chapter, requires "the repeated exercises of the senses, or reflections on those kinds of objects which at first occasioned them" if we are to arrest the decay of our ideas, but not all of our objects.

Acknowledgments

I thank the Wenner-Gren Foundation for Anthropological Research for the invitation to participate in the "Engaging all the senses" conference conceptualized and driven by Chris Gosden, Elizabeth Edwards, and Ruth Phillips. They, the participants at the conference, Mariane Ferme, Kathryn Mathers, the University of Pretoria's Anthropology Department seminar group and UC Berkeley's 2004 Material Culture seminar participants are thanked for constructive criticism. Graham Avery at the South African Museum kindly facilitated access to archival correspondence on the Linton Fragment, and photography of the Fragment. Research Funding was provided by the Horace Wilberforce Benevolent Fund, James A. Swan

Fund (UK), National Research Foundation (South Africa), the Lowie and Stahl Funds, UC Berkeley (USA), and the South African Archaeological Society Kent Bequest. Opinions expressed are not necessarily to be attributed to these institutions.

Notes

1. I use "artifact" and "object" interchangeably.
2. By "museum" I refer principally to institutions that archive and display human cultural history, though this type of history is often housed in "natural" history museums, art galleries and so forth. I use "archive" to refer to any systematic collection of artifacts from university collections to private hoards.
3. The second Linton fragment bears detailed antelope paintings.
4. San rock art is understood not as "imagery" but as an entity that connected ordinary and Spirit Worlds. This transgressing of boundaries and exploring of strange worlds is perhaps one object-centric way of understanding how Linton, through its exceptionally fine imagery, wanted to travel to new worlds, such as the South African Museum, rather than being collected solely by Péringuey's desire.
5. South Africa has 18 "Declared Cultural Institutions" that have national status. These institutions periodically are reordered, amalgamated and unbundled – an interesting taphonomic process in itself.
6. Though by no means exhaustively quantified, among the many many thousands of human figures in San rock art, a ratio of something like two male figures exist for every female figure with 8–9 "asexual" human figures existing for "male" and "female" categories combined.
7. I here experience a conflict between personal and situational ethics. Striking gong rocks with a hard object removes the patina that has formed over ancient percussion marks, thus damaging the potential to date the percussion episodes. Further, as a non-San may I strike a gong rock? On the other hand, a recording of the anvil-like metallic sound could be played on-site and evoke something of its past atmosphere.

References

Appadurai, Arjun. 1992 [1986]. "Introduction: Commodities and the Politics of Value." In *The Social Life of Things: Commodities in Cultural*

Perspective, ed. Arjun Appadurai. Cambridge: Cambridge University Press.

Arie, Sophie. 2003. "Bacterium Used to Clean Frescoes." *Mail & Guardian*, June 30.

Barnard, Alan. 2003. "!Ke e: /xarra //ke (People who are Different Come Together): Khoisan Imagery in the Reconstruction of South African National Identity." In *Diverse People Unite: Two Lectures on Khoisan Imagery and the State*, ed. Alan Barnard. Edinburgh: Center for African Studies Occasional Paper 94: 6–48.

Beck, James. and M. Daley. 1993. *Art Restoration: The Culture, the Business and the Scandal*. New York: W.W. Norton.

Behrensmeyer, A. Kay and A.P. Hill (eds). 1980. *Fossils in the Making: Vertebrate Taphonomy and Paleoecology*. Chicago: University of Chicago Press.

Belk, Russell. 2001. *Collecting in a Consumer Society*. London: Routledge.

Bender, Barbara and Margot Winer. 2001. *Contested Landscapes: Movement, Exile and Place*. Oxford: Berg.

Benjamin, Walter. 1968. "The Work of Art in the Age of Mechanical Reproduction." In *Illuminations*, trans. Harry Zohn. New York Shocken.

——. 2002. "A Berlin Childhood around the Turn of the Century." In *Walter Benjamin: Selected Writings, Vol.3: 1935–1938*, ed. Howard Eiland and Michael W. Jennings. New Haven, CT: Yale University Press.

Bennet, Tony. 1995. *The Birth of the Museum*. London: Routledge.

Bhabha, Homi. 1994. *The Location of Culture*. London: Routledge.

Blacking, John. 1965. "The Role of Music in the Culture of the Venda of the Northern Transvaal." In *Studies in Ethnomusicology*, ed. M. Kolinski. New York: Oak Publications.

Brodie, Neil. 2003. "Stolen History: Looting and Illicit Trade." *Museum* 55: 10–22.

Brown, Michael. 2003. *Who Owns Native Culture?* Cambridge, MA: Harvard University Press.

Bruder, William. 1997. "Deer Valley Rock Art Museum." In *The Architecture of Museums*, ed. Asensio Cerver. New York: Arco.

Buchli, Victor and Gavin Lucas (eds). 2001. *Archaeologies of the Contemporary Past*. London: Routledge.

Buck, Susan. 1998. *The Global Commons: An Introduction*. Washington, DC: Island Press.

Burström, Mats. 2003. "The value of junk." *Axess Magazine*. http://www.axess.se/english/currentissue/theme_junk.php. Site accessed May 10, 2003.

Butler, Judith. 1993. *Bodies that Matter: on the Discursive Limits of "Sex."* New York: Routledge.

Clifford, James. 1988. "On Ethnographic Surrealism." In *The Predicament of Culture: Twentieth-century Ethnography, Literature, and Art*, ed. James Clifford. Cambridge, MA: Harvard University Press.

———. 1997. "Museums as Contact Zones." In *Routes: Travel and Translation in the Late Twentieth Century*, ed. James Clifford. Cambridge MA: Harvard University Press.

Coombes, Annie E. 2001. "The Object of Translation: Notes on "Art" and Autonomy in a Postcolonial Context." In *The Empire of Things: Regimes of Value and Material Culture*, ed. Fred Myers. Sante Fe, NM: School of American Research Press.

———. 2002. *History after Apartheid: Visual Culture and Public Memory in a Democratic South Africa*. Durham, NC: Duke University Press.

Crew, Spencer, R. and James. E. Sims. 1991. "Locating Authenticity: Fragments of a Dialogue." In *Exhibiting Cultures: the Poetics and Politics of Museum Display*, ed. Ivan Karp and Steven D. Lavine. Washington, DC: Smithsonian Institution Press.

Cronon, William. 1995. "Introduction: In Search of Nature." In *Uncommon Ground: Toward Reinventing Nature*, ed. William Cronon. New York: W.W. Norton.

Daniels, Glenda. 2000. "Guess What's Missing?" *Mail and Guardian*, May 5.

Davison, Patricia. 1998. "Museums and the Re-shaping of Memory." In *Negotiating the Past: the Making of Memory in South Africa*, ed. Sarah Nuttall and Carli Coetzee. Cape Town: Oxford University Press.

———. 2001. "Typecast: Representations of the Bushmen at the South African Museum." *Public Archaeology* 1: 3–20.

Debord, Guy. 1994 [1970]. *The Society of the Spectacle*. New York: Zone books.

de Certeau, Michel. 1984. *The Practice of Everyday Life*. Berkeley: University of California Press.

Dekkers, Midas. 2000 [1997]. *The Way of All Flesh*. New York: Farrar, Straus and Giroux.

Dicks, Bella. 2003. *Culture on Display*. New York: McGraw-Hill.

Dolf-Bonekämper, Gabi. 2002. "Sites of Hurtful Memory." *Conservation* 17(2).

Dundes, Alan. (ed.) 1984. *Sacred Narrative: Readings in the Theory of Myth*. Berkeley: University of California Press.

Eco, Umberto. 1986. *Faith in Fakes: Travels in Hyperreality*. London: Minerva.

Elkins, James, J. 1997. *Our Beautiful, Dry and Distant Texts: Art History as Writing*. London: Routledge.

——. 2000. *How to Use Your Eyes*. New York: Routledge.

Fabian, Johannes. 2001. *Anthropology with an Attitude: Critical Essays*. Stanford: Stanford University Press.

Fehr, Michael. 2000. "A Museum and its Memory: the Art of Recovering History." In: *Museums and Memory*, ed. S. Crane. Stanford: University of Stanford Press.

Forty, Adrian and Susan Küchler (eds.). 2001. *The Art of Forgetting*. Oxford: Berg.

Friedman, Jonathan. 2002. "From Roots to Routes: Tropes for Trippers." *Anthropological Theory* 2(1): 21–36.

Gosden, Chris. 1999. *Anthropology and Archaeology: A Changing Relationship*. London: Routledge.

——. 2001. "Postcolonial Archaeology: Issues of Culture, Identity, and Knowledge." In *Archaeological Theory Today*, ed. Ian Hodder. Cambridge: Polity.

Gudde, Erwin G. 1998. *California Place Names: The Origin and Etymology of Current Geographical Names*. Berkeley: University of California Press.

Hamilakis, Yannis. 2003. "Iraq, Stewardship and 'the record': an Ethical Crisis for Archaeology." *Public Archaeology* 3: 104–11.

Haraway, Donna J. 1991. "Situated Knowledges: the Science Question in Feminism and the Privilege of Partial Perspective." In *Simians, Cyborgs and Women: the Reinvention of Nature*, ed. Donna Haraway. London: Routledge.

Harley, J. Brian. 2001. *The New Nature of Maps: Essays in the History of Cartography*. Baltimore: Johns Hopkins University Press.

Herzfeld, Michael. 1996. "Monumental Indifference?" *Archaeological Dialogues* 3: 120–33.

Hobsbawn, Eric and Terence Ranger (eds). 1992. *The Invention of Tradition*. Cambridge: Cambridge University Press.

Hooper-Greenhill. Eilean. 1992. *Museums and the Shaping of Knowledge*. London: Routledge.

Hoskins, Janet. 1998. *Biographical Objects: How Things Tell the Stories of People's Lives*. London: Routledge.

Howes, David. 2003. *Sensual Relations: Engaging the Senses in Culture and Social Theory*. Ann Arbor, MI: University of Michigan Press.

Ingold, Tim. 2000. *The Perception of the Environment: Essays on Livelihood, Dwelling and Skill*. London: Routledge.

Jay, Martin. 1994. *Downcast Eyes: The Denigration of Vision in Twentieth-century French Thought*. Berkeley: University of California Press.

Joyce, Rosemary. 2002. *The Languages of Archaeology: Dialogue, Narrative and Writing*. Oxford: Blackwell.

Karp, Ivan and Steven D. Lavine (eds.). 1991. *Exhibiting Cultures: The Poetics and Politics of Museum Display*. Washington, DC: Smithsonian Institution Press.

Kirshenblatt-Gimblett, Barbara. 1998. *Destination Culture: Tourism, Museums, and Heritage*. Berkeley: University of California Press.

Kopytoff, Igor. 1992 [1986]. "The Cultural Biography of Things: Commoditization as Process." In *The Social Life of Things: Commodities in Cultural Perspective*, ed. Appadurai, Arjun. Cambridge: Cambridge University Press.

Kusimba, C.M. 1996. "Archaeology in African Museums." *African Archaeological Review* 13: 165–70.

Lakoff, George and Mark Johnson. 1999. *Philosophy in the Flesh: The Embodied Mind and its Challenge to Western Thought*. New York: Basic Books.

Latour, Bruno. 1993. *We Have Never Been Modern*. Cambridge, MA: Harvard University Press.

Lewis-Williams, J. David 1988. *The World of Man and the World of Spirit: An Interpretation of the Linton Rock Paintings*. Margaret Shaw Lecture 2. Cape Town: South African Museum.

——. 2000. *Stories that Float from Afar: Ancestral Folklore of the San of Southern Africa*. Johannesburg: Witwatersrand University Press.

—— and Thomas A. Dowson. 1993. "Myths, Museums and Southern African Rock Art." *South African Historical Journal* 29: 44–60.

Marx, Karl. 1967. [1867]. "The Fetishism of Commodities and the Secret Thereof." In *Capital: a Critique of Political Economy*, Vol. 1, *The Process of Capitalist Production*, ed. Frederick Engels, Section 4. New York: International Publishers.

Mayer, Carol. 1998. "Empty Museums: the Politics of Silence." *Journal of Museum Education* 23(1): 21–3.

McCracken, Grant. 1991. *Culture and Consumption: New Approaches to the Symbolic Character of Goods and Activities*. Bloomington, IN: Indiana University Press.

Merton, Robert, K. 1973. "The Normative Structure of Science." In *The Sociology of Science: Theoretical and Empirical Investigations*, ed. N.W. Storer. Chicago: University of Chicago Press.

Murray, Tim (ed.). 2001. *Encyclopedia of Archaeology: History and Discoveries*. Santa Barbara, CA: ABC-Clio.

Okley, Judith. 2001. "Visualism and Landscape: Looking and Seeing in Normandy." *Ethnos* 66(1): 99–120.

Omland, Atle. 1997. "World Heritage and the Relationships Between the Global and the Local." http://folk.uio.no/atleom/master/contents. htm. Site accessed June 21, 2003.

Ouspensky, Peter, D. 1949. In *Search of the Miraculous: Fragments of an Unknown Teaching*. New York: Harcourt Brace.

Ouzman, S. (ed.) 1995. *The Wind Blows Dust ... Traces of the /Xam and other San of the Central Interior*. Bloemfontein: Quali-Press.

———. 1997. "Between Margin and Center : the Archaeology of Southern African Bored Stones." In *Our Gendered Past: Archaeological Studies of Gender in Southern Africa*, ed. Lyn Wadley. Johannesburg: Witwatersrand University Press.

———. 2001. "Seeing is Deceiving: Rock-art and the Non-visual." *World Archaeology* 33(2): 237–56.

———. 2003. "Is Audit our Object? Archaeology, Conservation, Sovereignty." *Antiquity* 77(297). http://antiquity.ac.uk/wac5/ouzman.html.

Page, Max and Randall Mason (eds). 2003. *Giving Preservation a History*. London: Routledge.

Palasmaa, Juhani. 1996. *The Eyes of the Skin: Architecture and the Senses*. London: Academy Editions.

Pearce, Susan. 1992. *Museums, Objects and Collections: a Cultural Study*. Leicester: Leicester University Press.

———. 1999. *On Collecting: an Investigation into Collecting in the European Tradition*. London: Routledge.

Pietz, William. 1987. "The Problem of the Fetish II." *RES* 13: 23–45.

Pluciennik, Mark. 1999. "Archaeological Narratives and Other Ways of Telling." *Current Anthropology* 40(5): 653–78.

Polanyi, Michael. 1962. "The republic of science." *Minerva* 1: 54–73.

Pollan, Michael. 2001. *Botany of Desire: a Plant's Eye View of the World*. London: Random House.

Renfrew, Colin. 2001. *Loot, Legitimacy and Ownership: The Ethical Dilemma in Archaeology*. London: Duckworth.

Said, Edward W. 1989. "Representing the Colonized: Anthropology's Interlocutors." *Critical Inquiry* 15: 205–25.

Samuel, R. 1994. *Theatres of Memory*. London: Verso.

SAPA. 2003. "Frozen Fritz Ready for the Big Chill in Italy." *Independent*, December 2.

Scarry, Elaine. 1999. *On Beauty and Being Just*. Princeton, NJ: Princeton University Press.

Shanks, Michael. 2001. "Culture/Archaeology: the Dispersion of a Discipline and its Objects." In *Archaeological Theory Today: Breaking the Boundaries*: ed. Ian Hodder. Cambridge: Polity.

Shepherd, Nick J. 2003. "'When the Hand that Holds the Trowel is Black...': Disciplinary Practices of Self-representation and the Issue of 'Native' Labour in Archaeology." *Journal of Social Archaeology* 3(3): 334–52.

Simmel, Georg. 1950 [1908]. *The Sociology of Georg Simmel*. Trans. and ed. K. Wolff. Glencoe, IL: Free Press.

Simpson, Moira, G. 2001. *Making Representations: Museums in the Postcolonial Era*. London: Routledge.

Skotnes, Pippa. (ed). 1996. *Miscast: Negotiating the Presence of the Bushmen*. Cape Town: University of Cape Town Press.

Smit, Estelle. 2002. *Form Function and Animation at Three Southern African Rock Art Sites*. Unpublished MA dissertation, University of the Free State, South Africa.

Smith, Benjamin, J. David Lewis-Williams, Geoff Blundell, and Christopher Chippindale. 2000. "Archaeology and Symbolism in the New South African Coat of Arms." *Antiquity* 74: 467–8.

Solnit. Rebecca. 2000. *Wanderlust: a History of Walking*. New York: Viking.

Spinney, Laura. 2004. "Restoration Tragedy." *New Scientist*.

Stahl, Ann Brower. 2002. "Colonial Entanglements and the Practice of Taste: an Alternative to Logocentric Approaches." *American Anthropologist* 104 (3): 827–45.

Stocking, George W. (ed). 1985. *Objects and Others: Essays on Museums and Material Culture*. Madison, WI: University of Wisconsin Press.

Stone, Christopher D. 1973. *Should Trees have Standing? Toward Legal Rights for Natural Objects*. Los Altos, CA: William Kaufmann.

Strathern, Marilyn. (ed.). 2000. *Audit Cultures: Anthropological Studies in Accountability, Ethics and the Academy*. London: Routledge.

Suzuki, Shunryu. 1999. *Branching Streams Flow in the Darkness: Zen Talks on the Sandokai*. Berkeley, CA: University of California Press.

Thomas, Nicholas. 1991. *Entangled Objects: Exchange, Material Culture, and Colonialism in the Pacific*. Cambridge, MA: Harvard University Press.

Tilley, Christopher, Y. 1991. *Material Culture as Text: The Art of Ambiguity*. London: Routledge.

Trigger, Bruce. 1989. *A History of Archaeological Thought*. Cambridge: Cambridge University Press.

Tuhiwa-Smith, Linda. 1999. *Decolonizing Methodologies: Research and Indigenous Peoples*. London: Zed Books.

Tuzin, D. 1984. "Miraculous Voices: The Auditory Experience of Numinous Objects." *Current Anthropology* 25: 579–96.

UNESCO. 2003. Intercultural Dialogue: the Slave Route. http://www.unesco.org/culture/dialogue/slave. Website accessed April 2003.

Vail, Amanda. 2001. "The work of Mark Dion." *Knot Magazine* http://www.knotmag.com/?article=212. Website accessed July 2003.

Weiner, Annette B. 1985. "Inalienable Wealth". *American Ethnologist* 12(2): 210–27.

Weisman Art Museum. 2001. *Mark Dion: Cabinet of Curiosities*. Exhibition, 24 February – 27 May. http://hudson.acad.umn.edu/Dion. Website accessed June 2003.

Werbart, B. 1996. "All Those Fantastic Cultures? Concepts of Archaeological Cultures, Identity and Ethnicity." *Archaeologia Polona* 34: 97–128.

Wilson, Fred. 2002–2003. *Fred Wilson: Objects and installations 1979–2000*. Retrospective Exhibition 2002–2003, Berkeley Art Museum.

Index